WHAT THE CRIT
ATLANTA JOBS
and STEVE HINES

"[*Atlanta Jobs*] The **best** of the local job search books."
Susan Harte, *The Atlanta Journal-Constitution*

"…*Atlanta Jobs* is the best book produced chiefly for Atlanta job seekers. Employers and consultants prefer *Atlanta Jobs*."
Nick Vance, *Atlanta Employment Weekly*

"No one knows the Atlanta job market quite like … Steve Hines."
Kitsy Rose, *Northside Neighbor*
Atlanta Journal-Constitution

"What people really need in ha
"If you want a job and feel you must have a book to use as a guide, then buy Mr. Hines' [*Atlanta Jobs*]… The book is well-organized, realistic, full of usable resources and heavy on good sense."
Susan Harte, *The* rd times is guidance…that's what Mr. Hines offers in step-by-step fashion."
Tom Walker, *The Atlanta Journal Constitution*

"Hines is the only writer with personnel experience writing for the Atlanta unemployed, and his advice works!"
Sara Moore, *Dunwoody Crier*

The clear choice among those who know is . . .

ATLANTA JOBS

ATLANTA JOBS

featuring the

CAREER SEARCH SYSTEM . . .

Your source to Atlanta jobs!

Not a vague, indiscriminate list of companies, but a **complete strategy** to uncover and utilize **every available source** to your advantage:

- Atlanta's primary hiring companies
- Personnel agencies, both permanent and temporary
- Classified Want Ads
- Government positions
- Job Fairs

- Professional and trade associations
- Network and support groups
- Free job assistance organizations
- Computer online services

And more!

- Resume, cover letter, broadcast letter, and salary history preparation, with examples of each

- Interviewing strategies, including questions and answers

- Detailed company profiles, employment data, and hiring procedures

NOW with still more: www.ajobs.com

The *ONLY* employment guide to include a companion web site that allows you to perform quickly and easily many of the tasks required for your job search – FREE! Special dialogue boxes are highlighted throughout *Atlanta Jobs* alerting you to ajobs.com opportunities!

Links to job sites, company home pages, travel directions, salary comparisons, professional associations, networking groups, etc.

BOOKS AND SERVICES

ATLANTA JOBS ON CD v. 2.0   *$27.95*
The most technologically advanced job search system available anywhere!
- Video and Audio clips explaining job search techniques
- Instant links to hundreds of helpful internet sites, including
  - **Top Job Sites** ▪ **Companies** ▪**Travel Directions** ▪ **Salary comparisons** ▪ **Network Groups** ▪ **Professional Associations** ▪ **Personnel Agencies** ▪ **Government**
- *New:* Web-friendly layout <u>and</u> includes workbook pages

JOB SEARCH COACHING BY STEVE HINES
- Finding a job is not that hard – if you know what to do!
- With more than 25 years in personnel recruiting and placement, well-known author and job search coach **STEVE HINES** knows how to get a job -- and he can show you how too!
- Individual, group, and seminar rates, call (404) 262-7131 or email JobGuru@ajobs.com for information

ATLANTA JOBS WORKBOOK   *$19.95*
- More than 75 forms and pages on floppy disk to guide you through each step in your job search
- Three-ring binder with dividers for organization
- Sample resumes and business templates with blank forms

WHO'S HIRING IN ATLANTA   *$15.95*
- All new THIRD EDITION includes job search tips and strategies
- More than 3,000 companies with complete addresses, including fax, web site, and email – Plus 300+ personnel agencies.
- Available on CD formatted for mail merge and search features

TABLE OF CONTENTS
Chapters:

ATLANTA JOBS + www.ajobs.com =

The fastest job search possible!

The only employment guide to include a companion web site that allows you to perform quickly and easily many of the tasks required for your job search. Special dialogue boxes are highlighted throughout *Atlanta Jobs* alerting you to ajobs.com opportunities.

- Apply online to hundreds of Atlanta companies and employment search firms.

- Links to helpful web sites giving company information, salary comparisons, directions to interviews, cost of living information, and more.

- Links to job sites, including WorkAtlanta, Monster, CareerPath, Career Builder, Office of Personnel Management, *The Atlanta Journal-Constitution*, et al.

- Updated information keeps *Atlanta Jobs* <u>always</u> current.

www.ajobs.com

ATLANTA

JOBS

featuring the

CAREER SEARCH SYSTEM

Steve Hines

CareerSource Publications
Atlanta, Georgia
(404) 262-7131

Published by CareerSource Publications,
P O Box 52291, Atlanta, GA 30355.
(404) 262-7131;   (404) 842-1815 fax
E-mail addresses: JobGuru@ajobs.com
                   hines@ajobs.com

World Wide Web site: http://www.ajobs.com

Manufactured in the United States of America.

Graphics and cover design by West Paces Publishing, Atlanta, GA.

All information herein is believed to be accurate and reliable. However, neither the author nor CareerSource Publications assumes any responsibility thereof. Correction requests should be mailed to CareerSource Publications.

The companies and services included herein do not in any way constitute an endorsement or recommendation by CareerSource Publications or the author.

ISBN: 0-929255-28-3

Also available from CareerSource Publications:

Who's Hiring in Atlanta (all new **Third Edition**)

- More than 3000 companies with web sites, email addresses, fax numbers, etc., plus 300 Atlanta permanent and temporary agencies.
- Job search strategies and Interviewing tips.
- $15.95

How To Get A Job On A Cruise Ship

Make money and have fun at the same time! Learn how to apply for exciting jobs on more than 100 cruise ships. Written by former cruise ship staff officer. All new Second Edition, $14.95

CHAPTER I

"I WISH I'D HAD

A BOOK LIKE THIS!"

INTRODUCING THE

CAREER SEARCH SYSTEM

Good News:
Atlanta is a great place to live and has thousands of job waiting!

Bad News:
The word is out and thousands of job seekers now have descended on Atlanta.

Good News:
There is a job in Atlanta for you!

CHAPTER I

"I WISH I'D HAD A BOOK LIKE THIS!"

INTRODUCING THE CAREER SEARCH SYSTEM

Even in the current recession, Atlanta indeed does have innumerable career opportunities available, but the catch is how to find the right one for you. And that's not really a problem; it just takes knowledge, a plan of action, and the commitment to see the plan through.

Many years ago, I moved to Atlanta, ready to seek fame and fortune in the business world. I had been teaching high school social studies for the previous three years, and thus coddled in the world of academia, I had no concept of what was in the "real world." I did not know what jobs were out there, or what companies offered them, and least of all, I didn't have the slightest idea how, where, or what to do to find my new career.

I wish I'd had a book like this!

In the years since that summer, I have worked in personnel re-cruiting and placement. I have seen thousands of applicants struggle and stumble, trying to advance their careers – expending too much time, energy, and money, and going in pointless directions. Finding a job is just not that hard – if you know what to do!

But of course, most people don't. The purpose of the **CAREER SEARCH SYSTEM** is to fill this vacuum of misinformation and lack of information, and to provide job seekers with the knowledge needed to successfully conduct a job search. This System represents more than twenty years of knowledge, gained almost entirely from that best teacher, experience. I have compiled the arcana, simplified and methodized it, and the result is the CAREER SEARCH SYSTEM.

The CAREER SEARCH SYSTEM will give you the tools you need to apply in your job search, and now *Atlanta Jobs* offers you even more: a companion web site **http://www.ajobs.com.** This site allows you to perform many of the functions online that are described in the CAREER SEARCH SYSTEM. Special dialogue boxes are highlighted throughout this text alerting you to **ajobs.com** opportunities. Watch for these helpers and take advantage of this new technology offered only through *Atlanta Jobs* and CareerSource Publications.

Combining the information in *Atlanta Jobs* with **ajobs.com** will save you many, many hours of frustration and work. And since most of us would rather play than work, let's get into the spirit of job hunting with a little game, on pages 14 and 15.

(Refer to pp. 14 - 15)

The Career Search System

ajobs.com
This is your first dialogue box. Play the expanded job game online.

The CAREER SEARCH SYSTEM consists of five basic steps that will lead to job offers. Each step is explained fully, describing in detail exactly what you should do, and the dialogue boxes will highlight shortcuts on the internet.

Step #1 is organization. As your job hunt progresses, you will come to see the value of the systems and procedures I suggest. For best results, order the **Atlanta Jobs Workbook** by calling (404) 262-7131 or order online at ajobs.com; at only $19.95, it's a bargain and will save you hours of time.

Step #2 in your job search is to prepare your resumes, written and oral, and business cards. Even if you have a service prepare your resume, carefully read this chapter, so that you can give them the layout

12

and standards you expect to be followed. Numerous examples are shown in Appendix A.

Now you are ready for **_Step #3_**, developing a marketing strategy to obtain interviews. The System describes more sources from which to develop leads and interviews than you probably will use, but they are all here if you need them. Start with the ones that are the simplest and easiest for you, and if you are not satisfied with those results, add the others. The System even indicates which sources work best for different backgrounds, and you can choose ones best suited for you.

Even with on-line job postings, more applicants find their jobs through some form of job networking. The **CAREER SEARCH SYSTEM** explains several networking procedures in complete detail, outlining exactly what you should do and say.

Step #4 contains information on the preparation you must do before an interview, as well as the interview itself. Numerous questions, suggested answers, and the reasoning behind the questions and answers are discussed fully. **Ajobs.com** will be invaluable here, providing links to reference sites, travel directions, etc.

If you have always thought that once you finished the interview, your work was over, then think again. **_Step #5_** covers the follow-up procedure you should do after the interview, to give you an extra push. The "thank-you note" is discussed, as well as additional research and sources you can employ.

In addition to the five basic steps outlined in Chapters II – VI, additional chapters cover other information to apply in your job search.

"Chapter VII: Salary Negotiating" explains how salaries most often are determined by companies. When you should and should not consider negotiating is explained, and if you do wish to negotiate your salary offer, several suggestions and procedures are outlined.

Start Here!
Move 1 space.

ASSESS YOUR ABILITIES:
Objectively—Move 2 spaces.
Non-objectively—Move 1 space.

STAY HERE UNTIL YOU TRY ANOTHER SOURCE

MARKET RESUME:
Move 1 space for
each marketing tool you use.

MOVE BACK & FORTH A WHILE, THEN MOVE 1 SPACE

2 sources are better than one, but use another source, then move 1 space.

Getting the Idea?
Use another source
and keep moving.

DITTO DITTO DITTO DITTO DITTO DITTO DITTO

JOB OFFER
YOU WIN!

Go to church and pray no one
else has both good interview
and good follow-up!

GO BACK TO START. GET HELP AND TRY AGAIN.

ASSESS NEEDS & WANTS
Realistically—Move 2 spaces.
Unrealistically—Move 1 space.

Stay Here Until You Come to your Senses!

ORGANIZE
Skip Organization—
Move Back 1 Space
Organize equipment, time, records & resources—
Move 1 Space
Organize emotional support systems—
Move 1 More Space!

PREPARE RESUME
Ordinary Resume—Move 1 space.
"Power" Resume—Move 2 spaces.

GET DEPRESSED
Wallow in self-pity!
Organize emotional support systems—
Then Move On—

CONGRATULATIONS!
You Got an Interview
Prepared for interview—move 1 space.
Unprepared for interview—move back 12 spaces.

PREPARATION
Research only—
Move 1 space.
Research & Rehearse—
Move 2 spaces.

CLOSE
but we're not playing horseshoes! Move back 1 space.

GOOD INTERVIEW!
FOLLOW-UP—Move 2 spaces.
NO FOLLOW-UP—Move 1 space.

Correspondence is covered in Chapter VIII. The basic format for cover letters is given here, followed by the variations used for specific instances. What to include in your "thank-you note" is clarified, with suggestions for making yours stand out. How to report your salary information or write a salary history is also detailed. In addition, you can find numerous examples of these correspondences in Appendix B.

"What am I doing wrong?" is a question I frequently encounter, and I have the answers. Chapter IX discusses what to do should you find your job search at a standstill. I can help you evaluate your job search and pinpoint problems, then find the solutions. I have recommendations to energize your search and to help you avoid the common mistakes I so often observe.

Lastly, Chapter X concludes with a few more suggestions, even using rejection as an asset.

Conclusion

In the twenty-five years that I have been in personnel placement in Atlanta, I have dealt with hundreds of companies and their personnel representatives, interviewed thousands of applicants, and read tens of thousands of resumes. I stress my experience so you will understand that I indeed do know how to win the "job game." I have encountered the problems you're facing many times, and I can help you find the solutions.

Step #1 in your job search is organization. Let's get started!

CHAPTER II

STEP ONE:

ORGANIZING YOUR JOB SEARCH

*Atlanta has 13 Fortune 500 firms headquartered
here, behind only New York and Houston:*

**BellSouth Corporation
Coca-Cola Company
Coca-Cola Enterprises
Cox Communications
Delta Air Lines
Genuine Parts Company
Georgia-Pacific Corporation
Home Depot
Mirant Corporation
Newell Rubbermaid
Southern Company
SunTrust Banks
United Parcel Service**

CHAPTER II:

Step One: Organizing Your Job Search

Before you write the first word on your resume and well before you make your first company contact, you must organize. This is the first of the five steps in your job search, and it is the foundation on which the rest of your job search is built.

Set Up an In-House Office

Create an environment similar to which you have been accustomed in the past or expect to have in the future.

Organize your space. You should have a well-lighted space with a desk and comfortable chair, and with your phone convenient. At the end of every day, strive to clear your desk of all papers and materials, so that you will start each day with a neat, clean work space.

Phone books and other reference materials should be within easy reach. Keep a copy of *Atlanta Jobs* close at hand, since you will refer to it often. Think of this book as a workbook, similar to the ones you used in school. Underline or highlight passages, write in the margins, fold down the edges of pages you want to refer to later – anything that will help you derive the most from the information contained here. By the end of your job search, this book should be thoroughly worn out.

Organize your records. If your desk does not have a least one file drawer, you will need a small file cabinet. Place in the file drawer several folders with topics that will help you store and organize your information and records, so that you can quickly retrieve information. For example, use a file folder to hold information on each company you have targeted. Include in the folder a copy of your correspondences with the company, annual reports you have obtained, information downloaded from the internet, etc. Should the company call you, all this information can be quickly retrieved; the caller will be impressed with your organizational skills and you will be relaxed. Use other folders to hold older information or any other topic you find helpful.

Next you will need a three-ring binder and a package of eight dividers to hold your current information. You can set this up yourself, but ordering the **Atlanta Jobs Workbook** through **ajobs.com** will save you time and it includes more than 50 forms and pages you will need.

Label the dividers with these titles:

- Time management
- Classified ads
- Networking contacts
- Information interviews
- Company "cold calls"
- Personnel agencies
- Professional associations
- News articles

Have business cards printed with your name, contact data, and your employment objective or expertise, but do not attempt to condense your resume onto this small card (see Appendix A for examples). You will use these cards extensively during your search, especially when job networking.

Organize your equipment. You must have either a telephone answering device or voice mail service with remote access ability, so that you will not miss any calls for information or an interview. Remember that first impressions are very important, and thus your recorded message should sound professional; this is not the time for a funny message or your children's voices.[1]

Computer Access

Just as a typewriter was essential in years past, the most effective job search today requires a computer with a modem to fax and to access the internet, and a quality printer. However, if that expense is prohibitive, several sources are available for free or low-cost computer usage. For example, state employment offices, public libraries, and college placement

> **Atlanta Jobs on CD**
> Completely interactive with hundreds of web hyperlinks. Order on line at ajobs.com or phone 404/262-7131.

departments have computers available free for job seekers. The local branches of Kinko's Copy Centers all have Macs and PCs for a low hourly rate.

If you are not computer literate, now is an ideal time to learn at least the basics. Every company and every discipline are becoming more dependent on computers, and your lack of computer skills will severely hinder your career. Consider taking free or low cost classes through a local college or adult education program.

With a computer, you can easily personalize your correspondence and resume to fit each situation. You can store vast amounts of data, and with internet connection, research any subject in minutes.

But the most important reason for having access to a computer during your job search is the ability to take advantage of **Atlanta Jobs Online** (www.ajobs.com). For example, **ajobs.com** contains links to hundreds of Atlanta companies, their current job vacancies, and the

---

[1] While on the subject of voice mail, let me say that my pet peeve has become people who leave a message on my voice mail, but speak so rapidly and/or enunciate so poorly that I cannot decipher the information, especially the phone number. When leaving messages, always repeat your name and phone number so that the receiver will have no difficulty returning your call. If your message is difficult to understand, you likely will not have your call returned.

ability to email your resume to their corporate recruiters. Personnel agencies are listed with their specialties, and also with the ability to email your resume. We have links to web sites that guide you to your interview location, evaluate a salary offer, search for government jobs, and much more. **Ajobs.com** has been designed as a complement and companion to *Atlanta Jobs*, and you should consider it to be part of this book and your job search.

Time Management

"*Dost thou love life? Then squander not time, for that's the stuff it's made of.*" -- Benjamin Franklin

How much time can you spend on your job search? If you are currently employed, you must budget your time wisely, conducting your search in the evenings, weekends, and during the workday when possible. If you are unemployed, you should plan to spend at least 40 hours per week in your search, and you should plan your schedule just as effectively as you would in your employment.

During your unemployment, strive to maintain the same agenda to which you have become accustomed. Don't allow yourself to wallow in bed every morning, or you will be wasting valuable time. In addition, when you begin your new employment, you will have difficulty readjusting to the work regimen.

Discuss with your family the need to maintain this work schedule. Don't carpool or baby-sit when you should be working on your job search. If you have been a member of a health spa, continue your workouts just as before, since exercise is an excellent way to cope with stress.

If you find yourself with extra time, use it constructively by establishing new contacts through volunteer work (see Job Networking in Chapter IV), enrolling in career enhancement classes, or acquiring certification in your field. Now is an excellent time to study up on new industry trends and advancements, especially computer-related developments. Include in your resume that you are currently attending

22

these job-related classes; companies will be impressed that you are using your time wisely and developing additional skills.

Suggested Schedule

You may not yet understand all the terms used here, and they are explained in detail in later chapters, especially "Chapter IV: Get the Interview."

Hours/week	Task
3	Newspaper classified ads (read and respond)
2	Personnel agencies (read and respond)
5	Surfing the net (commercial and company job sites)
4	Reading and research (AJ-C Business section, *Atlanta Business Chronicle*, trade journals, general research, identifying target companies)
2	Mail-outs (mass mailing, broadcast letters, general correspondence, thank-you notes, etc.)
2	Maintaining organization, updating information
2	Planning, evaluation, and analysis
20	Networking (to include at least one information interview/week and one networking meeting/week)

Note the emphasis on networking. More job seekers find new employment through some form of job networking than through all other sources combined, so plan to spend at least half your time on this part of your search. Chapter IV will give you all the information you need to develop a job network.

In addition to those tasks, you will also need to schedule time for interviews, including preparation, research, and evaluation; job fairs; agency visits; and any other needs. Try to think of these additional tasks as "overtime," while completing as many of the basic hours as possible.

Start each work day at your desk, allowing 10-15 minutes to plan your day. List the tasks you want to complete, set reasonable goals for your productivity, and then prioritize them. At the end of the day, evaluate your success: did you meet your goals for the day: If not, what interfered and why?

Really hold your feet to the fire and don't allow yourself to waste time. This may be the hardest job you have ever had and may test your mettle – are you up to the challenge?

Support Network

Some time ago, I spoke with an applicant who had 15 years experience in commercial real estate. Unfortunately, that field was depressed and his job search had stretched into seven months. His exact words to me were, "I sit across from my wife at breakfast every morning and I know she is thinking 'What is wrong with him?'." Of course, what he really meant to say was "What is wrong with me?"

Even in the best of economic times, conducting a job search is a highly traumatic and stressful endeavor. Maintaining a positive attitude through this most trying of times is painfully difficult, and you must recognize your need for the support of close friends and family, including your children. Let them know what you are doing every step of the way and what they can do to help you. Tell them of your frustrations and anxieties, fears and depression. Those are normal feelings and nothing to be ashamed of or suppressed.

Open your lines of communication and keep them open at all times. Unfortunately, I have witnessed too many divorces and dissolution of friendships that resulted from this stressful period. This is a strange and confusing time for family and friends as well, and oftentimes their puzzlement will exhibit itself in anger. Discussing openly your emotions will allow them to understand better your situation, and then free them to vent their feelings as well.

In addition, you should keep your friends and family informed of the positive aspects of your job search – your progress and up-coming interviews, your research and what you have learned. Many experiences will be very interesting and you will enjoy sharing them.

Join organizations, both those pertaining to your profession as well as non-profit charity associations. Become active and volunteer your time. This will give you needed diversions and new purposes, and also introduce you to another set of networking contacts, some of whom may be helpful in your job search.

Attend the job networking groups included in Chapter IV. You will have the opportunity to discuss your situation with fellow job seekers, and the camaraderie can be uplifting. In addition to the practical aspects of job search, these groups often address ways to deal with the emotional and stressful part of being unemployed.

Prepare yourself, too, by adjusting your attitude. Nothing can ruin a beautiful, sunny day faster than receiving a rejection letter in the mail. Accept the fact that you will be experiencing some let-downs and rejections, and don't be overwhelmed. When you begin to feel yourself slipping into a depression, that is the signal to pull out your emotional support systems and get back on track.

On the positive side, this time can be an opportunity for reflection, a time when you can sit back and evaluate your life and career direction. Are you really happy with your current occupation? What would you like to do differently? What are your goals? Most importantly, what are your priorities? What is important to you, in your personal life as well as your career?

All of this organization is vital to a successful job search, as you will come to see. Best of all, remember you are far ahead in the career search game already: You bought and are reading *Atlanta Jobs*!

CHAPTER III

STEP TWO:

PREPARING YOUR RESUMES AND BUSINESS CARDS

Part 1: The "Power Resume"

Part 2: The "30-Second Resume"

Part 3: Business Cards

What makes a resume stand out?

• Most importantly, I look for a neat, well-organized, clean resume. Poor layout or smudges will take me to the next resume immediately. I also discard the flashy resumes that look more like a sales brochure.

• Misspelled words or other inaccuracies make me question the applicant's attention to detail, and I will put the resume aside.

• Because my time is limited, I prefer a one-page resume, especially if the applicant has only a few years experience. I also avoid verbose resumes that have too much information crammed onto the pages or those that have reduced the type size to squeeze in more information.

• I look for a clear job focus or objective. If I can't determine quickly why this job seeker has sent me a resume, I don't waste time trying to second guess the applicant.

• I scan for "buzz-words" – those acronyms, titles, hardware, software, certain degrees, etc. that relate specifically to the position for which I am recruiting. If one or more catch my attention, I likely will read the entire resume.

• All recruiters will want to know what you have accomplished thus far in your career. What have you contributed to your company's "bottom line"? How have you excelled in your jobs? I favor resumes that contain actual figures or percentages proving your achievements.

When composing your resume, constantly remind yourself that this piece of paper is the first impression a personnel recruiter will have of you. If it is too long or too wordy, you will be judged as longwinded. If the resume lacks focus, you will be perceived as undirected or uncertain of your career goals. If you fail to include achievements and accomplishments, the readers will question what you can contribute to their organizations.

Worst of all, if your resume is messy, you can bet you will never be called for an interview.

CHAPTER III

Step Two: Preparing Your Resumes and Business Cards

Part 1: The Written Word – The "Power Resume"

It's not what you know, but how well you present it. Let me explain.

I recently ran a three-line classified ad in the local newspaper for a manufacturing plant manager. In response to that one tiny ad, I received more than 100 resumes; a larger ad would probably have elicited more. Obviously, I did not have time to interview all of these applicants, or even to call them all. Many of them had the right background and experience, so what criteria did I use in deciding which to interview first? I used the same test that every other recruiter uses: the quality of the resume.

> **ajobs.com**
> Check on other job search experts' advice about the resume.

And what happens to the applicants with poor resumes? I don't know, since I never call them.

Thus, you see that a resume has both positive and negative potential, and we can draw two conclusions:

1) A resume can get you an interview, which may ultimately result in a job.

2) But a resume also can *prevent* you from having an interview, and thus you will never have the opportunity to show why you should be employed there.

The importance of a good resume cannot be over stressed. Even if you have exactly the right background the company is seeking; even if you can interview perfectly; and even if you would make an ideal employee for the company, you will never get in the door if the company's first impression of you is negative, based on a poorly prepared resume.

Wow! Did you ever think that one sheet of paper could have so much power over your life and career?

But not only does your resume need to be "good," it also needs to be "better," that is, better than your competition. Imagine reviewing hundreds of resumes for just one opening. Most recruiters spend approximately 30 seconds on a resume, and if it does not grab their attention in that short time, they move on to the next.

How can you be certain yours will be among the chosen ones? Read on.

How to begin

Wondering what to do first? Here is a short exercise to start the ball rolling. It's purpose is four-fold:

1) To help you understand your strengths and weaknesses

2) To re-cap your career so that you have all the facts about your accomplishments written in front of you

3) To begin developing a job objective or summary statement

4) To start you thinking toward the interviewing process

On a sheet of paper, write down 15 accomplishments for each of your last three jobs or the past ten years of your career. Recent graduates can record 15 accomplishments during their high school and college years. Since most readers tend to scan vertically down the left side of the page, you should include either a percentage or dollar amount in the first few words of each description.

You likely will have difficulty in coming up with fifteen items. The first three or four may be easy, but those last ten or so will take some extra thought. You might be tempted to skip those last ones, but this exercise is an important step in understanding your strengths and values.

Spend several days to think this through fully and to allow your mind enough time to sort through all you have accomplished in your career. Review your performance appraisals; you may have over-looked some of your past activities. List your former bosses to see if forgotten assignments come to mind.

Soon you will begin to notice patterns developing: activities in which you excel, assignments you enjoy, projects of which you are proud, responsibilities you handled well. Conversely, you will remember what you disliked in your past employment, as well as those tasks you did not perform well.

As these patterns become more defined, you will observe a job focus emerging, and this will become the summary statement or job objective for your resume. Although you may be tempted to narrow your job objective down to the tasks you most enjoy, take care not to make this statement too specific, lest you eliminate other possibilities.

You also will begin to have a better understanding of your abilities and motivations, and this will translate into better answers to interviewers' questions such as
- What are your strengths? Weaknesses?
- What did you enjoy in your last job?
- Which accomplishment gives you the most pride?
- What are your looking for in your next job?

When you come to the parts of your resume calling for accomplishments, select only a few from the many you have written. Choose those that demonstrate your best efforts, keeping in mind that companies seek employees who can streamline operations, reduce expenses, or add revenue. Also remember that including too many achievements will dilute power from the top ones.

Writing a resume should not be a quick afternoon's throw-together. Allow it to be a time of soul-searching, to determine those tasks you enjoy the most and thus accomplish the most.

Assembling your resume

After you have completed the work pages, you can begin to assemble your resume, using the guidelines listed below. There are many ways to format your resume, and refer to Appendix A for illustrations of several methods.

There is no one universal format used by all job-seekers, but rather basic sections that can be worded and assembled to fit each person's background. The information I have outlined here is very general in nature, and will result in a functional/chronological resume, the type most commonly accepted and preferred by personnel recruiters. However, under certain circum-stances, you may wish to use a topical format, which will be discussed later in this chapter. Plain text or ASCII formats are often requested when emailing your resume, and that format is also discussed later in the chapter.

Most importantly, as you write your descriptions, keep in mind why you are writing this resume: to impress a potential employer and gain an interview. Thus, you want to include not only your basic qualifications and past responsibilities, but also distinctions and honors that put you ahead of your peers. These awards, accomplishments, and achievements should be emphasized in your resume, either in a separate listing after your job responsibilities or in some other conspicuous manner. The resumes included in Appendix A illustrate this principle.

Name and address: At the top of your resume, place your name, address, phone number, and email address. Professional certifications, such as C.P.A., should be included on the line with your name (John A. Doe, C.P.A.).

If you have a temporary address (*e.g.*, a student) you can use that address and include a permanent address at the bottom or elsewhere, noting when it will be effective. If you are moving soon, you can use either your old or new address and phone number; just be certain that you always can be contacted by prospective employers. Needless to say, update your resume with the new address as soon as possible.

> According to a recent article in *HR Atlanta*, 85% of resumes now are sent over the internet. Only 5% are mailed and 10% are faxed. Thus, be certain your email address is formatted to hyperlink. This allows the reader to contact you immediately after reading your resume online.

If you feel comfortable receiving phone calls at work, you may list both your home and work phone numbers. When you type in your email address, format it to hyperlink; most resumes are now sent via email, and this will allow your reader to send you an email after opening it online. Do not include a fax number.

Objective: Recruiters must be able to quickly know what employment you are seeking. Including "Objective" as your first topic is an easy way to establish this focus. Remember, however, that if your resume states a specific objective (*e.g.*, sales) and you are applying for another (*e.g.*, management), you likely will not be considered. Thus, if you are not so sure about a specific objective, you can make it more open in nature, but still showing focus. An alternative used by many applicants is to prepare two or more resumes with different objectives, and use the one most appropriate.

One of the biggest advantages to having your resume stored in your computer is that you can modify it to appeal to whatever needs you feel the company may have. Thus, if you are sending your resume in response to a classified ad, either from the newspaper or online, or if you have some inside information on what they are seeking, tailor your objective to fit. However, don't try to match perfectly, lest you seem too opportunistic. Also, the company may have another vacancy in a similar category for which you might be qualified.

Lastly, if you have no idea what the company might be seeking and you want your resume to be less specific, you can omit Objective altogether and open your resume with a Summary paragraph.

Summary: Including a Summary paragraph is optional, but it can accomplish several purposes, especially when using the functional/chronological format:

- Summarize your abilities, so the reader will quickly know your background and focus
- Highlight the qualifications that propel you ahead of your peer group
- Include key words and phrases[1] for database scanning and later retrieval
- Show how you fit the job requirements (if known)

The Summary can be used with or without an Objective, or you can incorporate the Objective within this section. It should be very positive and up-beat, with an emphasis on skills, abilities, and achievements. Do not defeat its purpose by making it too long and thus lose its impact. Here are three examples, and more are included on the sample resumes in Appendix A:

Proven success in solution-oriented Sales and active Sales Management. Consistently promoted or recruited as a result of

---

[1] What are key words and phrases? The purpose of scanning resumes into an artificial intelligence database is to be able to later ask of the computer to show all the resumes that contain specific data. For example, the company is seeking a Distribution Manager in Atlanta with MRP software experience: the recruiter could ask the computer for applicants with the key words distribution, manage, MRP, and GA (since Atlanta has many suburbs). The computer will produce all the resumes that contain those key words.

outstanding sales performance. Assembled highly effective and cohesive sales teams.

Recent college graduate in Business Administration with proven record of initiative and accomplishment. Completely financed all education costs through full-time employment, thus gaining five years of business experience. Skilled in numerous Microsoft applications, including MS Office 2002, FrontPage, and PowerPoint. Seeking Management Development Program utilizing practical experience and academics.

Accounting/Finance graduate with more than four years accounting and auditing experience. Thorough knowledge of current federal tax policies and procedures. Experienced with automated invoice systems using Lotus 1-2-3 software, plus all MS Office applications (Word, Access, Excel, PowerPoint). Seeking position as either Staff Accountant or Accounting Manager.

More and more companies are converting to resume scanning equipment, which allows them to store thousands of resumes in a computer database to be retrieved at any time using "key word" searches. In writing your resume, be certain to include those key words and phrases, and a summary paragraph is sometimes a convenient place to incorporate them. In addition, having this information at the beginning of your résumé will allow the reader to quickly understand your background and focus, and be enticed to read further.

Your resume must always . . .

- **Be focused**
- **Emphasize accomplishments**
- **Be concise and to-the-point**
- **Appear neat and clean**
- **Include key words and phrases**
- **Answer the question "What can you do for my company?"**

Whether you use an Objective and/or a Summary section, your resume must have direction and focus. Don't try to make your resume so open that it seems as though you have no idea what career you are pursuing. Recruiters will assume that is exactly the case and will pass over your resume for one that is focused more clearly.

Employment: This is generally your next section, although if you have limited work experience or very strong academics from a highly regarded institution, you may include Education before Employment. For example, recent grads with no relevant experience can place Education first; however, if you were a co-op student or intern, or have some other good business experience, list that first and Education next.

You may call this section "Experience" if you wish, especially if you are including experience gained through unpaid employment (*e.g.*, volunteer work), temporary assignments, or part-time jobs.

All potential employers want to see some work experience, even for recent grads, and the more successful and relevant it is to your job objective, the better your chances of securing employment. List your job title, company name, dates of employment and description of job duties. That seems simple enough, but since it is the most important part of your resume, it must be perfect. Follow these guidelines, and refer to Appendix A for examples:

- Use reverse chronology (last job first).

- Be concise, and thus hold your resume to one page, if possible, and never more than two.

- Don't get bogged down in details and don't feel you must include everything you have done. Save something for the interview.

- Since your resume may be scanned into a computer database for later "key word" retrieval, be certain to include those key words and phrases for which a recruiter would likely search.

- Titles can sometimes be misleading; use functional, descriptive titles when necessary. For example, I recently prepared a resume for an individual who was managing the company's entire personnel function, although his title was only Personnel Administrator; I used Personnel Director as his title, to emphasize the scope of his responsibilities.

- Always include management and supervisory responsibilities.

- Emphasize accomplishments, awards, and achievements. Underline and/or use boldface on only the most important.

- You may list your last or current job date as "present," even if you are no longer with the company, unless many months have passed since your departure. That may sound strange, but it is an accepted practice, since revealing your unemployment raises questions which probably could be explained best during an interview. However, you can clarify your employment status in your cover letter, if you wish, or wait for your first contact with a company representative.

- The most recent experience generally should have the longest description; experience more than ten years ago can be combined for brevity.

- Percentages are usually more easily understood than exact figures, since the relevance of large and small amounts varies from industry to industry. Unless you are certain your readers will understand and/or be impressed with your figures, consider using percentages instead.

- Do not list your reasons for leaving an employer, unless it makes a very positive point or explains several recent job changes.

- Do not use acronyms or arcana that may be unfamiliar to most readers.

- Include a brief description of your company(s) and its products/services, if most readers might not be familiar with it. Sales figures may give perspective on the size of the company.

- Numbers less than 10 should be written out.

- Do not state your salary on the resume. However, some classified ads may request your current salary or a salary history, which can be included in your cover letter or on a separate page. (See "Chapter VIII: Correspondence.")

- Since many companies shy away from individuals who have been self-employed, I suggest you avoid direct references to that. For example, you could describe your job title as "General Manager," rather than "Owner."

- Use mostly "non-sentences" without a pronoun subject, and avoid using personal pronouns. Definitely do not write in the third person and avoid using the passive voice.

Education: As you gain more experience, this section will continue to shrink, as the Employment section grows. For the recent college graduate with limited career-related experience, academics will be paramount and thus will incorporate a large part of the resume. State the name of your college, the type of degree you will be receiving, major and minor concentrations, and month and year you expect to graduate. If you

> ### *Your resume must never . . .*
>
> - **Seem too vague or undirected**
> - **Run more than two pages**
> - **Look like a brochure**
> - **Include too much detail**

had a high Grade Point Average (above 3.0 on a 4.0 scale) and/or

38

graduated in the top one-half of your class, include that information. Then list a few relevant courses that you have taken or plan to take. Earning a large part of your tuition and expenses shows initiative and should be mentioned. Definitely include honors, activities and elected positions. If you have more than one degree to include, list the most recent first.

Applicants with relevant work experience will list most of the same education information, eliminating less important data with each new job and subsequent resume. Course titles will be the first to be eliminated, followed by activities and minor honors. For about ten years, continue to include a good Grade Point Average, important honors and elected positions. By then, your recent achievements will be more indicative of your abilities.

If you are not a college graduate, I suggest you omit "Education" entirely, although you can include a reference to your academics in a Personal section, such as "Attended ABC University for three years, majoring in Business Administration" or "Currently enrolled at ABC University, pursuing a Bachelor's degree in Marketing. Graduation expected in June 2004."

After your academic institutions, list relevant seminars and courses taken, and the dates. Add computer knowledge (hardware, software programs, etc.) here if you have not mentioned it earlier. Also, include any professional certifications (C.P.A., Professional Engineer, etc.) or awards gained through additional studies, and the dates bestowed. However, do not include certifications from previous careers that are not germane to your current job search; for example, omit references to real estate courses, if you are no longer pursuing that career.

Personal: In the past, this was generally included on resumes, but now rarely is. The reason is that your personal data should not affect your job performance, and therefore it should not be a consideration in your job application. In addition, some personal information could lend itself to possible discrimination.

Frankly, I prefer the resumes I receive to have a Personal section, since it often can yield a more complete picture of the candidate. Nevertheless, I do not include one on the resumes I prepare, in deference to the above reasoning, and I recommend you also omit a personal section.

However, if you have some special information to convey that you feel is relevant to your job objective, or if you simply feel that the information will yield a more thorough appraisal of you, this is some of the information that may be included: birth date (not age, since that may change during your job search), marital status, height/weight and if you are available for travel and relocation.

Do not mention potential negatives (*e.g.*, obesity) or restrictions (*e.g.*, geographic). Some states restrict including age, and you may omit that if you feel it could be a handicap, and the same is true for marital status. Never state your race or religion, but do include citizenship status, if you sense it may be in question.

Next mention a few hobbies and interests (reading, sports, music, etc.), that you are actively pursuing and that can be used to "break the ice" during an interview. (Then be ready to discuss them; for example, if you list reading as an interest, be prepared for the question, "What have you read lately?") If you are multilingual, add that here; if you are not quite fluent, you can describe yourself as "proficient." If you have several years of college, but did not graduate, you may mention that here. If you have excellent career experience and have decided to stress that in lieu of a separate Education section, you should list your college degree here. Finally, include memberships in professional associations and your civic involvement; however, do not include more than three, lest your priorities be called into question.

References: You may end your resume with "References available on request." If you get to the bottom of your resume and will have to crowd to add this final sentence, just omit it.

I recently read an article that described this closing line as "utterly useless" and suggested omitting it, and I have also discussed this with several professional resume writers whose opinions I respect. Frankly, I agree that it is stating the obvious – of course you will have references! – but it is also a good method of saying "The End" in more tactful terms, and it can be a good balance in your layout. Whether you include it or not is your decision; your resume will not rise or fall on that sentence.

Do not list your references on the resume, but do prepare a separate "References" page to have should they be requested of you; see Appendix A for examples.

Other optional sections: Adding a separate "Skills" section is often a convenient place to include software and/or hardware knowledge, language proficiency, and other special and important information. Include this section at the top of your resume after "Objective" or "Summary," or as a part of your "Education." This will allow resume scanners to pick up on important data and for recruiters to quickly determine your qualifications.

Professional and civic affiliations are important and should be included, especially if you have held office. Include them at the end of your resume, just before "References."

Topical Format

As I stated earlier, the functional/chronological resume is the most widely used and accepted form because it is simple and easy to under-stand. Under certain circumstances, however, the topical format may be better suited for your use.

The topical format differs from the functional/chronological format in that it includes an Experience section, either in addition to or in lieu of the Employment section. It can be especially helpful when you are changing careers or re-entering the job market, and want to emphasize knowledge you have gained that is relevant to your new job objective. It also can be used to summarize what might otherwise be a very lengthy resume by combining many jobs into skill categories. And finally, it can be used simply to emphasize certain points or expertise

41

you feel important. Several examples of this format are shown in Appendix A.

I often use a variation of this format, combining it with the functional/chronological. When doing so, I generally choose the two or three abilities that best summarize my applicant's experiences or abilities, and include them under the heading "Qualifications." For example, I did a Communications Specialist's resume by summarizing her experiences in Marketing, Public Relations, and Copywriting, and then listing her employment and a very brief description of the responsibilities and accomplishments in each position.

Synopsis/Amplification Format

This resume version consists of a synopsis page that includes all the basic information and sections, but with no details. The details of employment and experience are placed on a separate page, called an "Amplification." I receive these occasionally, and they are acceptable. I don't recommend them, however, because invariably they get too long and so bogged down in detail that they are difficult to read, not to mention boring. As I have stated before, save the details for an interview, when you have the opportunity to explain personally your experiences.

The Finished Product

In Appendix A, I have included many examples of excellent resumes, and I have tried to illustrate as many diverse situations and back-grounds as possible. But because each person's experience is unique, do not try to copy too closely any example given. There are many acceptable variations of the basic format, and if you keep in mind your purpose in constructing a resume, you can vary the format to fit your needs.

Since this is a resume, not a sales brochure, do not adopt any format that looks "gimmicky." Use separate sheets of standard size 8 1/2" x 11" paper, printed on one side only. Print your resume using a laser printer or high-quality ink jet printer. Do not use a dot-matrix printer.

After you have finished typing, carefully proofread for errors and misspellings. Ask two or three friends to read it also, for suggestions and further proofreading.

When you are satisfied with your product, print it on a good quality of cream, light beige, or buff-colored paper for best results, although plain white is certainly acceptable. Do not use green, pink, or any other brightly colored paper. Also, do not use parchment paper, which does not photocopy well and because of its density, does not fax well either. Buy extra blank pages to use for cover letters, and envelopes that match your stationery. Above all, be certain the resume is neat and clean; remember, it represents you.

Finally, here are a few common grammatical mistakes I have observed through the years on the resumes I have reviewed:

1) Without question, the most frequently misspelled word on resumes is "liaison," probably misspelled on a third of the resumes I receive. Another word often misspelled and misused is "Bachelor." It does not contain a "t" (batchelor), and the degree is a Bachelor of Whatever or a Bachelor's degree, not a Bachelor's of Whatever. The same is true of Master's degrees.

2) The most commonly misspelled and overused abbreviation is "etc." (not ect.), and note the correct punctuation of the abbreviation "et al." (a period after "al," not "et").[1]

3) The most common punctuation errors I observe are in the misuse of periods, commas, semicolons, and colons, and the misplacement of quotation marks. The correct usage of these punctuation marks is generally misunderstood, and unless you are positive you have used them correctly, I advise you to check with a grammar reference book. Three primary examples are these:

---

[1] Incidentally, the correct punctuation for foreign words used in print is to underline or italicize them. However, the Latin abbreviations "etc." and "et al." have become so commonly accepted that we no longer treat them differently. Other foreign words, such as *cum laude,* should continue to be underlined or italicized.

- Commas and periods are always placed *inside* quotation marks, and the reverse is true for colons and semicolons. The placement of question marks and exclamation points varies, depending on the usage. (Now that you know this, notice how often it is done incorrectly.)

- The word "however" is preceded by a *semicolon*, not a comma, when used as a conjunctive adverb, separating clauses of a compound sentence; however, a comma is correct when using "however" as a simple conjunction or adverb. If this sounds confusing – and it does to me! – just notice how I have correctly used "however" throughout this book.

- Colons should be used at the end of a complete sentence, not a phrase.

4) Other frequent grammatical mistakes are inconsistencies in verb tense and in parallel structure.

If you still have questions regarding correct word usage, spelling, or grammar, you can call Georgia State University's Grammar Hot Line at (404) 651-2906. This free service is staffed by professors who work the hot line on a volunteer basis between their regular schedule of classes. If your question cannot be immediately answered, the staffer will research the information and call you back.

Resume Scanning

Pity the poor resume: Unloved and unwanted. It's difficult and time-consuming to prepare, and almost as time-consuming to read. A well constructed resume can be an asset in your job search, but a badly prepared one will destroy you. It can be expensive, when you add up the preparation fee, cost of paper, printing, etc. On the other end, a company must pay someone to open it, then read it, toss it, file it, scan it, or add it to the resume stack.

I sometimes wonder how many forests would remain if there were an alternative to the resume shuffle. Nevertheless, it is universally acknowledged that all job applicants must have at least one version of their resume, and oftentimes several different variations to meet specific objectives. How else can you show your background and experiences?

A high-tech development has made resumes easier to reference and store, and ultimately will cut down on the use of paper. Many corporations have developed or purchased resume database software with artificial intelligence that allows the resume to be electronically scanned into the company's computer system and then retrieved later when needed. These remarkable systems allow a recruiter to conduct a computer search for specific key words or phrases, and then present the recruiter with the resumes that contain the background needed for a current job vacancy.

Many companies already have installed such systems, and I am certain more will follow soon. Unfortunately, these systems work best with an unformatted, plain text (ASCII) resume rather than the one you will have prepared to show to prospective employers, so you need to have another version of your resume. In addition, I have observed many companies now require that you email your resume in plain text format in the email message box, rather than attach your resume in MS Word which would then have to be downloaded and opened.

After you finish preparing your resume, convert a copy into simple ASCII text format to be used for scanning and emailing when ASCII is preferred. Converting is simple:
- Use Arial or Helvetica font, all in 12-point type
- make it entirely flush left; and
- remove all formatting, including tabs, bullets, margin changes, italics/boldface/underlining, centering, etc.

The resume will be bland, looking like the resumes twenty or more years ago, but it will transmit correctly in the email message box and it is what resume scanning equipment is best able to read. An example is included in Appendix A. After you convert your resume, take it for a test run by sending it to several friends to confirm it will email correctly.

Incidentally, because your resume will be scanned for specific key words and phrases, a one-page broadcast letter with the key words will work as well as a resume when you are sure it will be scanned.

Conclusion

"What can you do for me?"

> ## *Keep your resume current!*
> Within a few weeks of your new employment, update your resume, and always have an updated version available. Every time you receive a promotion or achieve some distinction, add it to your resume. If you are doing a good job, your reputation will spread, and sooner or later someone will call you with a possible new job.

Whether or not that question is directly asked of you, it is what every recruiter and hiring authority wants to know. When writing your resume, keep this question in mind and when you have finished your resume, review it to see if it answers the question. Later when preparing for an interview, continue to remember that question and plan your answers with it in mind.

Follow the outline and guidelines presented here, and your resume will have answered the question. My knowledge on resume preparation is first-hand, having read many thousands of resumes, written at least a thousand more, and consulted with other personnel recruiters to obtain their input as well. Thus, you can rest assured that your better and more powerful resume will get the best results possible.

P. S.

Now that you know what is involved in preparing your own resume, you may be concerned that it is too difficult and time-consuming for you, and you may be planning to have a professional resume service prepare it for you. Considering some of the home-made products I receive, I might encourage that also – but with definite reservations and qualifications.

In the past, I have been hesitant to recommend the use of resume services, because I have seen so many poor results. In fact, I recently discussed this with the former Director of Employment for a major Atlanta corporation, and who is now a training consultant. We were talking about resumes – specifically, the bad ones – and we agreed that some of the worst were "professionally" prepared.

Let me quickly add, however, that although I most remember those bad examples, I have also reviewed many excellent resumes that were prepared by resume services. A good, experienced resume service can be extremely helpful; just be careful with your choice. Insist on editorial approval and be certain it meets our standards before you accept it. Ask the background and experience of the person who will be preparing your resume, and request to see actual copies of recent work. Show them some of the samples I have included in Appendix A, to use as a pattern for your resume.

Although the layout and appearance are important, the paramount factor is the content of your resume. You can help in this preparation (and probably save money) by composing most of the content of your resume beforehand, and simply have the service do the re-typing and lay-out correctly.

Whatever you decide, remember that this resume represents *you*. If you have the time and feel competent, use the information I have outlined here and make your own resume. It's really not as difficult as you might imagine. Otherwise, pay to have it prepared for you, but be satisfied that it is an accurate depiction of you, and that it does you justice.

Part 2

The Oral Synopsis:
The "30-Second Resume"

How many times have you been at a party, seminar, or meeting when someone turned to you and said, "Tell me about yourself," or "What do you do?" or "What is your background?" What did you answer?

"Well, I was an accountant, but now I'm between jobs," or "I used to be an accountant, but was laid off. Do you know of any job openings?" Worse yet, did you ramble on for several minutes and bore your listeners so badly that they were wishing to be in another room, another place, another time?

Wouldn't you have been more successful if you had a short, prepared answer that covered your background highlights and job objective, and still kept your listener's attention?

During your job search, you will encounter many networking opportunities when you will be called upon to relate your qualifications and objectives. Some of these situations you will have created through your specific networking efforts, but there also will be other times when someone simply will turn to you and ask, "What do you do?"

Be prepared for these opportunities with a short, oral synopsis of your background and career objective. Since you may have only a few moments of your listeners' time, you need an answer that will quickly stress the most important factors you want your listeners to know while you have their undivided attention. You cannot hope to relate all of your background, experiences, and achievements at once, but rather you will reveal just enough of your background to hold your their interest and hopefully lead to further dialogue.

What you need is a "30-Second Resume."

I recently attended a seminar in which the speaker commented that the average person has an attention span of approximately thirty seconds! I do not know the accuracy of his source, but that generally confirmed my suspicions and experiences. Perhaps if you will be honest, that may be true for you too.

When I receive phone calls from job seekers asking for advice, I always ask, "What is your background?" or "Tell me about yourself," and their answer reveals much of what is right or wrong in their job search. If they are unable to relay quickly and concisely their background, or if they ramble on until I cut them off, then I know what they should do first: they must compose their "30-second resume."

Composing your "30-Second Resume"[1]

When writing your "30-second resume," bear in mind when and how you will use it, remembering its two primary purposes:

1) to relay only the most important facets of your background

2) to arouse enough interest to lead to further dialogue.

Note that its purpose is not to include all the information you want to relate, and since you want to involve your listener in dialogue, you should keep your discourse upbeat and non-technical.

---

[1] Forms to plan your oral resume are included in the **Atlanta Jobs Workbook**.

What should you include? First answer these questions:
- What are the requirements for the job I am seeking?
- What in my background fits those requirements?

With that information, you can begin to separate relevant material from information that can be discussed later. Then plan how you will encapsulate the most relevant material into a very short time span – approximately 30 seconds. If your listeners seem interested in hearing more, you can elaborate and give details then. But first, you must gain their attention with your "30-second resume."

Preparing this oral resume may take as much time as your written one, and it is equally as important. Probably the worst mistake job seekers make with their written resume is making it too long and detailed, boring the readers and losing their attention. I assume you already know that the purpose of a resume is not to get you a job, but to arouse just enough interest to obtain an interview.

The same is true regarding your oral resume. Keep it short and relevant to your job objective, saying just enough to show you are qualified and to keep your listener's attention. What would you want to hear if you were the listener? What can you say that will arouse interest and perhaps lead to further discussion?

Most importantly, plan this well in advance and then rehearse it aloud or with a friend. Here are some factors to consider:

> *Job objective:* In as few words as possible, explain the field or type of job you are seeking. Probably this should be the first item in your oral resume, but you also can explain your qualifications first and then show how it fits into your career plans.

> *Education and training:* Some professions emphasize academics, and if you have the right degree, you should mention it. (For example, a science degree may be helpful in a pharmaceutical or chemical sales position; a degree in industrial management is good preparation for a manufacturing management position; a marketing MBA is usually vital to a

staff marketing position; etc.) Familiarity with computer hardware and software programs is becoming a necessity in most professions, and you probably will want to indicate your proficiency. Certification is nearly always an important asset and should be stressed. Career-related seminars and training programs also may be added, if they are well-known.

Skills: Some examples are good communicator, self-motivated, well-organized, aggressive, etc. Keep in mind that you may be called upon to give specific instances showing how you exemplify these characteristics, so be prepared with some good illustrations.

Accomplishments and achievements: This is an integral part of both your written and oral resumes, and must always be included. Of what in your life and career are you the proudest? Choose the most important one or two and mention them. Remembering that corporations are all "bottom-line"-oriented, you also should stress any increases in revenue or decreases in expenses due to your efforts.

Prior employment: If you seek to advance your current career path, then your past and current employment may be the most important information to stress. Condense it into a few sentences, stating job titles or descriptive titles and the responsibilities you have had.

Other experience: If your objective is to change careers, mention specific experiences that relate to your new field. For example, if outside sales is your objective, stress your familiarity with the product line, through experience, academics, or whatever. Volunteer experience and civic involvement may have given you some experience relevant to your new career. Prior employment could have yielded some transferable skills or knowledge.

I realize that this may be an enormous amount of information to condense into thirty-or-so seconds, but you must.

If you still are having difficulty filtering down enough material to reach the 30-second point, try this exercise: Take fifteen pieces of paper and write on each piece an item of information you would want to relay if you had all the time you wanted and could hold your party's attention level. Then remove the four least important, then another three, another two, and finally one more. The remaining five items probably will be the core of your oral resume.

Then organize your information into a clear, concise "30-second resume." Practice it aloud many times until you are comfortable repeating it and then try it with a friend for critique.

You may wish to end your oral resume with a "tickler," such as "What more would you like to know?" or "Is there something you would like for me to explain further?" This also has the advantage of beginning a dialogue and allows you to add information you may have wanted to include earlier.

In an informal or social setting, you also could ask, "Are you familiar with that industry?" or "Do you know someone who does that type of work?" If your listener does know someone, you are off to a fast start in your information gathering.

Just as you can vary your "tickler," you also may need to develop variations of your "30-second resume" to fit specific situations. For example, should you be talking with an authority in your industry, you could be more technical in your description than you would at a social gathering. In your "cold calling," you might wish to stress your ability to reduce costs or increase profits.

As your job search progresses, you undoubtedly will be surprised how often you will need this oral resume. Not only will it form the foundation of your networking campaign, but you also will use it on many other occasions. When you contact companies for the first time, when you attend networking meetings, when you are asked the standard interview question, "Tell me about yourself" – these are only a few of the many times you will use your "30-second resume," so take the time to prepare it well.

Part 3

Business Cards

Why do you need business cards, even when you are unemployed?

There will be many occasions, especially in your networking efforts, when you will have the opportunity to discuss your job search with someone. Many of these meetings will be planned, but more often they will occur simply by chance. You want to leave your listener with contact data as well as a short summary of your expertise or job objective, and you cannot possibly carry copies of your resume at all times.

Oftentimes you will want to leave information with several persons, but when a full resume would be inappropriate. For example, when attending a professional association meeting, passing out your resume to many members would be viewed as obnoxious and criticized severely. Certainly you would not want to distribute your resume at a party or other social gathering. However, exchanging business cards is an accepted practice on nearly all occasions.

As your job search progresses, you will find still more uses for this card. For example, you may wish to include it with much of your business correspondence, especially in your thank-you notes.

Another advantage to offering your business card is that it usually will elicit a card in return. As soon as possible, make a note on the back of the card to help you remember that person (where you met, appearance, etc.), and record what help the person might have for you later. Set up a file for these cards so you can refer back to them when you need specific information.

There are other, more practical reasons, too. Resumes cost more to print than business cards, and business cards are far easier to carry than an 8 1/2" x 11" pile of resumes. You can keep your business card in your pockets, wallet, purse, attaché case, car, or virtually anywhere. Furthermore, business cards are not only easier for you to handle, but your recipients are more likely to keep this small card than a bulky resume.

In order to give a longer lasting impression when exchanging your business card, a good practice is to personalize your card when possible. For example, write your nickname or most recent employer on the card when you hand it out.

In Appendix A, I have included some sample business cards. Note their simplicity, with only name, contact data, and employment objective, experience summary, or expertise. Do not attempt to condense your resume onto this small card, lest it look crowded and messy. However, do include one or two items that show you are a high achiever, such as a strong Grade Point Average or recent company award. As with your resume, do not design a flashy format or use colored paper. Again, this card is a reflection of you.

> **ajobs.com**
> Use a business card template to prepare your card online, then take to a printer.

Keep your business cards in an easily accessible place (*e.g.*, pocket or purse) and don't hesitate to exchange cards whenever you feel there is a possibility to develop a lead.

CHAPTER IV

STEP THREE:

GET THE INTERVIEW!

Part 1: The "Visible Market"

Part 2: Job Networking

Part 3: Useful Resources

Total employment in Atlanta is 2,136,600, divided into these:

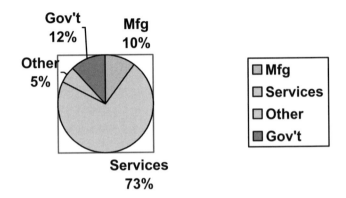

Almost three of every four employees in Atlanta is in a Service Producing Industry (excluding government employees):

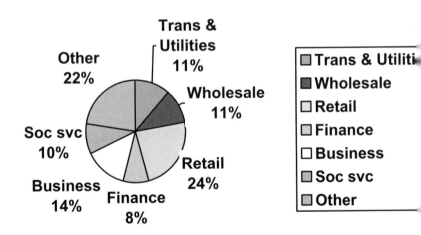

CHAPTER IV

Step Three: Get That Interview!

Plan your attack!

I hesitate for this to sound like a battle plan, but maybe that is a good analogy. At any rate, this must be as well-planned and organized as any military assault. Get out the armaments – that is, the supplies I listed in Chapter II; you will need them now.

In our case, the military assault becomes a marketing assault. Every company develops a strategy for positioning its product or service in front of its buying public. Likewise, you will plan how to spotlight yourself and/or your resume in order to obtain interviews, the next step toward your new job.

The CAREER SEARCH SYSTEM includes fifteen marketing tools with which to develop your marketing plan. Depending on your background, you most likely will not need all fifteen, but if you do, the System is here to help. Each tool works best for certain types or levels of applicants, and I have indicated that information at the beginning of the discussion of each tool under *"Pro's"* and *"Con's."* In addition, each tool also has certain advantages and disadvantages, and those also are discussed.

Beginning your job search

There are essentially two approaches to conducting a job search, depending on which "job market" you utilize:

- the "Visible Job Market," when the employer looks for you

- the "Hidden Job Market," when you look for the employer

The "Visible Job Market"

Career counselors generally agree that approximately 25% of all job vacancies fall into the first category, the "visible job market," which consists of those jobs that are
- advertised in classified want ads and web sites,
- recruited for by personnel agencies,
- available through job fairs,
- sought by corporate human resources departments, or
- available with federal, state, and local governments.

Locating these openings is the fastest and easiest course of action, and depending on your background, it may be all you will need to do. Individuals with experience in health care, computer science, or food service, for example, will find countless openings in their field through these sources. Applicants with between two and four years of career-related experience are always the most marketable, and they too may need only to tap into the "visible job market."

Nearly all job seekers will utilize these sources, and since they are easy and inexpensive, you too should use them. The CAREER SEARCH SYSTEM describes fully how to obtain the best results from each source, and you need only to follow the instructions.

The first eight sources described in this chapter address the correct procedure you should follow in order to

- mass-mail your resume or background data to companies

- establish direct contact with companies, either through their personnel department or with a department manager,

- utilize permanent and temporary personnel agencies and the services they offer,

- stand out from the crowd at job fairs,

- respond to classified want ads and jobs posted by companies and on web sites (Cover letters, salary histories, and other correspondences are discussed later in "Chapter VIII: Correspondence" and examples are given in Appendix B.), and

- apply for government positions.

Job Networking

In addition to this "visible job market," there are many other jobs available with companies, but as yet unadvertised and generally unknown, even within the company. There may be a planned addition, promotion, retirement, or replacement for which management has not yet begun a search. These plans may be only in the consideration stage now, awaiting further developments. In addition, companies often will create a new position if and when they find the "right" person.

These unpublicized openings are referred to as the **"Hidden Job Market,"** and experts generally agree that at least three-fourths of the jobs available at any time are part of this gray area. The primary way to locate them is through job networking, and Part 2 of this chapter details four methods to uncover them:
- Establishing a Job Network
- Attending networking clubs and meetings
- Networking through professional associations
- Using the "Information Interview"

Job networking is the most time-consuming and laborious method of job search, and to most job seekers, the most mysterious. Too few job seekers understand the importance of job networking, and even those who do, have little knowledge of how or where to begin. *And yet more applicants find their job through some form of job networking than all other sources combined!*

The importance of job networking cannot be over-stressed. At least 70% (and I have read articles suggesting 85%) of all applicants will obtain new employment through this method, and thus you must incorporate it into your job search. The CAREER SEARCH SYSTEM leads you through it step-by-step, and you will be surprised how easily your networking progresses.

The sooner you begin developing your job network the sooner you will be employed!

Other useful resources

Part 3 of this chapter describes three more tools and how to use them in your search:
- Public agencies
- Privately funded organizations
- Useful publications

Organizing your job search

If you have not yet organized according to the suggestions I outlined in Chapter II, you should do so now. Either order the **Atlanta Jobs Workbook** through CareerSource Publications, or download some of the forms online at **ajobs.com**. The **Atlanta Jobs Workbook** is a bargain at $19.95 and consists of a 3-ring binder with dividers and up to 75 useful forms which can be photocopied if you need more. Call for information or order by phone at (404) 262-7131, or order online at ajobs.com. This organization is more important than you may think, so don't shortcut.

Now have your business cards and resumes prepared, especially your oral, "30-second resume." Chapter III detailed why you need these documents and how to prepare them, and examples of written resumes and business cards are included in Appendix A. All three are vital to the success of your efforts throughout the job hunt, so prepare them well.

Next, plan your time. This is especially important if you are currently employed, since you will be limited in the amount of time you will have available for job search, and you must prioritize your efforts to maximize your results.[1]

If you are currently unemployed, how much time do you plan to spend job hunting? If your answer is other than at least 40 hours/week, think again! Perhaps being unemployed is an advantage here, since you will have enough time to conduct a thorough campaign. Continue to conduct your work-week as though you were still employed – which you are, only now your new job is finding a job. Refer back to Chapter II for a suggested weekly and daily time schedule.

You now are ready to begin your marketing assault. Read through every tool at least once, and then decide when and how you will use each one.

---

[1] For several reasons, companies prefer to hire individuals who are currently employed, and so I urge you not to resign your position in order to job hunt. Even if you are very unhappy with your job, I suggest you stick with it as long as possible, unless it becomes too difficult to conduct your job search effectively.

PART 1:

THE "VISIBLE JOB MARKET"

Tool #1: Mass Mailing

Tool #2: Internet Services and Web Sites

Tool #3: Direct Contact

Tool #4: Classified Advertising

Tool #5: Permanent Employment Agencies

Tool #6: Temporary Personnel Agencies

Tool #7: Job Fairs

Tool #8: Government Jobs

Tool #1: Direct Marketing

Pro's: Contacts a large number of companies, easy to do, minimal expense, can be done during non-business hours.

Con's: Least effective job search method, time and labor intensive.

Direct marketing, often referred to as "mass mailing," is the oldest and simplest method of job search, and undoubtedly the most popular. It can be done at your convenience during evenings, weekends, or at any time you are not busy with other activities. Since it requires no face-to-face or verbal contact, it feels comfortable or at least non-threatening. Thus, this approach is tried by almost every job seeker.

The down side is that it is far less productive than other methods. Nevertheless, since some applicants will find it successful and since you can plan it around your other job tools, you can use it also.

Resume with cover letter vs. "broadcast letter"

Most mass mailings include a resume with cover letter. This cover letter mentions information not included in your resume (*e.g.*, why you have chosen to contact them, salary requirements, geographic restrictions, etc.) and emphasizes highlights in your background that will encourage the reader to peruse your resume. (See "Chapter VIII: Correspondence" for a full description and Appendix B for examples.)

An alternative method, the "broadcast letter," has gained popularity. Essentially, the broadcast letter is a one page merger of the cover letter and the highlights of your resume. It tends to be more "reader friendly" by not including all of your experiences, but just the parts most likely to catch the reader's attention. It emphasizes accomplishments and achievements, and stresses what you can offer the company. Contact data is readily found and the reader is encouraged to call you for more information or an interview. Examples are included in "Appendix B: Correspondence."

The advantages to the broadcast letter are obvious. Since only one page is involved, it is simpler to handle and send. Since any correspondence with a resume attached is generally forwarded directly to Human Resources, this letter may be read more often by department managers. The primary disadvantage is of course that the reader has only limited information presented.

In speaking with applicants who have tried both methods, I have concluded that for most mass-mailing, the broadcast letter is equally as successful as the resume with cover letter, especially when you are contacting a hiring authority or department manager, not in human resources. Thus, use the broadcast letter with most of your mass-mailing, but use the resume/cover letter approach when you have reason to believe the company may have an opening for your experience.

Procedure

Determining which companies are more likely to have vacancies for your background will require some research on your part, but the pay-off will be worth the effort. You probably already know many companies and the detailed company profiles I have included in Appendix C will provide more. Using the reference materials in the last section of this chapter will help you identify still more.

As part of your overall organization, you should maintain a record of every company you contact and the results. You can make a list if you wish, but the simplest method is to keep a copy of your correspondence. This copy will include the date and the person you contacted, and you can write notes on the page regarding your activity there. Keep the pages in alphabetical order in a folder in your desk so that you can refer to it quickly when a representative of the company calls.

To whom should you address your correspondence? Most job seekers will send it to the generic "personnel department," where it will be added to the pile of resumes already received. The more enterprising job seekers will send it to a specific department that will be more likely to need their background. But the job seekers who will be employed first will seek out the name or at least the title of the person responsible for hiring their experience.

However, if you don't know the name or title and don't have the time or ability to research the data, send your letter to "Human Resources." Later when you have more time or better information, you can re-contact the company, directing your information to a more appropriate source.

Conclusion

I have included this job search technique as Tool #1 because it is the most popular approach and the one most job seekers try first. That is unfortunate, since it really should be your last effort, to be used only after you have tried other more productive tools.

Why is a "resume blizzard" so unproductive? There are several reasons:

• In Atlanta, almost every job seeker will contact Coca-Cola, Home Depot, BellSouth, et al. Can you imagine the number of unsolicited resumes these large companies receive daily? Do you really think their personnel recruiters have the time to review all those resumes? In fact, a corporate recruiter recently confided with me that her Human Resources department has cases of unopened letters.

• Determining to whom you will direct your information is very difficult. There may be several persons within the company who sometimes seek your expertise, and you cannot hope to contact each of them. Human Resources should know of all job vacancies, but that is often not the case. And unless you indicate some person or department on your envelope, your resume could end up anywhere in the organization.

• Most of the new jobs being created in today's economy are not with major corporations. In fact, one reads daily about down-sizing and lay-offs at the Fortune 500-type corporations. The growing job markets are in small- to medium-sized companies, generally not included on any list of companies you may locate.

Mass mailings work best for only certain types of job applicants, generally those with highly desirable experience. Otherwise, the more years of experience you have, the more frustrating you will find this method.

Now relax. The CAREER SEARCH SYSTEM describes at least sixteen basic sources, with variations and additions to each one. If this is not the right one for you, several others will be.

Tool #2: Internet Services and Web Sites

Pro's: Free or low cost, many job listings for Atlanta and nationwide, useful at all levels and disciplines, good research tool and easier than traveling to local library, will have many useful articles, most have resume database

Con's: Must have access to computer with modem or Internet access, jobs posted are just like other classified ads, so many sites and too little time

If you are not using ajobs.com as an integral part of your job search, you are running at half-pace!

Our site (www.ajobs.com) will link you to hundreds of extremely helpful web sites, all free. We include company web sites and their Atlanta job vacancies lists; commercial sites such as Monster, HotJobs, CareerBuilder, etc; government job sites; *The Atlanta Journal-Constitution* classifieds; Atlanta personnel agencies and their specialties; job networking groups and directions; free downloads and job search tips; professional associations; and much more. To keep your spirits up, we also have links to several comic strips!

Free internet access is available at the metro-Atlanta public libraries, most colleges, and the Georgia Department of Labor's state employment offices. Also, you can use the super-fast T-1 lines at the US Government Store, operated by the General Services Administration at 675 Ponce de Leon Avenue (Atlanta's City Hall East). Their computers have links to all

ajobs.com
Links to the largest and most popular commercial sites, plus hundreds of Atlanta companies and their job vacancies.

sorts of information in addition to job sources. For a reasonable fee, you can access the internet at all metro-Kinko Copy Centers.

Internet Sites

Only four years ago, I began to include the internet as a tool to use in your job search. At that time, few companies had a web site and only a few commercial sites existed that listed job vacancies or maintained a resume database.

Now every company has a site, usually including their job vacancies, and many encourage you to apply on-line or provide you with an e-mail address. I cannot even begin to count the number of commercial sites that now exist, both all-purpose and as well as for specific target groups. Then add in 300+ personnel agencies, all listing job vacancies at their sites. It's almost become too much of a good thing, and the problem now is that far more web sites exist than anyone could possibly utilize.

I cannot describe all the sites here, but I have included a critique of many on **ajobs.com**, with links to the most useful and easiest to use. I would greatly appreciate feedback concerning them and others you use successfully. Also consider using smaller, niche sites (e.g., professional associations) or local sites (e.g., **ajobs.com** which is Atlanta specific) if you find these sites overwhelming.

America's Job Bank (www.ajb.dni.us) Produced by the US Department of Labor, this site contains more than 1,500,000 current listings and 2,500,000 available job seekers.

The Monster Board (www.monster.com) Boasts the largest number of job vacancies, and includes employer profiles, a resume database, and online resume distribution. You may find it to be large and unwieldy.

HotJobs (www.hotjobs.com) Key word search again is good, but less convenient. Allows you to search by company.

Career Builder (www.careerbuilder.com) Searches 70+ other job sites. Parent of former headhunter, CareerMosaic, and CareerPath.

MonsterTrak (Formerly JobTrak, now owned by Monster) The dominant player in the college job listing and resume markets. However, in order to access the job listings submitted by the various career centers, you first must contact your college career center or student employment office for a password. (Most career centers allow "pathway" access from on-campus computers.)

Direct Employer Owned and managed by a non-profit association of employers, so supposedly is checked first by their member companies. Jobs posted by staffing firms and employers.

FlipDog Forbes Magazine's "Best of the Web -- Top Pick" Uses search engine to locate jobs from employer sites, claims faster postings.

All USA Jobs Although less well-known, probably the most user friendly (little verbage, right to the point), especially for locating jobs close to your home (allows search by zip code).

Atlanta Job Post New site exclusively for Atlanta job seekers. Allows keyword job search, resume posting, and job search robot.

Georgia Department of Labor Job Information System (**www.dol.state.ga.us**) Includes list of services offered by the Georgia Department of Labor, locations of local employment offices, and hundreds of job openings by profession and location.

Office of Personnel Management (**www.usajobs.opm.gov**) Lists thousands of federal government jobs and how to apply.

Other helpful web sites

Again, all of these sites can be quickly accessed through our web site at **www.ajobs.com**.

www.tripquest.com Now you have no excuse for being late to an interview because you could not find the company's office. This site allows you to type in your current address and the address you are seeking, and then shows maps of your location, the company's location, and an overall map of the area, plus text directions for every step of the way. It even gives the total distance in miles and the estimated driving time.

www.homefair.com This site contains everything you need to evaluate a relocation, including a salary assessment of your current location and potential location. It also ranks school districts, reveals local crime statistics, and lists real estate firms and mortgage brokers.

www.databaseamerica.com For a $3 fee, you can obtain a wealth of information on companies that will be helpful in preparing for interviews. It also offers a free people locator, allowing you to search for persons nationwide and obtain their address and phone number.

www.jobconnection.com This user friendly site lists the members of the Georgia Association of Personnel Services. Especially helpful is the ability to select agencies by their specialty.

www.vistaprint.com "Free" business cards – free except for the $5.95 shipping charge, still a good bargain.

Still more and newer sites are catagorized and grouped for easy use on **ajobs.com**. Keep me posted on any I have omitted and your comments about their helpfulness.

Posting your resume

All the commercial sites allow you to post your background for perusal by interested companies, and many companies encourage you to complete an online application form, "resume builder," or some other method of leaving your information in their database to be retrieved later when a need for your experience arises. Prioritize your time and complete these forms at night or some other spare time, leaving your days for networking or something else more productive. I have spoken with job seekers who have been contacted from this source, so do list with the largest commercial sites and companies in which you have a strong interest.

A few cautions however:

- <u>Never</u> include sensitive information such as Social Security number or date of birth, and be wary of any site that requests it.

- Before posting, find out when it will be deleted. You don't want it to remain after you have secured employment.

- If possible, mask confidential information such as telephone numbers and your name, and consider using a disposable email address which you can eliminate later.

Conclusion

Although you may think responding to online job postings is a constructive use of time, remember that only 3-5% of job seekers will find employment by blindly answering these ads. When you find a job opening, instead of sending your resume and hoping for the best, try to locate a source in the company who will take your resume to human resources or the hiring authority. This procedure is discussed further in the Job Networking section later.

Tool #3: Direct Contact

Pro's: Works best for first job changers, and persons seeking a specific industry or company. Good approach for individuals with experience and knowledge in one industry.

Con's: Labor intensive, especially in locating hiring authorities. Less effective for applicants with extensive experience that is not in one industry.

To cold call companies without having reason to suspect they might have an opening for your background is at best a long shot and a worst a total waste of your time. In today's voice-mail world, you are very unlikely to directly reach someone who could help you. Spend your time wisely, and only cold-call the companies that you suspect have occasional vacancies in your discipline.

Mounting a Direct Contact Campaign

Scan through the list of companies in Appendix C and then using a highlighting marking pen, mark those in which you have an interest and those that hire in your specialty. I have included a description of their operations and hiring procedures, as well as the types of applicants frequently sought and whether the company seeks entry-level and/or experienced personnel.

Next, add several pages in your notebook to record your efforts. Use the sample form "Company Cold Calling" or one similar, which you will have downloaded from **ajobs.com** – other forms are included in the **Atlanta Jobs Workbook**, as well In addition to the large corporations detailed in Appendix C, you may know of other companies who hire in your field or for your specialty and that you wish to contact.

Whom should I contact?[1]

This is a debatable question, with many career counselors giving one answer and personnel managers another. As with most debates, there are good reasons to support both sides.

Most, if not all, career counselors suggest that you should make your initial company contact with a "hiring authority," that is, a department manager who has control over the personnel requirements in that department. One reason is that this person may have current or projected personnel needs that have not been requisitioned from Human Resources or Personnel Recruiting. Secondly, this manager will most likely be the ultimate decision-maker with whom you would eventually interview, and thus you are a step ahead by starting here. This logic concludes that Personnel Departments are often another hurdle and should be by-passed when possible.

There are many reasons why Personnel Departments may not be aware of all the needs within their companies. A manager often will have plans to add to or alter the department in the future, and if your background fits the need, he/she may consider going ahead with the change now. Also, some department heads prefer to hire direct, rather than using their recruiting staff, who may be busy with other assignments. Furthermore, some companies are very decentralized and encourage managers to conduct their own personnel search and hiring. There are many other reasons, too, more than we can discuss here.

Most personnel managers would disagree with those assumptions, and strongly feel that you should contact them first. It is their function within the company to interview and screen applicants, following federal and local statutes, as well as company policies and procedures; these guidelines may be unknown to executives attempting to conduct their own hiring. These personnel professionals have been trained to

---

[1]Although the vogue designation for the generic term "Personnel Department" is now "Human Resources," not all companies use that name. In addition, larger companies will also have a separate Recruiting or Staffing specialty within Human Resources. Although there can be definite distinctions, I have used these terms fairly interchangeably, and for our purposes here, that is adequate.

73

interview carefully and thoroughly, and they should be more in tune to the overall needs of the company, not just one department.

In addition, some department managers may find your contact a nuisance, and you will be off to a bad start. Personnel may feel you are trying to short-circuit them, and they too will be annoyed. And finally, some companies have a firm policy that all initial contacts with applicants must be through Personnel.

But perhaps the best reason for contacting Personnel is simply expedience. Large companies will have many department managers over your specialty, and you cannot expect to contact all of them. Also, you may not have the time or resources to trace all the hiring authorities within a company. In these cases, you must utilize the company's Personnel Department.

Although in my practice I generally work with Personnel, I adhere more to the former reasoning. I understand Personnel's concerns, but tend to agree that contacting a hiring authority is more productive, especially when you have a friend or source within the company who can tell you whom to contact. (Of course, this person may also tell you that the company requires you to start with Personnel.)

Don't totally ignore Personnel, however. You can cover both bases by contacting a hiring authority and sending your resume to Personnel.

"Cold Calling"

Now comes the laborious part: "cold calling" each company. In your "cold calling" section, list the companies you plan to contact, using a form included in the **Atlanta Jobs Wookbook** or one you have created. Ideally, you should speak by phone personally with an official at each company, but that is not always possible. The company representative may not be available, or you may not have the time or facility, especially if you are currently employed. In these cases, you

jobs.com
Purchase the Workbook online or call (404) 262-7131. No shipping charges on phone orders.

74

should send a resume and include a cover letter. (The cover letter is explained in Chapter VIII.)

Many people have a fear of the phone, and if you are one of them, you need to overcome this dread. Preparing and rehearsing what you plan to say on the phone will help, as well as having your "30-Second Resume" prepared and ready to use. I mentioned earlier that you would be using this oral resume often, and now is one of those times. If you missed the discussion of this topic, it was described in Part 2 of "Chapter III: Preparing Your Resumes."

Procedure to follow

Regardless of whether you contact Personnel or a department manager, the procedure is the same. When the company receptionist answers your call, ask for the Whomever (the department or job you will to contact, or the department manager you are seeking). When Whomever's secretary answers, say, "Hello. My name is Whatever, and I am seeking a position in _____(or as a _____). May I speak with Whomever?" Most likely at this point, you will be instructed to send your resume, in which case ask for the name of the person to whom you should address it, and record the name in your notebook. Don't be upset, however, if you are not given the name; some companies have a policy forbidding the disclosure of employee names. For quicker turnaround, ask if you can fax or email your information.

If you actually do get the opportunity to speak with Whomever, you must be prepared. This is your chance to make a positive impression, have a brief telephone interview, and schedule a personal interview also. Fortunately, you are a tempo ahead, because you already have composed and rehearsed a brief summary of your qualifications – the "30-second resume." You may have only one shot here, so make it count.

If it appears that they do have an interest or need for your background, offer to come for a personal interview, if this is possible for you. If you are talking with the company's interviewer, you must be ready for this telephone interview. Prepare and practice your interviewing techniques in advance, and don't be caught by surprise. (See "Chapter V: Interviewing Techniques.")

If your contact states that there are no job opportunities available there, try to turn the call into a networking or information call. Ask for suggestions in your job search. Is he/she aware of openings with other companies for your background? Even better, would he/she consider spending a few minutes with you in an "information interview." This "information interview" is discussed later in the chapter as "Tool #9" and you should have read that section before beginning your "cold calling." (Actually, you should read this entire book at least once before beginning any part of your job search.)

Assuming you were instructed to send your resume, you will also need to include a cover letter or other appropriate form. Chapter VIII is a thorough discussion of correspondence, especially cover letters, email forms, and fax cover sheets, and several examples are included in Appendix B. In the closing paragraph of your correspondence, you will have said that you plan to telephone them in a few days. Definitely do so. You want to know if your resume was received or lost along the way, and if it has been reviewed. Does the company have an opening for someone with your credentials? Is it being routed to another department or department manager? Are there any questions they would like to ask or additional information they need? As always, record the results of your phone call in your notebook.

Finally, you will recall that I suggested you contact department managers whenever possible; but this is not to say that you should ignore Human Resources or Recruiting. In fact, if you are told by the department manager that no opening currently exists, I suggest you also contact Personnel. Individual departments and their managers seldom keep a resume file, but Human Resources often maintains a resume database, and another need for your background may arise later.

Even if the department manager does request your resume, you may wish to send one to Personnel as well, especially if you do not hear back from this manager within a reasonable time period. This is because the manager may be too busy with other projects to consider you now, but there may be another opening somewhere else within the company. Also, just as Personnel may not be aware of projected needs within all departments, those department managers may not be aware of upper management's plans.

In summary, don't look upon personnel departments as just another hurdle to be avoided whenever possible, but rather utilize them when necessary or expedient. They have a purpose within their companies, and you should make use of it.

Telephone Etiquette

On many of your phone calls, you may be connected with your party's voice mail, and you will be asked to leave your name, phone number, and "a brief message." I nearly always do leave a message and have been pleasantly surprised at the high rate of times I have had my call returned.

I too have voice mail, to cover the times when I am out of my office or otherwise unavailable to receive calls. My pet peeve has become the callers who leave an incoherent or inaudible message, and I am forced to replay the message several times. For example,

• they speak so rapidly that I cannot understand, especially in relaying their phone number;

• they have an unusual name or a foreign name that is difficult to understand or spell;

• their message is garbled or their thoughts are unorganized.

On those occasions when you are referred to an answering device, I suggest you do leave a message, but with the knowledge that a poor message will have created a poor impression, and that may result in your call not being returned. Thus, plan in advance what message you will leave. Speak your name and phone number clearly, leave your prepared message (short and well-enunciated), then repeat your name and phone number. End your message with "Thank you and I look forward to speaking with you soon." Unless your name is a very common name like Smith or Jones, you should spell it.

Conclusion

The CAREER SEARCH SYSTEM outlines many different and effective sources for obtaining interviews and job offers, and not all of them will apply to you. Quite frankly, the direct contact source has limited success unless you fit one of these categories:

1) You have extensive experience within one industry or discipline, and that experience would be useful to most companies within that industry or discipline.

2) You have less than five years experience and can still be cross-trained into other functions within your discipline.

3) You have highly desirable experience or academic background.

If you do not fit into one of those descriptions, the direct contact source is not the one where you should be concentrating your efforts. That is my major complaint with books that list thousands of companies and suggest that you call, contact, or send your resume to as many as possible. There are other sources in the CAREER SEARCH SYSTEM that will benefit you more.

Tool #4: Classified Advertisements

Pro's: Cheap and easy source of many listings, covering all disciplines and levels. Good place to start. Good source to locate personnel agencies, as well as companies not using agencies, and small companies with infrequent needs. Often quotes salary. Local companies can be quick interviews. Thousands of ads free online.

Con's: You can get lost in the crowd of responses. May be difficult to discern good opportunities.

For obtaining employment in Atlanta, the largest source of announced openings is contained in the classified ads section of the Sunday edition of *The Atlanta Journal-Constitution*. It is a "must" in your job search. If you are currently living in Atlanta, you probably already receive it; if not, here is the procedure to order a subscription:

> **ajobs.com**
> Use the link to the AJ-C classified ads and web sites listing job openings.

• In Atlanta, call (404) 522-4141. You will be billed or you can charge the fee on a credit card.

• Out of Atlanta, but in Georgia, call (800) 933-9771. Same procedure as above.

• Out of Georgia, call (800) 933-9771. Subscription rate varies by location and you must pay in advance or charge to a credit card.

This Sunday section is by far the largest in the Southeast. Within the fifty or so pages of ads will be up to 10,000 job openings, advertised by both companies and personnel agencies. These openings are listed alphabetically, by job category (accountants, data processing, engineers, sales, etc.).

In addition to locating current job openings, perusing these ads can yield other information. You can determine which disciplines and industries are growing, because these will be mentioned most often. Conversely, shrinking job categories will be conspicuous by their absence. If you are contemplating a career change or undecided on which career to pursue (as so many recent college grads are), reviewing these ads can help you decide. Further, if there is a retailer near you who sells many newspapers from across the country, you can compare the size of the want ads from several cities to get an idea of the job prospects in each city. Not surprisingly, you will find that Atlanta's want ads are among the largest in the country.

In choosing which ads to consider, keep in mind that if the ad sounds too good to be true, it probably is. The newspaper tries to screen clients, but bogus or misleading ads sometimes slip by. Here is one clue: if you call a company, and someone answers with the phone number and then refuses to reveal the company's name, hang up!

Procedure

Peruse the job categories that apply to you and circle in red the openings, both company and personnel agency, for which you plan to apply. If the ad is an internet listing, download the information. After you have finished scrutinizing the ads, cut out the company (not personnel agency) ads you circled and tape them onto blank pages to put in your notebook, in the section you labeled "Classified Ads." Leave lots of empty space beside the ads, to record your activity with them, including dates contacted and results.

Next, cut out the personnel agency (permanent and temporary) ads. You may notice that one agency is advertising several jobs for which you will want to apply. Write the name of each agency at the top of a page and then tape the corresponding ads to the page, and include it in your "Personnel Agencies" section. Leave space on the page to record activity with that agency.

Now go back to the company ads and contact each one. If the company included its phone number or did not specifically forbid phone calls, I suggest you call them and ask if you can speak with someone regarding the opening. If you do get through to the recruiter, you must be prepared for an interview then, so before calling, you should study "Chapter V: Interviewing Techniques." Also, here is another opportunity to use your "30-second resume"!

Most likely, however, you will be instructed to mail your resume before you speak with anyone personally regarding the position. Politely ask to whom you should address the resume, and record the information in your notebook. Including that person's name on your cover page or envelope is an optional but personal touch, and some recruiters will note it. Don't be surprised, however, if the receptionist has been instructed not to give out that information. In this case, be certain to include on the cover page or envelope "Attn: Engineering Recruiter," or whatever corporate function you are seeking. Always ask if you can fax or email your information.

Along with your resume, you will include a cover letter or other fact sheet. Refer to Chapter VIII for a description and to Appendix B for illustrations. In your notebook, record the date you sent your resume, when you called to follow-up, and the results.

If you have sent your resume to a company, plan to call them in a few days to confirm that your resume was received. Ask if there are questions or additional information needed to complete your application. And, of course, offer to come for an interview at their convenience.

Just as you would prepare for a face-to-face interview, be ready for a phone screening also. Telephone interviews are usually short and cover only basic information. Typical questions will revolve around why you are seeking new employment and if you have the background needed for the job. If you pass this quick test, you will be invited for an interview.

Personnel Services Ads

Responding to personnel agency advertisements will be slightly dif-ferent, and after reading the next two sections describing permanent and temporary agencies, you will better understand the distinctions.

Whenever possible, call them before sending a resume. By talking with them first, you can ascertain if you fit their available openings and whether or not that particular agency will be able to help you. Operating procedures vary from agency to agency, some requiring that you send a resume first, others requesting you to come in for a personal interview and bring your resume. If you are instructed to send your resume, ask to whose attention it should be sent and record that name in your notebook on the page for that agency. Some agencies will have several persons handling the same opening, and so there may not be a specific contact person.

A formal cover letter is not necessary to send to agencies, although you may if that is convenient. Just a short typed or handwritten note with your salary requirements and restrictions (if any) is sufficient. Keep in mind, however, that this note is the agency's first impression of you and you must impress them in order to be referred to their client. Additional information on the use of these interview sources is contained in the next two sections of this chapter.

"Blind Ads"

Oftentimes companies advertise their job vacancies without identifying themselves, and you are instructed to mail your resume to a post office box number. These are called "blind ads," since they do not reveal the name of the employer. You may be interested in the openings but hesitant to reveal your name and information without knowing whom you are contacting. I have heard of individuals who responded to a blind ad, only to learn that the ad was submitted by their own company! Unfortunately, their employment was terminated as a result.

Other Sources of Classified Advertising

In addition to newspapers, another excellent source of classified ads is professional and trade magazines. If you have access to any periodicals in your field, review them and answer any classified ads that seem fruitful; these ads are usually on the last few pages of the publication. Respond to them as you would a newspaper ad. This source is especially helpful in determining which personnel agencies specialize in your field, since they are the ones that would place advertisements in specific trade journals.

Internet Web Sites

In the past few years, numerous computer on-line services have emerged to help job seekers. Most of them include a large section of classified ads, boasting upwards of a half-million job vacancies nationally and internationally. Refer to "Tool #2: Computer Services" earlier in this chapter for a description of several of the largest of these on-line firms and for their web addresses. These job postings are essentially the same as classified ads, and you should treat them as such.

| **ajobs.com** |
| Links you to the Atlanta-specific areas of these sites. |

The easiest way to link up with these databases is through ajobs.com. Our site includes comments about the contents of these gigantic and unwieldy web sites and will allow you to connect directly to the Atlanta-specific areas.

Most corporations now list their current needs and career opportunities on their web site, many encouraging you to apply on line. When you respond to a classified ad or job listing you found on the Internet, definitely mention that in your cover letter. Companies are looking for applicants who are computer savvy and that will be a significant boost to your application.

| **ajobs.com** |
| Provides a direct link to the Atlanta-specific job listings for hundreds of local companies. |

Conclusion

Here's a final word on classified ads, and this applies to direct contact and personnel agencies as well. A personal, face-to-face interview is always preferable to indirect contact, regardless of how good your resume looks. Thus, whenever possible, try to be seen, rather than just heard. If you are very interested in a specific position and have been able to speak with a company interviewer on the phone, press for an interview time or at least offer to bring by your resume in person. And if you do deliver your resume in person, ask to simply meet the interviewer, if he/she is available.

Tool #5: Permanent Employment Agencies

Pro's: Probably the largest source of job openings. Easy and convenient. Good agencies will supply you not only with interviews, but also information on the company, the job, and the interviewer. Can work well at all levels and fields. Usually free. Good source for quick interviews.

Con's: Not usually successful for hard-to-place applicants. Not easy to find most useful agencies. Fee sometimes involved, especially at lower-level openings.

The number of job openings represented collectively by the various personnel agencies in Atlanta can be numbered in the tens of thousands. There are several hundred of these agencies in Atlanta – more than twenty pages in the BellSouth Yellow Pages and in at least three different listing categories. Because they represent so many companies and opportunities, they should be an invaluable source for you.

> **ajobs.com**
> Lists agencies, their specialites, addresses, and web links when available.

Oftentimes, this industry receives a lot of bad press, much of it deservedly so. Some of these firms are excellent and do a very creditable job, and thus they are highly regarded and utilized by their client companies. But unfortunately, some agencies are downright awful. How do you select one?

First of all, don't select one; select several. Every agency would like to have you as its exclusive applicant, but "putting all your eggs in one basket" is not in your best interest. Be suspicious of an agency that asks you to wait in their office several hours while they attempt to arrange an interview; they are preventing you from maximum exposure. Rather, make yourself available to whichever agencies can present you to the best companies and positions.

Understand, too, that every agency specializes in a certain level (entry, middle management, executive, etc.) or areas (clerical, management, engineering, etc.), and there are probably personnel agencies or individuals within an agency that specialize in your field. Your task is to zero in on the ones that handle applicants at your level and in your field of specialty, without trying to call every personnel agency listed in the phone book.

Selecting your agencies

The Georgia Association of Personnel Services (GAPS) publishes a directory of their membership, including the specialties of each member. I have included that information in Appendix D, although you can order an updated copy for $6.95 by calling (770) 952-3178 and following instructions. However, there are excellent agencies who are not members of GAPS and thus I suggest you follow this procedure:

> **ajobs.com**
> GAPS is linked and you can download the membership roster.

• *Call corporate human resources departments.* The best method for locating older, more established agencies is to call the personnel department (or a specific department manager) of a few major Atlanta companies and ask which permanent employment firms they use for your discipline and if they would recommend a specific recruiter there. This has the advantage of not only finding an agency, but also talking with a corporate personnel professional who may have other suggestions as well. In addition, when you then call the agencies that were recommended, be certain to mention the company and/or the individual who recommended them, and I guarantee you will get a warm reception!

• *Read the classified ads.* You also should contact newer agencies, since they often are more aggressive and may give you more attention. These agencies probably will advertise in the Sunday classified section of *The Atlanta Journal-Constitution.* Pick out the agencies that are advertising for positions that interest you and contact two or three.

• _Network._ Ask friends and business associates which agencies they have used and would recommend. When attending job networking or professional association meetings, ask several people if they have used an agency or recommend one. This is especially helpful if the person you ask has a background similar to your own.

• _Check with college career placement departments._ If you graduated from a local college, check with the Career Placement Department and ask for recommendations. In addition, you can call a university's academic department that covers your background, and ask if they are aware of agencies that specialize in your field.

• _Review the telephone Yellow Pages._ Although you should not waste your time calling every agency in the phone book, nevertheless you should peruse the Yellow Pages under the headings "Employment Agencies" and "Executive Search Consultants" to see if there are agencies who specialize in your field. Oftentimes these agencies will have your industry as part of their name (_e.g._, "Restaurant Recruiters" or "Insurance Personnel Search") or they may have a display ad that mentions your specialty.

• _Locate specialized periodicals._ Still another excellent source is the back pages of trade newspapers and magazines. Agencies who advertise in these specialized journals usually concentrate on that discipline in their recruiting.

Lastly, to inquire if there are complaints about any agencies in general or specifically about the one(s) you are considering, call the Atlanta Better Business Bureau at (404) 688-4910.

Contacting your agencies

Once you have selected the agencies that you plan to useand if you are in Atlanta, you should visit them personally for two reasons:

1) to determine if they can adequately represent you or if you want them to represent you, and

2) to make a personal impression on them, so they can better present you to their clients.

If you are not local, call them to see if they can help you. If you are asked to send in a resume, do so, and then call back in a few days to check on the activity in your behalf. Ask them frankly if they will be able to arrange interviews and in what time frame. Be polite, but persistent. Can they help you or are you wasting your time? When would they like for you to call again? Do they have any suggestions for you? Since they have reviewed your resume, ask for their opinion.

Types of Personnel Agencies

Understanding the nature of personnel agencies and how they work will enable you to better utilize their services. Most importantly, realize that they are not philanthropic organizations; they are in business to make a profit. Their income is derived entirely from fees collected through their efforts at matching applicants with client companies.

Agencies can be broadly categorized into three groups, related to their primary sources of income:
- Executive search firms
- Temporary agencies
- Contingency agencies

Executive search firms, sometimes called "headhunters," are retained by companies to search for specific personnel needs, generally upper-level executives, and are paid in advance by the retaining company. Since they work on a limited number of specific cases, they generally are not a good source for entry- and mid-level positions. Senior-level executives, however, may benefit from search firms that specialize in their area of expertise.

Temporary agencies derive their income from providing companies with contract labor, for which the company pays the agency and the agency in turn pays the laborers. Oftentimes these contracts will be long-term and many positions may become permanent at some

88

future date. The use of temporary agencies has increased tremendously in the past few years, and thus a detailed discussion explaining how to use these agencies is included in the next section as Tool #5.

By far the largest number of agencies falls into the third group, called **contingency agencies**, and these will be your best source to call. These firms are paid only when one of their applicants accepts employment through their efforts with one of their client companies, and thus, their fee is contingent upon making the placement. These agencies will have many job openings in many diverse industries and with many different companies, and some of these companies also may have listed the same opening with other agencies.

Remember that since they are paid only when they make a job placement, they are most interested in applicants who fit the current needs of their clients, and if you are more difficult to place than another applicant, you will not get as much attention. When talking with them, state your employment objective, but be as flexible as possible and listen to their suggestions. However, you are under no obligation to accept any interview that does not meet your standards.

Interview with the agency as though it is the company with whom you hope to be employed. Many companies have established a strong rapport with the agency(s) they use and have great confidence in the agency's opinion. Thus, you must impress the agency enough to be referred on to these key clients.

At the end of your interview, ask how soon you can expect to hear from them and when you will be sent on an interview. Also, seek their frank appraisal of your resume and interviewing skills, and ask if they have any suggestions or recommendations for you to consider.

During this interview, you should ask questions that will help you to evaluate the agency, the agency interviewer, and the assistance they can offer you. Personnel agencies have notoriously high employee turnover, and it is not unlikely that this interviewer has been at the job for only a very short while. If this is the case, an opinion of your resume and interviewing skills may be totally useless. In addition, this trainee may not understand your background and experience, and will not be able to present you to potential clients.

Working with Agencies

You have every reason to expect the agencies you select to treat you honestly and fairly. They should never send you on interviews for which you are not qualified[1] or refer you to positions in which you have no interest. You should be briefed before each interview regarding the nature of the position, promotional potential, salary range, and company background. The best agencies will maintain files in their office of company literature for you to peruse, including annual reports and recruiting information, especially for their best clients. Many agencies also know their client's interviewers and interviewing techniques.

In return, you should treat your agencies with the same respect you expect from them. If you are not interested in a specific interview, tell the agency why; this will help your recruiter to be more selective for future interviews. Always show up for your interviews or advise the agency well in advance to cancel; most agencies will not work with you once you have failed to show for an scheduled interview. Call your agency recruiter immediately after each interview to relay your impressions of the interview.

Your personnel agencies' recruiters can become good, professional friends, and you should treat them as you would other professionals. I still talk with applicants I placed more than twenty years ago!

Agency Contracts and Fees

---

[1] Over the years, I have had many candidates insist that if I would just set the interview for them, they would "sell themselves" enough to get the job, regardless of their lack of qualifications. I never would waste their time or my clients' time in such a fruitless arrangement, and they often could not understand why. Believe me, an agency that somehow finagles you an interview for which you are not at all qualified is not doing you any favors. They are wasting your time and their (soon-to-be-former) clients' patience.

If the agency requires you to sign a contract, read it carefully before you sign and be sure to get a copy. Agency contracts are fairly standard, and generally speaking, you need not worry about signing one. The important facts to know are these:

1) You do not have to accept any offer extended unless you are sure it is what you are seeking. Do not allow the agency to pressure you into accepting a position you do not want.

2) No fee is involved until you do accept employment as a result of their service.[1]

However, before you accept a position through a personnel agency, be certain you understand your legal liability, if any, to the agency. For example, are there any circumstances under which you may be held responsible for all or part of the fee? Are you required to remain with the company for a period of time before your liability to the agency expires? If the company defaults on the fee, are you obligated for it? If you are uncomfortable with any part of the contract, get a written waiver from the agency before you accept the position.

When I first began agency recruiting twenty years ago, most personnel agencies accepted job openings that were both "fee paid" (*i.e.*, the hiring company pays the agency fee) and "non-fee paid" (*i.e.*, the applicant pays the fee). Times have changed, and now most professional-level personnel agencies now handle only positions in which the hiring company pays the agency's fee, and these "fee paid" positions cost you nothing. I strongly recommend that you restrict your initial agency contacts to those handling only "fee paid" openings, and if necessary, you can call the other agencies later.

---

[1] There is one extenuating circumstance of which you should be aware. In the past, I have seen agency contracts that required a portion of your salary increase, should you accept a counter-offer from your present company. The basis for this is that your increase is a direct result of their efforts in obtaining you other employment, which then forced your present company to make you the counter-offer. Thus, before accepting a counter-offer, confirm that you are under no contractual obligation to the agency or that your present company will pay the fee.

However, if you have limited qualifications (and this often happens to trainees), you may find yourself in the uncomfortable position of considering a position that requires you to pay a fee. I personally have a strong disdain for companies that will not pay an agency fee and yet willingly hire through personnel agencies, knowing that the high expense of the agency fee will be passed on to their new employee. Nevertheless, if you find yourself in this situation, be absolutely, 100% certain you want that job before you saddle yourself with the large financial burden of an agency fee. Try to negotiate with the agency for a lesser amount or with the company for a reimbursement later. Better still, stay away from this situation to begin with.

Agency Scams

There is one more situation you unfortunately may encounter: the "up-front fee" agency or some other business that requires you to pay a fee in advance of any job assistance. This fee can soar up to several thousand dollars for "counseling" or resume distribution. Outlawed in many states, some of these scams will pose as personnel agencies and sell you lists of alleged job openings, guarantee you employment after their fee is paid, or some other useless "service."

Atlanta has had its share of these operations. Just recently I read of an FBI sting on a business here that guaranteed overseas employment for a fee of $295, but in fact had no jobs to offer and kept the money. Beware of these crooks and before you hand over your money, ask for references or call the Better Business Bureau.[1]

Summary

Personnel agencies, both permanent and temporary, can be an excellent source and you should use them when possible, but recognize they do have limitations. If you are seeking employment in a very narrow field (*e.g.*, public relations or staff marketing), they likely will

---

[1] I must make a distinction between these shams and legitimate "outplacement" firms and reputable job coaches. Those firms can be very helpful and are often part of a severance package offered by employers. If you have doubts as to a firm's legitimacy, check their references.

be of little help. If there is something in your background that makes you less marketable than their other applicants, you will not have good results with them. As I stated before, the best approach with agencies is to ask for a frank analysis of the help they can offer you.

I frequently speak with applicants who have been offended by a personnel agency – not that they were really mistreated, but rather they were made to feel like one of the herd, impersonal and dehumanized. Instead of "good-bye," they wanted to say "moo" or "baa." Perhaps their interview was cold, short, and perfunctory, or frequently interrupted. Another major complaint I often hear is that phone calls were not returned promptly, or even at all.

I won't make excuses for this behavior on the part of agencies, but I will explain why it happens, and I even will admit some guilt myself. Remember back to the resume chapter when I stated that I often receive up to 100 or so responses per advertisement. Then you must understand that each personnel agent will be handling many, many applicants at all times. Unfortunately, we often do not have enough time to appease everyone and still do our work.

So don't let yourself be offended to the point of cutting yourself off from any possible source of leads and interviews. Your purpose is to use the agencies for your benefit, and don't lose sight of that objective, regardless of how you may feel toward the agency. I assure you that they mean no personal affront.

However, should you have a complaint regarding the ethics of a specific agency, you may seek redress through the Georgia Association of Personnel Services. Members of GAPS supposedly adhere to a code of ethics and you can register your complaint by calling their Atlanta office at (770) 952-3178.

And remember, this source is only one of the many you have available. Don't make the mistake of waiting for an agency to find you a job when you have other sources to tap.

Tool #6: Temporary Employment Agencies

Pro's: Quick source of income, offers possibility of permanent job, good networking source, variety of companies and assignments, maintains skills.

Con's: Often low salary, difficult to explore other companies while employed, not permanent, limited benefits, no promotional opportunity.

Companies sometimes need additional help, but for many reasons are reluctant to take on new, permanent employees. An increasingly popular solution to this dilemma is to hire temporary employees, utilizing the services of a temporary employment agency.

Temporary agencies derive their income from providing companies with contract labor, for which the company pays the agency and the agency in turn pays the laborers. Most often this is for hourly or clerical work, but some firms offer long-term contracts, especially for engineers, computer technicians, and other specialized workers. There are also temporary agencies specializing in short-term professional-level openings, most often in accounting and data processing.

Many companies have discovered the advantages of hiring temporaries. Labor costs are cut, since the company does not pay benefits or payroll taxes and does not need to maintain personnel records. "Temps," as they are euphemistically termed, are hired only for as long as needed or to fill a short-term replacement. There usually is no interviewing process and temps are available almost instantly.

Some individuals maintain a career working temp. They cite the variety of jobs and companies, the freedom to work when they want, and the knowledge gained from working different assignments as the advantages of this career path. However, for our discussion we will consider temporary employment only as a stepping stone to permanent positions.

In a recent report aired on National Public Radio, the reporter stated that of the total new jobs created in the past year, one in five was for a temporary employee. Moreover, in my recent survey of Atlanta's largest employers, 90+% indicated they regularly employ temps.

Working a temporary assignment offers you three new options for finding other employment:

(1) The position may be "temp-to-hire."

(2) While on the assignment, you can job network through other company employees, vendors, or clients.

(3) Once inside the company, you can review the company's in-house job postings and apply for other employment there.

"Temp-to-hire"

"Temp-to-hire," also called "temp-to-perm," positions are jobs that are classified by the company as temporary, but may become permanent within a short period. These positions may be for any discipline, including clerical, accounting, engineering, data processing, marketing, etc., and can be for short- or long-term assignments. When applying through a temporary agency, always ask what they have available in "temp-to-hire."

Oftentimes, a company will want to test an employee before committing to a definite job. For example, I am aware of a major Atlanta corporation that regularly hires several temps for customer service positions. After a few months, those temps who have performed their tasks well are offered permanent employment. Those temps who have difficulty with the assignments are not retained.

Another example is a growing company that needs additional help but is not ready to hire a new employee. A temp can fill the current urgency, and if the expansion continues, the position can become permanent.

Networking

Since you were hired as a temporary employee, the company should have no objection to tactful efforts at job networking. Comparing job search techniques and information with other temps can be a useful exchange of ideas. Permanent employees may be aware of vacancies within their company or openings they learned about through clients. You also may be able to discuss your job search with vendors or clients, but be discreet.

For example, I know of an accountant whose supervisor on a temporary assignment referred him to the company's CPA firm for placement. Also, we recently hired a temporary receptionist who was seeking a sales position in the hospitality industry; I know the personnel manager with a major hotel here and referred her to them. As with all job networking, the possibilities are infinite.

Remember, however, that you have been employed to perform a specific task. Do not allow your job networking efforts to interfere with your assigned duties.

In-house job postings

One of the advantages of working temp, especially at a large company, is that you will be privy to the company's "in-house job postings," i.e., listings of jobs currently available with the company, including functional descriptions and basic requirements. You can peruse the information and then apply for positions for which you qualify.

Every corporation strives to fill new job vacancies with current employees whenever possible, especially promotions. Promoting from within is good for company morale, and there are financial and practical advantages as well. But the best reason for promoting current employees is that the employee's work performance has been carefully observed by supervisors, who are in a position to offer critical comments and recommendations.

As a temporary employee, you also will report to a supervisor, who will be familiar with the quality of your work and who will be called upon for a recommendation (or rejection!) of your application for permanent employment. A good report from your supervisor will weigh heavily in the decision to hire you.

Thus, approach each temporary job as if it were a pre-employment test or part of the interviewing process. Even if the position for which you are applying has nothing to do with your temporary assignment, the quality of your work and the attitude you demonstrate can determine whether or not you are offered the job. Further, if you feel certain that your supervisor is pleased with your work, consider asking him/her to intercede in your behalf.

Other advantages

Another reason for working temp is the opportunity to learn new skills, or maintain and improve existing skills. For example, if your background is in data processing, working a temp position in your field might expose you to new software or new applications for procedures you already knew. At the very least, you would preserve your current level of competency.

Accepting a temporary position allows you to decide whether you like the company and the position, without needing to include this short stay on your resume.

Many temporary agencies offer training classes in the new, "hot" fields, especially in data processing. These classes are free and you can include the added knowledge on your resume.

In the past few years, several of Atlanta's largest corporations have established in-house temporary services that staff positions primarily for their firm.[1] Nearly all of these positions offer a route to permanent, full-time employment with that company, either through "temp-to-perm" or company job postings. If you have determined a specific company best fits your objectives, working through their temp agency affords an excellent opportunity to start a career there.

Conclusion

As you see, working temp offers many advantages. It provides you with income, skill and knowledge development, networking potential, and the possibility of permanent employment. Best of all, you can continue your job search in your time off, showing that you are currently employed.

One major downside, however, is that you will lose your unemployment benefits while working temp. But if your unemployment benefits have already expired or if the amount is less than you can earn working temporary, you should consider using this tool.

---

[1] Those of which I am currently aware are Coca-Cola, Turner Broadcasting System, Crawford & Co., Georgia Institute of Technology, and Georgia-Pacific. I have included contact information for these in Appendix C. If you find others, please let me know.

Tool #7: Job Fairs

Pro's: Exposure to multiple companies and/or job vacancies, free or low cost, good networking possibilities.

Con's: Can get lost in crowd, some job fairs have poor company representation, visibility may be a problem if currently employed.

Job fairs are large scale recruiting events. Their objective is to bring together qualified applicants and company recruiters at one time and in one location, hopefully leading to job offers. These gatherings often attract hundreds, even thousands, of job seekers and may have fifty or more companies represented.

For companies, this method could be cheaper than advertising expenses or personnel agency fees, and more time-efficient as well, since they can screen many applicants in a short period. For you, the job seeker, it offers the advantage of gaining exposure to a number of companies at one time, also saving time and money. In addition, you may encounter companies of which you were not aware or with whom you were unable to make contact.

In the past few years, I have noticed an increase in the number of job fairs offered in Atlanta. Since most of these are free or low cost, you should plan to attend some. The Sunday edition of *The Atlanta Journal-Constitution*'s Help Wanted classified advertising will include time and location in the Career Calendar section and there likely will be more information and details in a display ad further in the Help Wanted section.

Sponsors for these events may be non-profit or for-profit. Typical non-profit sponsors include professional associations, college alumni groups, professional service organizations, industry associations, and local media. Companies that have a large number of positions to fill often will conduct their own "open house" or job fair. In addition to these groups, there are many for-profit firms that conduct job fairs, often for specific target groups (*e.g.*, sales, engineering, ex-military, or computer backgrounds).

Preparation

Much of your preparation will be like preparing for an interview, which of course, is exactly what you are doing. Refer to "Chapter V: Interviewing Techniques" for a full discussion. As with interviewing, your success at the job fair will be largely determined by your planning and preparation. Take time to develop a game plan and start your planning early.

If possible, determine in advance which companies will be present, select the ones with whom you want to interview, and conduct some research into those companies. Rank them in order of importance to you and plan to visit them approximately in that order. The names of the companies planning to attend is usually listed in the display ad in *The Atlanta Journal-Constitution* or other advance notice, but if not, call the sponsor and request the information.

Check ahead for registration requirements or qualifications screening. You may be asked to send in your resume beforehand so that companies can peruse it prior to the event.

Have available many copies of your resume, at least 25. This is one occasion where you will be expected to distribute your resume freely. Of course, be certain it conforms with the principles we discussed earlier in "Chapter III: Preparing Your Resumes."

Carry an attaché case, which will keep your resume neat and clean, as well as have room to store the company literature you will receive.

JOB FAIR CHECK LIST

Before the fair
- ▶ Check registration requirements
- ▶ Determine location
- ▶ Research companies represented
- ▶ Prioritize companies to interview
- ▶ Pack and organize supplies:
  - ▶ Resume in attaché case
  - ▶ Business cards
  - ▶ Small note pad
  - ▶ Breath mints
- ▶ Plan attire

At the fair
- ▶ Visit most important companies first
- ▶ Take short breaks and refresh appearance
- ▶ Network at every opportunity
- ▶ Exchange business cards
- ▶ Use breath mints

After the fair
- ▶ Sort business cards
- ▶ Review and expand notes
- ▶ Send thank-you notes
- ▶ Recontact company representatives
- ▶ Plan follow-up
- ▶ Evaluate your performance and success

Include a notebook to record your activities or carry a small note pad in your coat pocket.

At the Fair

When you arrive at the fair, you will be given a program of participating companies. In addition to the ones you planned to contact, you may wish to seek out others as well.

Use your time wisely. You may have all day or just a few hours, but either way, you will be at your peak performance for only a few hours at best. Allow time for a short break and to recompose.

Many job fairs also offer seminars on job search techniques, but most of these classes are offered by other groups at other times. (See "Tool #9: Job Networking Groups.") Your focus should be to make company contacts, and thus I suggest you attend the seminars only after you have completed your mission or as a rest break between interviews.

Make notes regarding each company and their representative with whom you spoke personally, so that you will remember them later. You need not take complete notes, just enough to jog your memory later. You can use this note-taking time as a rest break or when you are waiting in line.

After the Job Fair

Send a thank-you note to the companies with whom you spoke and include some bit of information that will help them remember who you are. They will have spoken with many, many applicants and thus you will need to refresh their memory. In this note, you will indicate that you plan to recontact them in a few days.

In speaking with some company recruiters who have worked at these fairs, a common comment is that applicants must take the initiative in recontacting companies with whom they left their resume or interviewed. If you have mailed a thank-you note, you will have said that you will recontact them; definitely do so.

Evaluate your results from the fair. What did you gain from the experience? What could you have done differently that might have produced a better payoff?

Review your notes. What companies should you be recontacting? What actions should you take as a consequence of the fair? What follow-up needs tending? Do you have new leads to check?

Networking at Job Fairs

Job fairs offer an excellent opportunity to job network with other job seekers. For example, while standing in line, you can compare job search techniques and information with the people around you. Anyone you happen to meet is a potential source for leads. Use your "30-second resume" whenever you have the chance.

Save your resumes for the companies, but hand out your business cards freely and solicit others as well; you may wish to contact later some people that you meet. Don't just mill around waiting for an interview; use all of your time constructively.

Standing Out

As I stated earlier, there may be hundreds or thousands of job seekers at a job fair. How can you stand out from the crowd?

• Develop a game plan for what you plan to do at the fair and proceed accordingly. Not only will you accomplish more, but you also will feel less stressed and more relaxed with this preparation. Not surprisingly, you also will reflect that feeling and attitude.

• Be appropriately attired, with a professional, business image. Since you may be there several hours, plan to "freshen up" while there. For example, men should carry an electric shaver in their attaché case and women who wear make-up should also check their appearance often. Carry and use breath mints.

- Be organized. Don't fumble for papers or a resume, but have your materials readily accessible. Keep your business cards in a pocket easy to reach.

- Be prepared. If you know which companies you will be seeing, compile and learn information about them and be certain to relate it during your interview. Prepare for the interview, following all of the suggestions I have outlined in the next chapter on interviewing techniques.

- Take an occasional rest break, so that you will not seem tired.

- Use the check list I have prepared.

Conclusion

Why attend job fairs? Depending on the size of the fair, several hundred participants may receive offers then or later from the companies they met or interviewed. Even if you do not receive a job offer from the fair, the job networking opportunity is worth the time and effort. Moreover, since these events are either free or inexpensive and close by, you have no reason not to attend. This tool is still one more of the many you have learned about through the CAREER SEARCH SYSTEM.

Tool #8: Government

Pro's: Generally stable and secure. Local and many state jobs are generally permanent Atlanta. Many openings for recent grads.

Con's: Can be very long and complex procedures. Not good source if you need a job quickly.

Metro-Atlanta currently has nearly 288,500 government employees, up from 278,100 in 2002, and that figure is likely to grow. The approximate numbers are these[1]:
- Federal – 47,800
- State - 56,700
- Local (18-county metro) 184,00

Appendix F includes addresses and contact data divided into the above three groups.

If at all possible, I suggest you go to a Georgia Career Center, especially one of the five metro-Atlanta offices listed below, where you will find not only Georgia openings, but many Federal and local job lists as well. Call if you need directions.

ajobs.com
Link is provided to GA Dept. of Labor and the employment listings.

• North Atlanta/Fulton County: 2943 N. Druid Hills Rd NE (in Toco Hills Shopping Center); (404) 679-5200
• South Atlanta/Fulton County: 2636 Martin Luther King Jr Ave (across from MARTA's Hightower station); (404) 656-6000 (auto phone info)

---

[1] Source: *Georgia Labor Market Trends*, 03/03 issue, published by the Georgia Department of Labor, Workforce Information & Analysis. Estimates include all full- and part-time wage and salary workers. Proprietors, domestic servants, self-employed persons, unpaid family workers, and personnel of the armed forces are excluded.

- DeKalb County: 3879 Covington Hwy, Decatur, GA; (404) 298-3970
- Cobb/Cherokee County: 465 Big Shanty Road, Marietta; (770) 528-6100
- Gwinnett County: 2211 Beaver Ruin Rd, Norcross; (770) 840-2200
- Clayton County: 2450 Mt. Zion Parkway, Building 100, Suite 100, Southwood 75 Office Park, Jonesboro, GA 30236; 678-479-5886

If you are not in Atlanta or unable to go to one of the above offices, then

(1) go to your local US Office of Personnel Management (or in smaller cities, the Georgia Career Center, formerly known as State Employment Services Office) and request the Federal Job Opportunities List for Atlanta (out of state, ask for Georgia and peruse for Atlanta openings);

(2) write the Georgia State Merit System and request the pamphlet, "The State Employment Process" (Their address is included in the Merit System discussion in this chapter.);

(3) contact the local government offices listed in Appendix F.

U. S. (Federal) Government

Most federal government agencies hire through the Office of Personnel Management (OPM), formerly known long ago as the civil service commission, and their web site is www.usajobs.opm.gov (can be accessed through an automated telephone at 478-757-3000 or TDD 478-744-2299). Federal jobs often require a competitive exam, which may be all written, all experience-oriented, or a combination of both.

OPM has greatly streamlined its initial employment process and their web site is user friendly. You can search for positions by agency, position title, series, or profession. USAJOBS provides worldwide job vacancy information that is updated each day from a database of more than 17,000 worldwide job opportunities. In many instances, you can

106

apply for positions online or submit a resume online. Separate links are provided for student employment.

USAJOBS by Email: If you register your job search, you will be notified automatically by email of new job listings posted to the USAJOBS web site meeting your search criteria. These emails will also have a direct link to the vacancy's information. You can create and store up to three searches on this service.

USAJOBS Resume Builder: This service is designed to help you create a résumé that is acceptable for applying for most Federal jobs. You can print your résumé, store it on our site, or in some cases submit the résumé electronically to the hiring agency.

Many agencies do not hire through OPM, however, (e.g, departments of Treasury, Transportation, HUD; the IRS, FAA, Customs, et al.), but you can link to them through USAJOBS.

US Postal Service (www.usps.gov): The USPS is another federal organization that conducts its own hiring and has no contact with OPM. In Atlanta, the USPS employs more than 7,000, including some 3,000 at the managerial level. Interestingly, nearly all USPS employees start as clerks or carriers, and only the highest levels and technical positions (attorneys, engineers, etc.) are hired from outside the system. Thus, one would start entry-level, and then bid for higher-level positions after one year of employment. A test is required for all prospective new employees. Refer to their web site www.usps.gov, or call (404) 765-7234 for information on job application procedure.

General Accounting Office (www.gao.gov): Another federal agency conducting its own hiring is the General Accounting Office (GAO), a Congressional agency and not under the Executive Branch. Most of their hiring is for economics, public administration, accounting/finance, and computer-related degrees, both entry-level and experienced. A job announcement is published each fall, and applications are taken from September through April. They also offer several co-op programs and summer internships. Refer to their web site or call (404) 679-1900 for information.

Incidentally, the federal government offers its employees alternate work schedules, one of which allows an employee to work nine-hour days, Monday - Thursday, and then have Friday afternoon free. It's still a 40-hour week, but the half-day can make a nice, long weekend.

State of Georgia

> **ajobs.com**
> In addition to the GA DOL, a separate link is provided to the GA Merit System and its job vacancies.

The vast majority of state job vacancies are filled through the Georgia Merit System, which last year hired more than 5,000. An orientation class explaining the application process is offered daily at 9:30 a.m. at the Merit System office. The merit system office is open Monday - Friday, 8 - 4:30, but you are encouraged to arrive by 3:00. It is located downtown at 200 Piedmont Ave, Room 418, West Tower, and is in the same building as the MARTA Georgia State station. You also may call the Merit System office at (404) 656-2725 and ask to have mailed to you the pamphlet "The State Employment Process," which outlines the procedures for securing employment with the state.

The State of Georgia has created a new web site called "Applicant Resource Center," (www.thejobsite.org) which explains the employment process. Although all positions still pass through the Georgia Merit System, this site attempts to simplify the procedure as much as possible. Note that no faxes or emails are accepted.

A separate application is required for each job for which you wish to apply. You may submit additional information about your background on a resume with the application. Once your application is received, it will be evaluated to determine if you meet minimum employment qualifications for the position for which you are applying.

All applications must be submitted for a specific job title that is currently available. Some jobs are hired continuously and some are hired on a regularly scheduled basis. Other job vacancies that occur are detailed in a list published each Friday and is available at all Georgia state agencies and colleges, as well as the labor departments of all states. The list cannot be obtained by writing or calling; rather, you must go in person to an employment office or to the Merit System office.

If you are in Atlanta, I suggest you visit the state Career Centers for information on all current openings and help in the applications procedure. You also can call (404) 656-2724 for a recorded announcement of the hiring procedure.

One of the larger non-merit system agencies is the Department of Audits. It is divided into three sections, financial, performance, and Medicaid. Addresses and hiring needs are listed in Appendix F.

ajobs.com
Links to web sites of metro cities and counties, including job vacancies.

Local Governments

Appendix F lists the contact data and procedure followed by the five major metro counties, plus the City of Atlanta.

PART 2:

JOB NETWORKING

Tool #9: Developing a Job Network

Tool #10: Job Networking Groups

Tool #11: Professional and Trade Associations

Tool #12: The Information Interview

Tool #9: Developing a Job Network

Pro's: Most effective source overall. Works well for all experience levels, especially middle level. Best source for individuals changing fields, re-entering work force, or other difficult-to-place situations.

Con's: Slow, time-consuming, labor intensive, lots of "dead-end" leads.

Looking at all the "con's" to job networking might make you want to skip it, in favor of the easier and simpler methods. Before you do, consider this: More people find their jobs through networking than through any other source, at least 70%, and I have heard estimates of up to 85%. Perhaps this is a good example of the old adage, "You get what you pay for," because even though it is the most difficult, it is the most fruitful.

Now that everyone either owns or has access to a computer and letter-quality printer, everyone has a resume to quickly email, fax, or send via USPO. One the receiving end, there are hundreds of job posting sites and resume databases, plus nearly every company now lists job vacancies on their web site and often with one or more of the commercial job sites. The result is an avalanche of resumes, cover letters, broadcast letters, etc. at most companies. In fact, I have spoken with corporate recruiters who admit that they have boxes of unopened resumes. Blindly mailing your resume to major companies, hoping it will somehow result in an interview and job offer is like tossing coins into a wishing well.

Although logic would suggest that the Fortune 500 companies should have the most job vacancies, most of their hiring is for replacements, not new positions. On the other hand, companies with fewer than 100 employees will account for almost 80% of the new jobs. Further, firms with fewer than 20 employees are expected to add 57% of the new positions. As I stated earlier in this chapter, simply mailing your resume to the biggest companies will not find enough openings. Networking, however, will help you locate these smaller firms.

There are several approaches to job networking, all of which can generate many leads and interviews. This and the following three sections detail the most successful methods that you can incorporate in your job search.

Before starting to network, you already must have developed your "30-Second Resume," described in Part 2 of Chapter III. If for some reason, you skipped that discussion, refer back to it now. I stated that you will be using this oral resume often, and now is still another of those times. The "30-second resume" is just as important as your written one, so spend enough time to make it the best possible.

Developing A Job Network

Since job networking can be so productive, you should spend at least half of your time developing this source. I know what you are thinking: that it's too difficult or that you lack the skills or contacts from which to establish your base. Not true – once you start, you will be surprised how quickly your network will expand. As with so much of your job search, it simply requires planning and organization. Even if you are new to Atlanta, you can cultivate a networking system; the procedure is the same.

First, let me emphasize what job networking is not. It is not an excuse to abuse your friends and relatives by bombarding them with constant calls for contacts or by pressuring them to use their influence when you sense their reluctance. Certainly you will include them in your job networking, but there are so many other potential networking sources at your disposal that you should not test the patience of any person. If you find yourself calling the same people, then you are not conducting a correct job search.

SIX *EASY* STEPS TO DEVELOPING A JOB NETWORK

1) Start a list.

Which family and friends will I call first?
What questions will I ask?
What do I expect to achieve?

2) Expand the list.

Add business associates, clients, former co-workers and supervisors, professional and civic contacts, etc. Also, determine <u>why</u> I think each will be helpful in my job search. What information might I gain from each?

3) Act on the suggestions.

What courses of action do I plan to take? Direct contact? Information interviews?

4) Seek other sources of information.

Which professional associations will be helpful for me?
Which job networking groups do I plan to attend?
Other sources I will utilize and when: (job fairs, temporary employment, alumni associations, etc.)

5) Volunteer

In my spare time, where will I volunteer? (church, civic, charity, professional association, etc.)

6) Evaluate your efforts.

Of the methods I have used, which have been most helpful?
Which are not successful?
What should I do differently?

Start developing your job network by compiling a list of individuals you want to contact. Begin with friends and relatives, who should be the most sympathetic and supportive, and this will have you off to a good start. Expand this list to include business associates, then social, professional, civic, and church contacts, and anyone else you think could help. However, if you are currently employed and discretion is utmost, you may wish to contact only close, trusted associates.

In compiling this list you also should predetermine why you are including each person. How can they help you? What information do you think they may be able to share with you?

Now phone each one and state that you are actively seeking new employment. Conduct your calls seated at the desk of the new "job search area" you have set up, so you can record all of the information you are given and keep it organized. Be certain to ask specific questions which will yield helpful information.

Here are some questions to ask:

• "Do you have any job search suggestions?" They may have completed a job search recently and will have some good advice. Or they may know of others who have, and you can contact them to ask what they learned during the job search.

• "Do you have any contacts that could be of assistance?" Perhaps your contact may be friends with a Director of Human Resources that could be a good lead, or a department manager in the field you are seeking, or some other person who might be helpful.

• "Do you know an employee with ABC Company?" If you are targeting a specific company, ask if your source knows someone who works for that company. You can call that person and obtain information about the company, its job vacancies, and perhaps the name of an hiring authority or recruiter.

- "Is there a career consultant, personnel agent, or advisor you know and would recommend?" This is a good method for locating a reliable personnel agency or outplacement counselor.

- "Are you aware of any professional or job network groups that I should contact?" In addition to the local chapters of national trade and professional associations, Atlanta is fortunate to have several job networking groups. (Networking groups, professional associations, and privately funded job-search organizations are all discussed later in this chapter.)

In addition to your initial list, there are many other networking sources. When at social gatherings, listen out for people who might be able to lead you to a source. Call the appropriate academic department head at a local college and ask for suggestions. If possible, discuss your situation with current or former clients and vendors. Contact former co-workers and supervisors. When you prepared your written resume, you secured at least three persons who agreed to be your references. Definitely include them in your network list, and since they are familiar with the quality of your work, they likely will be able to suggest other persons to contact.

College alumni groups are an outstanding source, and you should locate the local chapter president of your alumni association and attend the meetings, planning to job network there. If you don't know who the local officers are, call the alumni office or the president's office at your alma mater and ask for the local contact. Ask if a membership directory or alumni magazine is published for your locale; it may contain the company and job title of alumni who could be helpful in your job search.

Many college alumni associations sponsor career seminars and job fairs, and they often have "young alumni" sub-groups. Try to locate alumni with backgrounds similar to yours and ask for career and job search advice. You also should discuss your job search with the chapter president and perhaps arrange an "information interview."[1] In

---

[1] The "information interview" is discussed later in this chapter as Tool #12.

fact, I recently spoke with an applicant who expects a job offer from Coca-Cola and whose interview was arranged through the president of her alumni association.

Still another valuable source of leads and contacts can be found through professional and trade associations. In researching this subject, I encountered many persons who obtained their jobs by networking at these monthly meetings, and thus I strongly urge you to try it also. This source is discussed in more detail in the next section, "Tool #11: Professional and Trade Associations," and Appendix E includes information on many of the most active of these groups locally.

> **ajobs.com**
> Links to 75+ national and local web sites.

If you are already a member of a society that covers your field, you should contact the president or job coordinator and consider arranging an informational interview. If you are contemplating a career change, these groups can be a tremendous help. Search out the one(s) that pertain to your newly chosen field, contact them and attend meetings.

Volunteer your time with a professional association, church, civic group, favorite charity, or any other organization where you will meet people. As you get to know these new friends, they may have suggestions or contacts, and you

Don't let your job network fade away!

After you have accepted new employment, send a thank-you letter to all the people who helped you or even tried to help, letting them know of your new assignment and new responsibilities. Add them to your holiday greeting card list, forward an interesting article you read, send an occasional email – anything to keep your network "warm." You may need their help in the future, plus they may alert you to other opportunities later.

likely will find persons who recently conducted their own job search. This is especially helpful if you are unemployed, since it keeps you active and involved, as well as adding to your emotional support systems and avoiding depression.

Conclusion

Don't expect instant results or that all of your efforts will be productive. Accept the fact that although most of your leads will not be useful, you must follow through on all of them anyway. That is the slow, time-consuming part of job networking.

But since networking is the most effective source overall, you should plan to spend half of your time cultivating leads and contacts, and then following through. Don't let all the dead ends deter you; sooner or later, one of your efforts will uncover that "right" lead that lands you a new job!

CASE EXAMPLE

I recently received a phone call from an accountant who had just located a new job, and since it is a great example of job networking, I want to share it with you.

John had joined the volunteer auxiliary of a well-know charity and then volunteered to assist the group's treasurer during their annual fund-raiser. In real life, the treasurer was the Controller with a large corporation, and he was so impressed with John's enthusiasm and abilities, he arranged an interview with his firm for a position in his department. With this recommendation, John was offered a job there.

All non-profits need volunteers. Choose one that you enjoy and then actively participate, especially in a function that will allow you to demonstrate your skills and abilities. This will keep you current in your field, and you will make many new friends and contacts – one of whom may be the source of your next job.

Tool #10: Job Networking Groups

Pro's: Most are free or little expense; offer emotional support, job search seminars, and sometimes job openings; excellent networking opportunity; good source for recent grads through middle-management.

Con's: Some volunteer instructors are not well-qualified; not best source for senior executives; very open and thus may not be good if you are currently employed.

Atlanta is fortunate to have several networking groups specifically aimed for job searchers. While their general purpose is to help job seekers through job networking, they often offer seminars on the practical aspects of getting a job (*e.g.*, interviewing, resume preparation, focusing your job objective, planning a job search, job networking, etc.). In addition, they maintain files of job openings sent to them by many metro employers, and these files can be perused at the weekly meetings.

ajobs.com Links provided to individual groups when available.

I am including here the current groups as of this writing, but since many new groups form and some cease operations or move, you should check with ajobs.com first. **Ajobs.com** includes all of the current groups, a link to the web site of each one if available, and another link for directions. Also, *The Atlanta Journal-Constitution's* "Career Calendar" section in the Sunday edition lists groups, and the *Atlanta Business Chronicle* devotes a page called "Networking Calendar" to listing upcoming meetings of professional associations, networking groups, civic associations, chambers of commerce, etc.

Although many of them meet in local churches, they are all non-sectarian and welcome all job seekers. While attending one of the meetings, I suggest you ask other participants which job networking groups they have visited and their comments. If you have time, you may wish to visit several groups to determine which ones will offer you the most help.

**Crossroads Career Network** (www.crossroads-career.net): This is a sort of franchise ministry, with 25± large local churches meeting on different days of the week, generally monthly. Some groups may have 75 or more participants, and with so many churches participating, you are likely to find a convenient one every week.

In addition to Crossroads, these groups meet weekly:

All Saints Episcopal Church in midtown Atlanta, 634 West Peachtree St NW, Atlanta. "New Dimensions" meets every Wednesday evening from 7 – 9pm. Job search experts, including myself, cover various topics each week. Emphasis is placed on specific goals and actions. (404) 881-0835 for directions.

Catholic Church of St. Ann at 4905 Roswell Rd, Marietta, GA. (Note: If you are not familiar with the Atlanta area, there is more than one "Roswell Road"; be certain you are on the right one.) Career Quest meets every Tuesday at 7:45 pm. For directions, call (770) 552-6402.

Career Mavens: Cobb County: Meets Tuesday from 7:15 - 9:30pm at Temple Kol Emeth; for info, call 770/973-3533 x209. DeKalb County: Meets Wednesday at 7:30pm at Congregation Beth Shalom; for info, call Bill Schwartz at 770/740-8552.

**JobSeekers USA** is a group of business executives who volunteer their time to help others in career transition. There are no charges or fees for participants. As many as 150 job seekers attend free weekly sessions where they find encouragement, job leads, mentoring, and tips for job hunting. In addition to addressing vocational needs, they are challenged to consider their spiritual and family relationships as well. Thousands of job seekers have been served and encouraged by JobSeekers since it began in 1991. Currently, there are four groups meeting in metro Atlanta, plus other cities.

- Dunwoody: Meets Friday morning, 7 – 9 am at Fuddrucker's Restaurant, 240 Perimeter Center Pkwy. Call

770/399-6041 for directions. Often has 150 participants, so they break down into small focus groups.

- Kennesaw: Meets Tuesday mornings, 7 – 9 am at the Varsity at Town Center Mall. Call 770/795-0802 for directions.

- Peachtree City: Meets Friday mornings from 7:30 – 9:30 am at Longhorn Restaurant, Hwy 74 x Hwy 54, 2633 Floy Farr Pkwy. Call 770/486-8791 for directions.

Layoff Lounge (www.layofflounge.com): National organization that sponsors highly effective monthly structured networking meetings; time and place varies. After a short talk from a job search expert, the participants break down into groups of four for fifteen minutes of networking, then move to another group for more networking. During the evening, you will have met with all the 50 or so people present. Have plenty of business cards and plan in advance what information you would like to obtain.

Mothers and More (www.mothersandmore.org) is an organization for "sequencing" women (i.e, moving from career to motherhood and back to career). Members meet for a variety of activities, including play groups, mothers' night out, charity drives, and discussions about topics from child safety to career networking. Atlanta currently has five groups. For information about a metro Atlanta chapter near you, call 770/326-6176 or their Chicago headquarters at 900/223-9399. Even easier, click the link at **ajobs.com.**

Sales and Marketing Seekers (SAMS) is a networking and support group, comprised mostly of career salespersons seeking employment. They meet Monday mornings at 7:00 for coffee and doughnuts at Roswell United Methodist Church. For information, call the church office at (770) 993-6218 or Richard Card at (770) 971-0848.

Other job networking groups are listed later in this chapter in the section called "Tool #13: Privately Funded Organizations." These bodies have a more specific purpose and constituency, as well as offering an opportunity for networking.

Procedure for attending networking meetings

A little preparation before the meetings and some understanding of the networking opportunities they offer will help you derive the most from these groups.

Plan ahead. Carry a few copies of your resume, but you should give one only to persons who request it. Far better is to pass out your business card, which will show your job objective or expertise and your contact data. This small card is easier to keep and less likely to be tossed in the trash. Casual attire is acceptable, but always neat, since you may receive more and better information if you project a professional image. Needless to say, be certain you know the time, date, and location.

Arrive early. Remember that the primary focus of these groups is to encourage job networking. Arriving promptly or a little early will allow more time to meet other job seekers and exchange information.

Set goals. An easy goal is to meet at least ten attendees and exchange business cards. Discuss what you have learned and ask for suggestions from them. An even better plan is to locate at least two attendees with backgrounds or objectives similar to your own. Trading job hunting tips with them will be especially helpful to your own search, as well as to theirs. Ask for suggestions in selecting personnel agencies.

Don't waste time. Don't spend too much time with one person. Keep moving and try to locate other participants who can address your needs. However, you should always exchange business cards and perhaps phone those persons later. Should you locate someone with very good information relative to your job search, get their name and contact data (a business card, for example) and ask if you can call or meet with them later, when there are fewer distractions and you can continue your dialogue.

Actively participate. Converse with as many people as you have time. This is a good place to try out your "30-second resume" and receive sympathetic, constructive feedback. If you are researching a specific company and seeking information or a contact there, mention it often. You likely will encounter someone who can help. Many of the classes allot time for this exchange of information and you should mention it then also. If you have questions or comments during the classes, speak up. The facilitators are glad to hear from you, if you don't monopolize their time.

Identify yourself. Each group has a sign-in table and you are given a name tag on which to write your name. Under your name and in only a few words, include your job objective or expertise in letters large enough for other attendees to read. If someone with a background or objective similar to yours sees this tag, you likely will have identified a useful source. For variety, you occasionally might write in your alma mater, home state, former employer, etc.

Take notes. The classes are generally informative, and you should take notes. You also will want to jot down details about some of the participants you meet and the information you obtain from them.

Exchange information. If everyone at these meetings only selfishly soaked up information from other attendees, there would be no purpose in participating. Offer your own ideas and experiences, and any other information helpful to others. Some weeks you may feel that you have given more than you have received, but it will all balance out later. However, don't allow yourself to be trapped by someone seeking too much information for the short period you have at the meeting. Should this be developing, ask if you can call them later when you both have more time for discussion.

Follow-up. All of the knowledge you obtained at the meeting will be useless, unless you incorporate it into your search. In addition, keep in contact with some of the participants you meet, especially those with backgrounds or objectives similar to your own. If someone provided you with information that resulted in some positive step in your search, send them a thank you note.

JOB NETWORKING MEETINGS
Check List

Before the meeting
- ▶ Decide attire
- ▶ Plan what to carry and how:
  - ▶ Resumes in folder or attaché
  - ▶ Business cards in pocket
  - ▶ Note pad convenient
- ▶ Rehearse "30-second resume"
- ▶ Confirm time and location
- ▶ Set objectives

At the meeting
- ▶ Arrive early
- ▶ Identify self and job objective
- ▶ Actively participate
- ▶ Achieve goals
- ▶ Don't waste time
- ▶ Take notes
- ▶ Exchange business cards

After the meeting
- ▶ Renew contacts
- ▶ Analyze results
- ▶ Determine follow-up
- ▶ Review notes

Conclusion

Although your results will vary from week to week, you will always come away with a boost in morale from commiserating with other job seekers like yourself. I also suggest you occasionally take your spouse or best friend with you, so that they will better understand what you are doing and feel more personally involved.

A word of caution: I have observed that many attendees seem to be hooked on the seminars offered and ignore the opportunity for networking. Although the seminars offered are very helpful indeed, that is only part of your reason for being there. If you only attend the seminars or only speak with your friends there, you will not be profiting from all you should.

Tool #11: Trade and Professional Associations

Pro's: Works well for middle- and upper-level executives, and somewhat for entry-level. Good source for changing careers.

Con's: May be costly if you must join first or pay to attend meetings. Can be slow and time-consuming getting to the source.

How do companies hire? Where do they find their applicants?

Companies find the vast majority of their applicants – 80% or more – through three primary sources:
- Professional Associations
- Company web sites (*not* the large commercial sites)
- Referrals

I have long encouraged job seekers to use professional associations as part of a job search. Moreover, you can use these groups in combination with the other two sources for even better success. For example, you can find a job opening at a company web site, and then attend an association meeting to locate someone who will give you the name of the hiring authority.   Even better, you might meet a member who knows of an opening his/her company and offers to be your reference within the company.

> **ajobs.com**
>
> ■ addition to the associations ▮sted here in Appendix E, ▮ore are listed online, along ▮ith links to their national and ▮cal web sites.

Your background and experience is covered by a least one major association, and more than likely, several associations. Determine which ones apply to you and visit their national web site to locate the local site. Reviewing their web site will help you determine if your background fits their membership, and also what job assistance you can expect to find. There is an organization covering virtually every conceivable job description, industry or academic discipline. Although you already may be a member of one or more of these associations, there likely are other associations of which you may not be aware, but from which you could benefit. *National Trade and Professional Associations of the United States* (published by Columbia Books, Inc., Washington, DC) is a catalogue that lists thousands of trade and professional associations and labor unions with national memberships. Even more complete is the *Encyclopedia of Associations*, a multi-volume work that includes detailed information.

Available at most public libraries, these books include not only addresses and descriptions of each organization, but also a cross reference section to access associations by subject. You likely will be surprised to learn that many disciplines are represented by numerous associations, some of which specialize in specific industries. For example, under the Subject Index heading "Marketing," there are 75+ specialty associations, in addition to the 52,000-member American Marketing Association. In the same section, there are many organizations listed for specific ethic or minority groups, such as "black," "women," "handicapped," etc. Thus, I urge you to incorporate these publications in your job search. (If you are not able to obtain these through a local public library, mail order information is included in "Tool #15: Useful Resources and Publications.")

Nearly all of the largest associations offer job assistance on the national level and include job vacancies on their sites. Moreover, many local chapters also list jobs online, and some have an "employment chair" to assist job seekers. If your association is not listed here or on ajobs.com, I suggest that you contact the national headquarters of your association and ask for the local Atlanta chapter president, and then inquire about their direct career assistance, if any.

In some cases, you must be a member of the association offering employment assistance before they will help you. However, I was pleased to find that many organizations are interested in helping an applicant secure employment now, assuming he/she will join the association later. Since membership dues can be expensive – prohibitively so if you are unemployed – I suggest you call the association contact I have listed to inquire if membership is a prerequisite.

If your association does not offer any formal job assistance, remember that you can attend their meetings and network there; in fact, many associations encourage networking, especially at the social hour before the program. And if the associations do offer job search assistance that you plan to use, you have even more reason for attending their meetings.

Most associations meet monthly and welcome visitors and potential members, in addition to their current members. Since there may be a fee involved or reservations required, you should check ahead. Appendix E also includes information on monthly meeting dates. If you are strapped for cash and don't want to stay for the meal, you can leave after the social hour or the business meeting.

Networking at Association Meetings

A friend of mine recently moved to Atlanta in search of an audit/accounting position. I suggested that he attend a meeting of the Institute of Internal Auditors, which he did, and he even sat beside a woman who had just found her job the previous month by networking at the I. I. A. meetings. Unfortunately, however, Ray is somewhat shy and felt uncomfortable in an unfamiliar setting where he knew no one. He spent the entire evening alone and gained nothing from the experience, except a fear of ever returning.

Many job seekers are like Ray, and you may be one of them. With a little preparation beforehand, however, you can overcome your reticence and successfully job network at any meeting – professional association, alumni group, business meeting, or whatever. The key word here is "preparation."

Although you often can make reservations online, I suggest you call the contact (usually the phone number is given) and explain your situation: you are new to the association and you would be most appreciative if the contact would meet you at the door and introduce you to some other members. Explain further that you are seeking employment and hope to make some useful contacts. You may be pleasantly surprised to hear your contact say that networking is encouraged and then give you the name of the person who handles their job assistance.

Now set your objectives for the meeting. What do you hope to accomplish? You will want to meet some officers, certainly the president and/or the job coordinator. Ask if there are members who recently completed a job search, and then try to locate them to discuss your current search and to ask for suggestions. Are there other specific members you want to meet, department managers with certain companies, etc.?

Plan what you will wear – business attire, of course. You should dress as though you were going on an interview, which is exactly what you are doing. Carry enough business cards to hand out, as well as a few resumes to give to key people. Take a small, pocket-size notebook to record quick information. Remember your "30-Second Resume"? You will use it often at the meeting, so rehearse it some more.

At the meeting, remember your objectives. Don't spend too much time with one person, or you may run out of time. Ask open-ended questions, and then listen; people are always more impressed with good listeners than they are with good talkers! I suggest you do not hand out any resumes, but if someone requests it, obtain their business card and send it immediately after the meeting. Record names and information in your notebook, but don't waste time recording too much now; you can do that later.

Current officers of professional associations are excellent sources for "Information Interviews" (discussed in the next section). They are generally the "movers and shakers" in the industry and are often among the first to hear of new job vacancies. Introduce yourself to several of them, especially the job coordinator, and exchange business cards. Plan to call them in a few days to set up a meeting.

If you have the inclination and the time available, volunteer to help out on a committee or such. You will make valuable contacts and begin to feel more comfortable at the meetings.

Immediately after the meeting, record your results. Whom did you meet (name, company, job title, association function, etc.)? What follow-up do you plan? Is there someone you met and with whom you would like to schedule an "information interview"? What would you want to do differently at the next meeting?

You should send a thank-you note to the person who introduced you at the meeting and enclose your business card. Are there others you need to write and/or send a resume?

Planning what you will do at these meetings will make you less nervous and self-conscious, plus you will accomplish more. You can use this procedure to network at other meetings as well (*e.g.*, college alumni groups, social gatherings, etc.) As with so much of your job search, it only takes organization and preparation.

Conclusion

I personally know of many people who found their jobs through associations, and so I am positive it works. Definitely plan to incorporate them in your search. In the "Professional Associations" section of your notebook, record the names of the associations you contact, the people with whom you speak, when you attended meetings, and the results. These contacts will be helpful now and later.

After you are employed, I strongly urge you to become active in your association, not only attending the meetings but also volunteering for committees and signing up for professional seminars. The knowledge you will gain from the meetings, programs, and classes will be very helpful in advancing your career, as will the professional contacts you make. Drawing from your own experiences will enable you to be very helpful to other job seekers – and then too, you never know when you might need their services again!

NETWORKING AT MEETINGS
Check List

Before the meeting
- ► Set objectives
- ► Establish contact(s)
- ► Determine time, location, and fees
- ► Put business cards and note pad in pocket (no folders or attaché cases)
- ► Rehearse "30-second resume"
- ► Decide attire

At the meeting
- ► Meet appropriate officers
- ► Achieve objectives
- ► Don't spend too much time with one person
- ► Volunteer time, if possible
- ► Ask open-ended questions and listen
- ► Record short notes
- ► Exchange business cards rather than pass out résumés
- ► Keep right hand free for handshakes

After the meeting
- ► Expand notes
- ► Send thank-you letters
- ► Analyze results
- ► Determine follow-up
- ► What will you do differently at the next meeting?

Tool #12: The Information Interview

Pro's: Especially helpful to change careers or re-enter the job market. Good way to re-energize a stale job search campaign. Provides more information than can be obtained in informal settings.

Con's: Very time consuming. Can be difficult to find right sources to contact. May not be feasible if you are not in the city where you are attempting to relocate.

The information interview is contacting individuals who have information useful to your job search and arranging a meeting time to discuss your job search face-to-face, rather than over the phone. It differs from a job interview in that your objective here is to gain information – suggestions, names, etc. - to help with your job search.

These individuals are most often successful and knowledgeable business executives or authorities in your field, but you can gain valuable search tips from fellow job seekers and others as well. Whomever you choose, they will become part of your job network. Their input can be helpful not only now, but you may wish to recontact them later in your job search for more suggestions.

Who can benefit from the "information interview"?
• Recent college graduates uncertain what career to pursue
• Individuals contemplating a mid-life career change
• Displaced homemakers or others re-entering the job market after an absence
• Job seekers in need of fresh input and suggestions to re-energize a stale job search.
• Anyone seeking ideas and information about an industry or job.

Whom to contact

There are two approaches to selecting authorities in your field:

1) Call business executives you already know either personally or by reputation.

2) Identify a position or job title that would have information you are seeking and then locate someone in that position. For example, determine who is the president of a professional association covering your field or call a department manager in your industry, and arrange an information interview with each of them.

I even know someone who was able to create his current job with a company that he "cold called" for an information interview. That, however, is the exception and you should not mislead your contact by saying you are seeking help when in fact you want a job interview. Your objective is to gain information – suggestions, names, etc. – and trying to turn your information interview into a job interview will destroy your credibility.

Nevertheless, if you do sense during your discussion that your source is asking questions that suggest you may be considered for a position within the company, be prepared for a full job interview. You should have read "Chapter V: Interviewing Techniques" and thus are ready for this pleasant turn of events!

Although you may think that a luncheon is a good idea for interviewing a busy executive, it really is not. There are too many distractions and the setting is too informal. Try to conduct your interviews in your source's office where you will have his/her undivided attention.

The main disadvantage to the information interview is that it is far more time-consuming than a phone call. If you are currently employed or not living in the same city as your potential sources, you may not be able to utilize this method. In addition, some of your contacts may feel inconvenienced, particularly if they are often called upon for this type of interview. Nevertheless, it is a good networking technique, and I suggest you consider it.

Procedure

Step 1: Compile a list. First make a list of persons to contact and why. Or you may need to use the reverse approach, and decide what information you want and then research the name of a specific authority who might have that knowledge.

Since information interviews are time-consuming, you should be selective in planning your list. What possible information can you obtain from each person on your list and how can you use it in your job search? Having answered that, you are ready to call your first authority.

Step 2: Contact your authorities. Depending on the amount of information you have, there are three approaches or possibilities. Whichever method you employ, when you do speak with your authority, ask for a fifteen minute interview at his/her convenience.

1) If you have the email address of your proposed contact, first send an email stating why you are making contact (You are seeking information as part of a job search.) and why you are targeting this authority. (You consider this person to be an expert on some subject related to your job search.) Perhaps you have been referred by someone, in which case include that. Immediately state that you are not calling for a job interview, but only for information that will be helpful in your job search. Then close with "I will be calling you in the next day or so, and look forward to speaking with you." Thus, your source will be expecting your call.

2) If you do not have the email address, then call your source at his/her office, never at home. Most likely, you will be directed into voice mail, so you must be ready with a prepared message, stating the same information as above. This could be your contact's first impression of you, so be certain your message is coherent and well-organized; repeat your name and phone number. If you leave a

rambling, poorly constructed message, you likely will not have your call returned.

3) In attempting to reach your sources at the office, you may speak with a secretary or receptionist. Remember that part of these employees' job is to screen unwanted calls for their bosses, so don't be upset if you are quizzed on the purpose of your call. On the contrary, these assistants can be your ally if approached correctly.

Stress that you are not seeking a job interview and that you will take up only a minute or two of the boss's time on the phone. If you have been referred to this authority by someone, say that so-and-so said you should call. If you are told that your authority is not available now, ask if you can leave a voice mail or when would be a convenient time to call back. Be polite, ask the secretary's name, and then thank him/her for the information. When you do call later, be certain you refer to the secretary by name.

Step 3: Prepare for the interview. After you have established an interview time, the next step is to plan what you will do in the interview, and understanding your respective roles will help. Even though you will be seated in the small chair in front of the big desk, nevertheless you are the interviewer now and your victim is the "interviewee." Thus, you will have prepared just as thoroughly as you would expect from one of your interviewers.

What questions should you ask? This will depend on why you have arranged the interview and what your objectives are. Decide what general and specific information you hope to learn, and then develop questions which may lead to that information.

For example, if you are considering a new career, you should ask questions such as these:
• Why did you pursue this career?
• What qualifications did you have for this career?
• What do you like most about your industry? What do you dislike?
• Would you encourage others to pursue this career? Why?
• To what do you attribute your success here? (A nice compliment)

If you are attempting to further your established career path, these questions could be helpful:
- What do you feel are the future trends in our industry?
- Which companies are experiencing the strongest growth in our field? Who are the "winners" and the "losers"?
- Of which professional associations are you a member? Who are the officers?
- If you were considering a job change, what companies or individuals would you contact?
- Why have you and your company been successful? (Again, a compliment)

Although you should not carry a notebook and take notes during a job interview, you will do so here, since you are the interviewer. Write your questions in a place that will be easily accessible during the interview (the first page of your notebook, on a separate note card, etc.). During the interview, you also will have spontaneous questions that arise from the conversation.

A day or so before the interview, plan what you will wear – professional attire, of course. Check out the location and be certain you know how to get there. Even still, on the day of the interview, allow extra travel time; there is no excuse for being late.

Step 4: Take charge of the interview. Remember your objective for the interview (to get as much information as possible) and don't waste too much time in incidental conversation. Thank your source for allowing you this time and for sharing his/her knowledge with you. Then get straight to the point. Your contact will appreciate your time concern and the interview will be off to a good start.

During the interview, don't feel that you must write down every bit of information now. Make the most of this short interview and record just enough information to jog your memory later, realizing your time constraints.

After your allotted time is over, thank your source for the time and information, and then end the interview. Let me repeat this: after your allotted time is over, thank your source and then end the interview. If you overextend and wear out your welcome, your source will be irritated and you will lose any empathy and support you may have developed. However, if your source offers to continue your time, you can accept if you wish. Be certain to ask if you may include this authority in your email "Buddy List," to contact occasionally in the future. (These "Buddy Lists" are discussed later in this chapter.)

Step 5: Review the interview. Immediately after the interview is concluded, record the information you did not have time to write during the interview. Then critique your performance. What would you like to have done differently if you had the opportunity? What will you do differently on your next information interview? Did you obtain the information you needed?

Step 6: Plan your follow-up. Now analyze the information you garnered and plan what you will do with it. Do you have new sources to contact? Did your source mention companies you now wish to call? Are there organizations and/or associations you plan to contact and meetings you plan to attend? Add this person to your email "Buddy List," if you cleared it with him/her, and stay in touch by email periodically.

Don't forget to send your source a thank-you note as soon as possible. A hand-written note is fine, if that is more convenient. If you have some item of information that you feel would be of interest, enclose it with your note. Be certain to include your address and phone number or a business card, should he/she recall some information later for you.

Carrying your resume

Should you carry your resume to an information interview? There are two theories on this, and since both have merit, use the approach that suits you.

You may have a copy of your resume, in case your source asks for it, but do not offer it yourself. You are there to obtain information to use in your job search, and offering your resume will both waste time that you could better use asking questions, as well as possibly offend your source who is expecting an information interview only.

Nevertheless, if during the interview, your source is impressed with your preparation, thoroughness, and/or subject knowledge, you may be considered for possible employment. Having your resume then allows you to seize this opportunity.

The other approach is *not* to carry a resume with you. If asked for it, state that you did not bring one, since you are only conducting an information interview. Then offer to bring one by later. This way, you may be able to have two interviews, one for information and another for possible employment.

Informal Information Interviews

In addition to a formal interview with these authorities in their offices, you should also have casual, informal meetings with fellow job seekers – for example, former co-workers also laid off, or individuals you met at a recent job networking meeting. Meeting for coffee at a local Starbucks or bookstore is a good suggestion.

Your purpose here is to exchange job search information. They may know of companies moving to town, planned expansions, useful personnel agencies, or any other information about your industry or potential employers. Be prepared to share your knowledge also.

Conclusion

Information interviews are another invaluable tool, and you must plan at least one every week, either formal or informal.

How successful this technique works for you will be determined by
1) how successful you are in selecting good sources to interview,
2) how prepared you are for the interview, and

3) how well you make use of the information you are given.

I am often called for an information interview, and I know from these experiences that the information I recall during the session is much better than that I would have given on the phone. People generally like to be helpful (especially when there is no tangible cost involved!), and I think you will be pleasantly surprised with the reception you receive. Even if your source is reluctant to commit to a personal interview, you likely will be given helpful data on the phone.

INFORMATION INTERVIEW
Check List

Before the interview
► Determine objectives
► Plan questions
► Decide attire
► Carry resume?
► Have business cards convenient
► Carry folder, not attaché case

During the interview
► Take charge of interview
► Remember and complete objectives
► Don't waste time
► Take short notes
► End interview on time

After the interview
► Critique performance
► Expand notes
► Send thank-you letter
► Plan follow-up

Tool #13: Internet Networking

Pro's: Free and easy source. Best method to obtain "insider information."

Con's: Must be computer literate. Success depends on number of contacts willing to help with your job search.

Like almost every aspect of our lives, the Internet has revolutionized job search. Hundreds of thousands of jobs nationwide are posted on thousands of web sites, and you are encouraged to apply online in most cases. I have written earlier about the pitfalls of over-reliance on those job vacancies, but you can find many other uses for the Internet to speed your job search.

Buddy Lists

At the onset of your search, start a Networking Buddy List, a group email of close friends and colleagues, those people who would help you if they knew what specific information could facilitate your search. Obtain their email addresses and ask permission to email them on occasion – not too often, since you don't want to alienate them by becoming more spam to delete. Send them an email explaining what you are looking for and attach a resume for them to keep stored in their computer. Ask for suggestions or any other help they might offer. As your job search progresses, add new contacts you develop through your networking efforts.

My most recent company survey found that nearly all large companies offer some sort of Employee Referral Bonus for applicants referred to the company and hired. From the company's standpoint, the $100 or so paid out for prescreened applicants is far cheaper than any advertising. For the employee, helping with recruiting is a way to stand out within the company, as well as pocketing some extra money. Even if no monetary incentive is offered, referring qualified applicants is an excellent way to show you are a "team player" and to advance in the company. Understanding that practice, here are two more ways to use your Buddy List:

First, through your research, you have determined a dozen or so companies that periodically have needs for your background and skills. Email your Buddy List and ask if they know someone employed at any of your target companies and if they would recommend you to the person. Call that person and using your Buddy's name, ask if your new contact would keep an eye open for future openings that fit your background and keep your resume in his/her computer to refer when the need occurs.

Secondly, you have found an opening on the internet or other classified advertising, and you want to apply. You also know that blindly sending your resume has little chance of succeeding, and probably will just be added to a resume heap somewhere or just drift in cyberspace. Here's the solution: email your Buddies and ask if they know someone at the company who you could call and who would take your resume to the hiring authority if possible or at least present it to the Human Resources recruiter in charge of filling the position. If you could meet with that new contact and make a positive impression, you might also have developed a reference inside the company.

Next create a Job Seekers' Buddy List for fellow job seekers you meet at job networking meetings or other sources. When you hear of a new opening, a job fair, a good networking group, or any other job tip, send it to your buddies here. (Start it off by telling them to buy a copy of *Atlanta Jobs*!) Even if the tip does not apply to someone in your group, they may refer it to a friend who can use it, and you also could be the recipient of this form of networking.

Still another use for your Buddy Lists is to get "insider information" on a company. For example, you have an interview scheduled with ABC Corp. Email your Buddies and ask if anyone knows the "culture" of the company or any other useful information.

Although a personal snail-mail thank-you note is correct after an interview, you should email anyone who has helped you in your job search. Keep your job network active by occasionally sending an email to update your contacts on your job search progress. And when you do find employment, be certain to email all your networking lists to let them know what you will be doing. You may need to call on them again later or they may hear of another available job for you to consider.

PART 3:

OTHER RESOURCES

Tool #14: Public Agencies

Tool #15: Privately Funded Organizations

Tool #16: Useful Resources and Publications

Tool #13: Public Agencies

Pro's: Free and easy source. Free testing and counseling available. Listings at all levels of experience. Includes jobs available in the public and private sectors.

Con's: Companies tend to shy away from public agencies, since there is limited applicant screening or matching.

Georgia Career Center

When is the last time you went to a state employment office?

If your answer is "years," you are in for a real shock. Gone are the dark, depressing "unemployment offices" with metal folding chairs, long lines, and impersonal bureaucrats. These offices are now state-of-the-art, offering on-line job databases, computers you can use, and with free access to the internet, plus many, many new services. Incidentally, you will also see several copies of *Atlanta Jobs*, as they use it extensively, as well as an interview video I recorded for Georgia Public Television.

> **ajobs.com**
> Link to GA Career Center offices and directions.

Go to an office in person (do not mail a resume) and have your Social Security card and valid driver's license to use for identification. Office hours generally are 8 a.m. - 4:30 p.m., Monday thru Friday, and some offices are open at nite. A brief orientation session is required first and is given at several different times during the day at each location; call and ask the times before you go to an office. Here are six metro branches, so pick the one closest to you. Call if you need directions or visit **ajobs.com** for direction links and maps.

- North Atlanta/Fulton County: 2943 N. Druid Hills Rd NE (in Toco Hills Shopping Center); (404) 679-5200
- South Atlanta/Fulton County: 2636 Martin Luther King Jr Ave (across from MARTA's Hightower station); (404) 656-6000 (auto phone info)
- DeKalb County: 3879 Covington Hwy, Decatur, GA; (404) 298-3970
- Cobb/Cherokee County: 465 Big Shanty Road, Marietta; (770) 528-6100
- Gwinnett County: 2211 Beaver Ruin Rd, Norcross; (770) 840-2200
- Clayton County: 2450 Mt. Zion Pkwy, Bldg 100, Jonesboro; (678) 479-5886

Services offered

The Georgia Department of Labor maintains computerized databases of job openings from corporations, the Georgia State Merit System, and many federal agencies. In addition, they offer information on the procedure to follow in applying for state and federal government positions. Their computerized job bank (JIS = job information system) is very user friendly and allows you to access job openings by industry, specialty, and geographic preference, including Atlanta only. You can access this database from your home computer as well.

Most offices will administer the "GSIS," an interest inventory to assist you with career directions and decisions. Skill tests for computer efficiency and typing speed are also given. Tutorials for computer proficiency are available, and English as Second Language is offered in Spanish, Russian, Greek, and Bosnian.

Seminars are conducted on every facet of the job search process and each office will have a large amount of free job search literature. The Professional Executives Networking Group (PEN) meets at the Toco Hills office each Wednesday at 1:30pm, attracting 100+ professional-level job seekers to exchange job information. Another group for aspiring entrepreneurs meets on Fridays, to learn about starting a business and covering topics such as financing, funding, and applying for SBA loans; call the Toco Hills office for more details.

Computers are available at no charge for writing or revising your resume (BYOD: bring your own disk) and certified resume writers are available at the larger offices; the North Metro Office on Toco Hills Avenue has three on staff.

Banks of computers with internet access are on hand, so you can "surf the net" and that includes **ajobs.com**. Fax machines, copiers, and phones are also available for your use.

Georgia Works

This program offers companies an opportunity to employ a job seeker at the state's expense for up to eight weeks, but not more than 24 hours/week. The applicant receives superised training by the company, and is paid a salary while continuing to draw unemployment benefits. Hopefully after this trial and training period, the company will hire the applicant full time. Discuss this program with your Career Center counselor for more details.

Re-employment Unit

The Georgia employment service also offers a specialized job placement program called the Re-employment Unit which includes a wealth of free information, seminars, and publications on finding employment. I have reviewed the information and generally recommend it highly.

You cannot request to be included in CAP; rather, you are assigned to participate when you file for your unemployment benefits. As part of this process, they administer a profiling test that identifies applicants who may need special help. (Incidentally, you can file at any of the state offices, regardless of the county in which you reside.) There generally are two criteria, although everyone can audit the classes:

(1) you must have been terminated as a result of a lay-off or reduction-in-force, and

(2) your prior company must have been in Georgia.

Veterans' Placement Unit

Federal law mandates that each state must have a job assistance program for veterans. Here in Georgia, each state employment office has at least one veteran (usually a disabled veteran) on staff responsible for administering this program. At the North Druid Hills office, the contact person is Robert Hurd at (404) 679-5200.

If you are a veteran and wish to participate in this service, you must visit one of the many state employment offices (no appointment necessary) and complete a veteran's application form. Then you will be assigned to a job counselor, who will offer job-search advice, make job development phone calls in your behalf, and attempt to arrange employment interviews. This group also conducts monthly job-related seminars at Fort McPherson.

Workforce Investment Act

The WIA is a federally funded program, offering grants to states for additional education. In Georgia, it is administered by the counties, and your Career Center counselor can help you with the procedures. This program offers free tuition to job seekers wishing to further their education to be more competitive in the job market. I know of several people who have benefited from it, and I highly recommend you explore the possibilities of obtaining certification in your field, additional skills, or some other education that will enhance your career. Some restrictions may apply, so discuss it with your counselor.

Tool #14: Privately Funded Organizations[1]

Pro's: Specialized help for specific target groups. Will more closely empathize with your problems. Often acts as non-profit personnel agency, arranging interviews, counseling, etc.

Con's: Often must be "minority" group member. Companies tend to shy away from non-selective referrals.

Atlanta has several privately funded groups that offer many forms of job assistance to a specific constituency. I have included several here, and I suspect there may be more. Please let me know if you encounter a group I have omitted.

ajobs.com
Internet links when available.

Atlanta Urban League

The Atlanta Urban League sponsors a free service called the "Employment Referral Program," which operates as a non-profit training center and personnel agency. They place up to 500 applicants annually in Atlanta, from hourly personnel to recent college grads to top-level executives.

The Urban League requires all applicants to come to their offices for a personal interview and evaluation with one of their counselors before they will refer you to companies. They accept applicants Monday - Thursday from 8:30 to 12:30 on a "first-come, first-served" basis. However, if you have a unique situation and need to reserve an appointment time, contact John Bray, Employment Referral Program Director, at (404) 659-1150.

100 Edgewood Avenue, Suite 600, Atlanta, GA 30303

---

[1] See also "Tool #9: Job Networking Groups," discussed earlier in this chapter.

Jewish Family and Career Services (www.jfcs-atlanta.org)

Non-profit agency offers employment counseling, resume assistance, interview coaching, vocational testing, and other general career help, including video recording and critique of your interviewing skills. There are nominal fees based on one's ability to pay, but I am told that no one is turned away for lack of funds. They maintain a Job Bank of current openings referred to them, and when appropriate, they make direct referrals of applicants to companies and arrange interviews.

Call for an appointment.
4549 Chamblee-Dunwoody Road, Atlanta, GA 30338
(770) 677-9300; 677-9400 fax

Seniors' Employment

Funded by the AARP, this is a free service, targeted for applicants age 50 and older. You must appear in person, and bring with you numerous documents, such as birth certificate, driver's license, etc. Call 404/609-9697 for more information and which documents you will need to bring. Located on the first floor of the Darlington Apartments at 2225 Peachtree Rd NE, Suite D, Atlanta.

Georgia Center for Non-Profits (www.nonprofitgeorgia.org)

Organization that offers various business assistance to Georgia non-profits. Job help is through "Opportunity NOCS," a free bi-weekly newsletter that lists job openings submitted by member associations, and is available by visiting the Foundation Center Resource Library in Suite 150 (Lobby level) of the Hurt Building at Edgewood Ave x Peachtree Center Ave. For more information, call Tinsley Waters at 404/688-4845 x3100.

Latin American Association (www.latinamericanassoc.org)

Funded by the United Way, this association offers job assistance to Hispanics and other Spanish bilingual applicants, both for professional and non-professional positions. Primarily, they serve as a referral agency, accepting job openings and referring applicants for employment. In addition, they conduct seminars on the basics of job search, including resume preparation, interviewing techniques, etc. There is no charge for their services.

For more information or to schedule an appointment, contact Patricia Rincon, Employment Director, at
2665 Buford Hwy., Atlanta, GA 30324.
(404) 638-1800; fax 638-1806

Southeast Employment Network (www.senetwork.com)

Unlike the other network groups I discussed as "Tool #8," this is not an "applicant-oriented" network. Rather, it is a private group of 150± technical recruiters representing mostly high tech companies, who meet monthly to discuss the personnel needs of their individual companies and to share resumes they have received, as well as any other helpful recruiting information. There is no charge to applicants for this service.

In addition, they sponsor semi-annual job fairs (March and September), which are attended by 50+ companies and where 100+ applicants generally will receive job offers. If your background is in MIS, high-tech engineering or telecommunications, or your objective is computer systems-oriented, or you have a non-technical background but have worked in a technical environment (_e.g._, human resources for a high tech company), you can have your resume made available to all 110± member companies simply by mailing one copy to
Jim McNabb
c/o Staff Tech Jobs, 11625 Rainwater Dr, Alpharetta, 30004
(678) 338-2067; jimm@stafftechjobs.com

> **ajobs.com**
> Review their site, job fair dates, and email your resume.

New Horizons

New Horizons is a for-profit computer learning center offering training for Mac and PC software, from beginners through high-end users. Many of their students are between jobs and using their time constructively by updating computer skills, something I also strongly encourage you to do. Some state financial aid is available to Georgia residents, so ask your New Horizons counselor. Also ask for financial aid or a discount.

As a service primarily to their students but also available to anyone, they maintain a free Job Book which lists 50± job vacancies in all computer areas, including graphic design, administration positions, Novell, LAN, etc. To review the Job Book, visit their offices at 4053 LaVista Rd., Atlanta, GA. No appointment or referral needed. Call (404) 270-2000 for directions.

USO of Georgia (www.uso.org)

For military members and their families, this organization offers free booklets and guides to Georgia job search and job training resources, job search tips, and other career transition information you should know. They also maintain a career resource library and hold career transition seminars. Call (404) 761-8061 and information will be mailed to you.

Career Calendar

The Sunday edition of *The Atlanta Journal and Constitution* includes a column called "Career Calendar," that lists many other privately funded or public job search assistance that is free or at a small cost. This column includes upcoming job fairs, job network groups, low-cost aptitude and intelligence testing offered by local colleges, free resume consultation, and other helpful assistance sponsored by non-profit agencies. "Career Calendar" is located at the beginning of the "Job Guide," which is generally one of the first pages of the classified want-ads.

Tool #15:   Useful Resources and Publications

Pro's: Sources smaller, specialized companies for specific industry experience, as well as larger corporations and employers. Most helpful for experienced applicants searching for companies in their industry.

Con's: Moderate expense or travel to a public library, some duplication from other sources.

I am including information on reference materials that you may order, although many are available at public libraries, and some comments regarding each. In contacting the companies that are included in these publications, treat them as a Direct Contact.

Atlanta Chamber of Commerce

Several helpful publications are available from the Atlanta Chamber of Commerce. You can order by phone and charge to Visa or MasterCard. You can also order by mail, but since there may be a postage charge, I suggest you call first. Prices and publication availability are subject to change.

> **ajobs.com**
> Much free info online, and can order online.

Atlanta Chamber of Commerce
235 International Blvd, N.W., Atlanta, GA 30303.
Attn: Public Information Dept.
(404) 880-9000; info/publications: (404) 586-8403

- Atlanta City Map - $2.00

- Atlanta's largest employers, Fortune 500 companies with offices in Atlanta, and Atlanta headquartered firms. $10

- Manufacturing Directory - Lists more than 1500 manufacturing firms in metro Atlanta, including Standard Industrial Classifications. Good source to locating companies in your manufacturing specialty.
- "Atlanta Quick Look" - Includes the Newcomers Guide, Employment Services and Larger Employers publications. Good start if you are not local. No charge.

Multi-national Corporations

If you are interested in foreign companies with facilities in Atlanta, you can peruse the *Georgia International Facilities* information free online, courtesy of the Georgia Department of Industry and Trade (www.georgia.org). More than 45 countries are listed, plus statistics on foreign operations and facilities in Georgia. The lists are in PDF format, and can be downloaded and/or printed.

Manufacturing Facilities in Georgia

The Georgia Department of Industry and Trade also has an outstanding web site that allows you to search for manufacturing facilities in Georgia by name, product, size, SIC code, city, county or any combination of those (www.georgia.org/manufacturing). You are given names of their top officers, number of employees, contact information, and more.

Book of Lists

The *Atlanta Business Chronicle* (www.atlanta.bizjournals.com) produces an annual publication called the *Book of Lists*, which includes the 25 or so largest companies in various categories, and information about their sales, number of employees, major clients, etc. It is interesting reading in general, and it could be helpful to you to locate companies within a specific industry or profession. The current edition lists 45+ categories, including accounting firms, architectural/engineering firms, auto dealerships, banks, travel agencies, ad and PR agencies, computer companies, credit unions, HMO's, hospitals, hotels, law firms, printers, telecommunications companies, real estate firms and agents, plus many more. To order for Atlanta or other cities, call Biz Books at 800/486-3289 and charge to credit card, or order online at www.bizjournals.com.

National Trade and Professional Associations of the U. S.

I made reference to this catalogue in "Tool #9: Professional and Trade Associations." It is available at most public libraries, but you may order it if you wish. Call (888) 265-0600 for current pricing.

Columbia Books, Inc., Publishers
1350 New York Ave NW, Suite 207
Washington, DC 20005-3286.

Physicians' Desk Reference (PDR)

The primary focus of this weighty book is to provide doctors with detailed information on all prescription drugs. In addition, it lists drug manufacturers, complete with the addresses and phone numbers of their corporate headquarters and regional offices, and even includes the names and contact data for their sales and operations managers. If you are seeking a job in some medical field, either sales or management, the PDR will supply you with names to contact and information on the products marketed by each company. The PDR is available at most public libraries, or if you have a friend who is a doctor or who works in a medical facility, you can probably borrow one.

Georgia Association of Personnel Consultants

> **ajobs.com**
> GAPS directory can be reviewed and downloaded.

The local chapter of the National Association of Personnel Services publishes a directory of their members with contact information and classified by specialty. Remember, however, that not all Atlanta

agencies are members of the association. To order, send a stamped, self-addressed envelope and a check for $6.95 to
   GAPS
   P O Box 500386
   Atlanta, GA 31150-0386.

Georgia Manufacturers' Register

Lists 11,000+ Georgia manufacturers, with contact data, sales figures, size, primary executives (including personnel, accounting managers, engineering managers, etc.), import status, brand of computer, etc. -- more than the free site offered by the Georgia Department of Industry and Trade. You can order a copy for $119.95 (no shipping charge), but I suggest you reference the free public library instead.
   Manufacturers' News, Inc.
   1633 Central Street, Evanston, IL 60201-9729
   (888) 752-5200 – To order directory on IBM disk

CHAPTER V

STEP FOUR:

INTERVIEWING TECHNIQUES

Top 10 Ways
to Blow Your Interview

10. Offer to add the company's logo to your body tattoos.

9. Tell the interviewer about your psychiatrist.

8. Brag about the affair you are having with the boss' spouse.

7. Discuss your sexual harassment suit.

6. List your grandparents as references.

5. Wink often at the interviewer.

4. Mention your spouse works for the IRS.

3. Wear enough perfume or cologne so your scent will linger for days.

2. List your last job title as "Party Animal."

And the top way to ruin the day . . .

1. Bring your mother to the interview.

CHAPTER V

Step Four: Interviewing Techniques

Congratulations!

The fact that you are being given an interview indicates that you obviously have presented yourself well so far and that the interviewer has at least some interest in you to grant you some time. You have worked hard to get to this point, but don't let up yet.

Preparation

Remember this quotation:

"The successful job-seeker is the one who is willing to do what the unsuccessful will not: Preparation."

Preparation is important in every part of your job search, and it is absolutely essential to a successful interview. Nervous? That could be because you haven't adequately prepared. Being prepared not only settles the stomach, it impresses the interviewer as well.

Research the company, and when possible, research the job and interviewer. Learn as much about the company as timely possible, but don't feel that you must know more than the interviewer. Here is the basic information to digest:

- Most importantly, know the company's products or services. What do they offer, provide, manufacture, or sell?

- What is their annual growth and how profitable are they?

- What can you find out about their industry in general, including competitors?

- What is their ranking within their industry?

- Research the company's history.

- Try to determine their reputation. Are they considered aggressive? What is their personnel turnover rate? How are they regarded by their customers? This information is subjective and may be difficult to obtain, but if you have a reliable source, it is good information to know.

- Every corporation has its individual "culture," a nebulous term to describe a company's philosophy, attitudes, dress codes, and the image it strives to project. Knowing these factors can direct you with your answers and behavior during the interview.

- Find out as much as you can about the interviewer(s), especially background and previous employment, interviewing techniques, hobbies, interests, etc. If your interview was arranged through an intermediary, that person may be able to relay good insight into the whims of the interviewer(s); good personnel agencies always should have this information. For example, does the interviewer have any favorite questions for which you can prepare?

Researching most of the company data is easy, and there are many sources. The simplest method is to go on-line to **ajobs.com**, which has direct links to several hundred company information web sites. You also can call the company and ask for an annual report, information brochure, or recruiting information to be mailed to you. If the company declines, as many privately-held companies will, or if you are short on time, go to your college placement center or the public library. Some good

> **ajobs.com**
> Several sources are available online. Check the company links first for a free source, then the link to Database American for more in depth info for a small fee.

reference books include *Standard and Poor's, Moody's, Million Dollar Directory, American Corporate Families* and *Thomas Register of American Manufacturers.* All these are readily available on the second floor at the Atlanta-Fulton County Library downtown (Take MARTA to Peachtree Center station; exit Ellis Street and then West Peachtree escalator), as well as the public libraries in the metro counties. The Gwinnett County library branch at Peachtree Corners is very good.

Networking is also a good source. Ask friends or business contacts if they are familiar with the company; however, keep in mind you may be hearing biased information or rumor, and treat this information accordingly. If you know some of the company's clients, you can carefully and discreetly call them for information.

Determine your past accomplishments and achievements. This personal inventory is a very important part of your preparation and you should form some plans how you can mention them during your interview. Write them down and then review them before each interview. Include not only major feats you can document, but also problems you encountered in your job and how you solved them.

Anticipate certain questions and be ready with your answers. I recently spoke with a Vice President of Human Resources who told me that for his last job search, he wrote down fifty questions an interviewer might ask. Then he wrote down his answers, and put it aside for a few days. Reading them later, he realized how bad some of his answers really were, and he thought them through again. That took a lot of time – but then too, his thoroughness paid off in a big way.

It is impossible to anticipate every question you might be asked, but knowing what your interviewers are seeking with their questions will help you plan your responses. Of course you must have the technical expertise required for the position, and the fact that you have been invited for an interview, suggests that you do or nearly so. Excluding that, employers will be probing three areas: your past, your present, and your future.

Past: What have been your life patterns so far? Have you excelled or just run with the pack? What accomplishments can you point to that show you to be an achiever or better yet, and over-achiever? How have you performed with your past employers? Interviews feel that your past is an indicator to your future, and if you have been successful in your past endeavors, you likely will continue to succeed.

Your resume will reflect your accomplishments and achievements, and you should plan how you will mention them and others during your interview. Carry letters of recommendation to your interview, and offer them to your interviewer. Have records that prove your past successes, such as certificates of awards, sales quotas, letters of commendation, etc.

Typical questions: Of your past successes, of what are you the proudest? In what percentile of your graduating class did you finish? How successful were you in your past employment? Why did you leave your past employers?

Present: How well do you "know yourself"? Do you understand your strengths and weaknesses, your abilities, and your limits? What skills and character traits do you possess that are needed in your career? Do you have a clear and certain job focus?

Typical questions: Why are you pursuing this career and how does this job fit into your overall career plan? How would your spouse or best friend describe you? What are the qualities needed to be a good accountant [or salesperson, engineer, programmer, etc.]? Give me three adjectives to describe yourself. In what do you excell? What are your shortcomings?

Future: Now you must "sell yourself" to the interviewer, that is, convince him/her that you are the one for the job. In my practice, I have seen more applicants rejected for failing this section of the interview, than for any other reason.

This is the part of the interview where you must take control. Just as you prepared a marketing plan to get interviews, now you must plan how you will present yourself in the most positive light, showing why the interviewer should hire you. Just before the interview, review your past accomplishments and be sure to stress the strongest and how they demonstrate you will perform as an employee. The questions you have prepared to ask also should show your strong points and your interest in excelling in the job. Ask questions such as "What would you like done differently by the next person in this job." "What seem to be the qualities that have been successful with past employees in this job." – then show how you possess those qualities.

Typical questions: What can you do for our company? How can you help improve our profits? Why should we hire you?

The "Stress Interview"

I recently read an article stating that the so-called "stress interview" is becoming popular again. It has been around for as many years as I have been in personnel, but had fallen into disfavor because of its essentially negative approach. According to the article, however, in today's stressful business environment, companies would like to put you in a stress situation and then judge how well you can perform. Although I doubt you will encounter this style of interviewing often, you should be prepared in the event you do.

In a stress interview, the interviewer will appear to disagree with nearly everything you say, in order to see how you react. His/her comments, questions, and general body language are geared to lead

161

you astray, to offer you opportunities to make mistakes, and to generally make you uncomfortable. Oftentimes, the interviewer will ask a question, and then after you have given your answer, will sit quietly as though expecting you to continue.

If you sense you are in this type of interview, stick to your guns, and above all, do not begin to contradict yourself or start to ramble in a vain attempt to please the interviewer. In particular, once you have answered a question to your own satisfaction, stop and wait for the interviewer to continue; in my practice, I have had many applicants rejected because they didn't know when to stop talking. If the silence becomes awkward, ask a question that forces the interviewer to break the silence.

Interviewing Styles

Over the years, interviewing styles and questions have changed. Many years ago, the vogue questions were "What are your strengths?" and conversely, "What are your weaknesses?" More recently, "Tell me about yourself" was the technique of choice, and it continues to be very popular with many interviewers, including myself.

Although you will still encounter those questions, the current fad in interviewing now revolves around open-ended questions asking for specific examples or instances of real life problems: "Give me an example of how you . . . ." Part of your preparation was to list your accomplishments and achievements, and to plan how you can include them in your interview. Using them to illustrate how you handled specific situations is an excellent way to respond to these questions.

The so-called "STAR System" of interviewing is a good example of this style of interviewing. STAR is the acronym for Situation or Task, Action, and Results. You will be asked a question – for example, "Tell me about a communications problem you have had with a former supervisor and how you overcame it." Break this type of question into three compents:

1) What was the situation at the time? *I felt a barrier between my supervisor and me.*

2) What was the action that I took? *I asked my supervisor if I could speak privately with him. I said that I felt I was not communicating well with him and asked for suggestions.*

3) What were the results of the action? *My supervisor made some constructive comments and we have communicated very well since then.*

That illustration is very simple, but should give you the general picture. When you are asked to discuss specific instances, pause a moment to collect your thoughts, remember "STAR," then reply accordingly.

Interviewing Tips

The following are frequently asked questions that you should anticipate and for which you should have planned an answer:

1) Tell me about yourself.

2) Why did you leave your past employers?

> More than 100 additional questions are included in *Atlanta Jobs on CD v.2.0*. Call 404/262-7131 to order, no shipping or handling charge.

3) Pick three adjectives to describe yourself.

4) Give me a specific example of a problem you overcame in your job.

5) What are the qualities of a good manager [salesperson, accountant, engineer, etc.]?

6) How would you rate your success with your job? Why were you successful?

7) What did you like [or dislike] most about your last job? If you could change anything about your last job, what would it be?

THE MOST FREQUENTLY ASKED
INTERVIEW QUESTION IS
"Tell me about yourself."

What will you say?

Your answer should be no more than
two minutes, and yet it will set the tenor
for the remaining part of the interview.
Plan your reply well in advance and rehearse
it often. If you wait until you're sitting in
front of the interviewer to come up with
an answer, you have blown the interview!

Here are some guidelines:
• Be concise, and keep your response to
  a maximum of two minutes.
• Be upbeat, emphasizing accomplishments
  and achievements.
• Include data you want to discuss further
  during the interview.

8) Rank these in order of preference: salary, location, nature of the job.

9) Where do you expect to be in your career in five years?

10) How did you choose your college? Why did you choose your major? What did you intend to do with that degree?

These traits are often used by interviewers to rate applicants:

Intelligence: Conceptual ability, breadth of knowledge, verbal expression, organized thoughts, analytical thought process, logical decision-making.

Energy and Enthusiasm: Animated, spontaneous, fast-paced throughout, positive attitude, optimistic outlook.

Results-orientation: Responses revolve around task accomplishment, gets to the point, emphasizes achievements, provides information relevant to interview objectives, able to give specific instances and examples.

Maturity: Acceptance of responsibility for one's actions, self-confident, ability to reflect on experiences, understands strengths and weaknesses, clear career goals, punctual.

Assertiveness: Responds in a forceful manner, does not ramble, speaks in a convincing tone, persuasive, good at selling self and ideas, good communicator.

Sensitivity: Sincere, friendly, tactful, responsive, not aloof, listens as well as speaks, asks relevant questions.

Openness: Discusses short-comings as well as strengths, is not preoccupied with saying the right thing, consistent responsiveness regardless of content.

Objectivity: Stands up to interviewer when there is disagreement, discusses persons and events critically, does not allow emotions to cloud perceptions.

Appearance: Properly attired, professional projection, minimum of fragrance and jewelry, appropriate accessories, attention to detail, shoes polished, nails clean.

11) What do you consider the major accomplishment(s) or achievements(s) in your life and/or career?

12) Give me an example of an unpopular policy you had to implement and how you did it.

13) Why are you considering a job change?

14) Evaluate your present and past supervisors. (Recent grads may be asked to evaluate their instructors.)

15) Why haven't you found a job after so many months?

16) What interests you about this job?

17) What can you contribute to our organization?

18) How well do you communicate with others? Give me an example of a communications problem you encountered and how you solved it.

19) What constructive criticism have former bosses made to you, and what did you do in response?

20) If you were hiring for this position, what would you look for?

21) Are you interviewing with other companies?

There are many "right" answers to those questions, and undoubtedly, there are just as many wrong ones. Before reading further, decide what your answers would be. If you have access to a tape or video recorder, record your answers now, and then review your performance. After you have read my suggested responses and reviewed your answers, repeat this exercise.

Here are some reasons behind the questions and some suggestions for your consideration:

1) *Tell me about yourself.*

You know you will encounter this question during nearly every interview, so you must have prepared and rehearsed it well in advance. There is no excuse for not being prepared for this standard question. Here is a general outline to follow:

Who you are: (20 seconds)
Your qualifications: education, years of relevant experience, etc.
Very little personal (married ok)

What you have been doing: (40 seconds)
Either topical or chronological
Most recent job first, experience and skills gained relevant to new position
Why left last employer

Where you want to go: (20 seconds)
Job objective, career path

Why you should be hired: (40 seconds)
Stress accomplishments and achievements, relevant experience and knowledge for the job, etc.

2) *Why did you leave your past employers?*

Never say anything derogatory about former employers. Rather, you left your previous employment for more responsibility, a greater challenge and a better career opportunity. If your departure was the result of a reduction-in-force, make that clear, and note that your position was not refilled. If you were part of a massive lay-off, your job performance is less likely to be an issue.

3) *Pick three adjectives to describe yourself.*

This must be the oldest and simplest question of all, but it still amazes me how many applicants are stunned when I ask it. There are other ways of phrasing this question, such as "What are your strong points?" or "How would your best friend (or employer) describe you?"

Remember, this is a business interview, so pick adjectives that are business-oriented. Unless you are pursuing a career in the Scouts, do not be "loyal, thrifty, brave, obedient, etc." Here are some good choices: aggressive, ambitious, assertive, self-motivated, goal-oriented, self-disciplined, persistent, good communicator, competitive, team player, etc. Having chosen your adjectives, now think of specific instances illustrating how you have used those qualities, and be prepared to relate them.

4) *Give me a specific example of a problem you overcame in your job.*

The interviewer is asking you what you have accomplished in your job. Choose an achievement that best illustrates your results-orientation.

5) *What are the qualities of a good manager [salesperson, accountant, engineer, etc.]?*

Obviously, you must exemplify the same qualities of a good whatever, so pick adjectives similar to the ones you chose in question #3. Then be prepared with several good illustrations.

6) *How would you rate your success with your job? Why were you successful?*

Always rate yourself highly, but not perfect. Even if you were fired from your last job, you should rate yourself well. On a scale of one to ten, you should pick eight or nine. Why were you successful? Because you possess the qualities of a good whatever that you identified in questions #3 and #5. Again, be prepared with specific examples.

7) *What did you like [or dislike] most about your last job? If you could change anything about your last job, what would it be?*

Since you knew what your job would be, there must have been something about it that you liked, or why else would you have taken it? Thus, you should have many items about your job that you like and only a few that you dislike, although these dislikes obviously outweigh the positive aspects of your job. Above all, do not blame your displeasure on any person, especially your supervisor; the interviewer will question your version of the conflict. Never make any references to location, personality conflicts, or any answer that would allow the interviewer to conclude that you could be the problem.

Let me stress, however, that you should not suppress your feelings about your present employment. If you are seriously considering a job change, then you must have serious misgivings about your job. You should discuss them tactfully, yet frankly and forcefully, showing that you have given this considerable thought and have concluded that your talents would be best used elsewhere. Your thoughts here must be organized and logical, and expressed well enough to convince the interviewer.

8) *Rank these in order of preference: salary, location, nature of the job.*

This is another easy question, but frequently missed. Always have location last, even if you really don't mean it. Should the location of the job – Atlanta or other – be highly desirable to you, don't mention it during your interview. Companies need to think you are more interested in them and their position than you are in where you are located, and thus, nature of the job should be first, except possibly in the case of commissioned salespersons.

9) *Where do you expect to be in your career in five years?*

This can be tough if you don't know the company's normal career path. Certainly you expect to have been promoted, perhaps more than once. I suggest you answer with a question such as, "I expect to have achieved at least one promotion, but I am not familiar with your company's career path for this position. What should I reasonably expect?" Do not give the impression that you expect too much too soon and might become a disgruntled employee. And don't say you expect to be in the interviewer's position; that weak answer went out years ago!

10) *How did you choose your college? Why did you choose your major? What did you intend to do with that degree?*

Even if you attended the University of Saint Playboy-in-the-Caribbean and majored in underwater basket-weaving, you must present a logical reason for doing so. Companies want to feel that you are and have been in control of your life, and that you made your decisions based on a logical career plan.

11) *What do you consider the major accomplishment(s) or achievement(s) in your life and career?*

Surely you must have thought about this many times, but I am always surprised at how often an applicant falls apart when this is asked. Here is your chance to really pat yourself on the back, and don't be shy!

12) *Give me an example of an unpopular policy you had to implement and how you did it.*

This question was recently asked to one of my applicants applying for a personnel management position, and it could also be asked of many other positions. For example, if you are a salesperson, how do you tell your clients about an expected price increase? How do manufacturing managers explain increased productivity goals?

This is a good example of the "STAR System" of interviewing that was discussed a few pages back. Your answer will reveal much about your intelligence, results-orientation, and sensitivity, so be prepared with a thoughtful answer.

13) *Why are you considering a job change?*

Your answer here will be similar to your response in question #2. Now, however, you will add current considerations such as these:

• you are seeking a more dynamic or aggressive company;

• you want to use your knowledge and experience to transfer into a faster-growing industry (avoid saying a more stable industry, which sounds as if you are running away);

• you are seeking a company that will allow you more personal input into daily operations;

• you are seeking a company that gives more personal responsibility for final results;

• you would like to be better compensated for your contribution (especially good for salespersons);

• you would like to be more challenged than you are in your current position.

Note that these answers are positive in tone (versus, "I am *not* being adequately compensated....," etc.) Again, do not denigrate an employer, past or present.

14) *Evaluate your present and past supervisors. (Recent grads may be asked to evaluate their instructors.)*

Here you are displaying your tough-mindedness and objectivity. Using specific examples, mention a few good and bad points about current or former bosses, and how you might have acted differently. Most of your supervisors were probably good, so be certain that your praise is greater than your fault-finding, lest you be considered too negative or possessing a "bad attitude." Also, do not be too derogatory and never personal – you are commenting on performance as a supervisor, not as a "person."

171

15) *Why haven't you found a job after so many months?*

The standard reply is this: "Finding a job is easy; finding the right job takes a while longer." Quite likely, this will not satisfy the interviewer, and you may be asked for more details regarding your prolonged job search. Since this is essentially a negative discussion, try to end it as soon as possible, without becoming defensive. If you have received job offers that you declined, explain why – with good, logical reasons.

16) *What interests you about this job?*

If you don't have a good answer to this question, your interview is over. Your preparation should have given you at least some information about the job, and you must show how your qualities match the nature of this job.

17) *What can you contribute to our organization?*

If you can't sell yourself now, you never will. From your preparation, you should already know how your background and experience will benefit them, so tell them now – be assertive and lay it on thick! Show how their needs mesh closely with your own qualities, and include several examples.

18) *How well do you communicate with others? Give me an example of a communications problem you encountered and how you solved it.*

Over the years, I have reviewed thousands of job requisition forms, and nearly all have listed good communicative skills as a requirement for the job. Spend some time reflecting on how well you communicate your thoughts and ideas, and have several examples ready that demonstrate your ability to overcome problems communicating with others (superiors, subordinates, peers, clients, etc.). A variation of this question was discussed earlier as part of the "STAR System" of interviewing.

19) *What constructive criticism have former bosses made to you, and what did you do in response?*

In other words, how well do you take criticism? This question is a variation of "What are your weak points?" or "What are your limitations?"

If your answer is that you never have been criticized, then I think you are lying and so will the interviewer! Since we are all imperfect, we all have made mistakes and thus encountered criticism. You must freely and openly admit your shortcomings (but not too many and not too severe) and give specific examples of what you have done to overcome them.

20) *If you were hiring for this position, what would you look for?*

This is too easy. Describe yourself, using a variation of the adjectives you used in questions #3 and #6.

21) *Are you interviewing with other companies?*

Suppress the urge to answer, "None of your business," even though that may be the case. Reply something like this: "Yes, and it is very important that I choose a position that I will both enjoy and find challenging, as well as a company where I feel comfortable and can establish my career. I would like this job search to be my last. I feel that what ABC Company has to offer is exactly what I am seeking, and I would like to be a part of your organization."

Some interviewers may ask for what positions or with what companies you are interviewing, to determine if you have established a solid job focus. Politely decline to reveal the name of any company, but you can reveal other positions for which you are interviewing, being certain that these positions are similar to the one for which you are being interviewed and thereby confirm your job focus.

These 21 questions and answers are only a few of the many you might encounter, and I do recommend that you write down as many questions and your answers as you can. Then rehearse your answers aloud, perhaps to a friend for criticism.

Networking can be used in your interviewing preparation. Ask other job seekers what unusual questions they have encountered or what questions caught them off guard.

Relocation

In addition to the above questions, you will undoubtedly be asked about your availability for relocation. How you handle the following questions can determine the result of your interview:

- Are you available for immediate relocation?

- Will you be open for relocation at a later date?

- Does your spouse also have a career and if so, will that pose a relocation problem?[1]

- Are there any potential problems that could affect your relocation, now or in the future?

ajobs.com
Homefair and Datamasters are two sites that yield cost-of-living comparisons, plus other valuable info for many metro areas. Homefair allows you to input your current salary, then compare its worth in other areas.

These are definitely some of the most important questions you will encounter during the interview. I know I may get redundant here, but I must emphasize the importance of how you handle this series of questions. It is paramount that the interviewer feel that your major concern is the job – its nature, responsibilities, scope and potential. Be careful that you say nothing that will give the interviewer the impression that location is more important, or even equally so. If you say anything that leads the

---

[1]Yes, this question is legal, although it must be carefully presented so it will not suggest sex discrimination. Usually, it will not be asked so straight-forwardly, but the information somehow will be gleaned.

174

interviewer to conclude that location will be a primary factor in your career, you likely will not be considered further.

Unless the company with whom you are interviewing has operations in only one location, you may be required to move to another locale, either now or later. Since restricting your geographic availability eliminates an infinite number of jobs for which you could be qualified, I strongly urge you to consider any relocation as just another part of the total package, and evaluate it accordingly. If you are happy with your job, you most likely will be happy regardless of the location. Plus, companies need to think you are promotable, which usually involves a transfer, even if you are then assigned in Atlanta. If you are just starting your career, you may want to consider other Sunbelt locations, planning to request a transfer or promotion to Atlanta when one occurs. In fact, if you really like the company and its career path, that plan is a very viable alternative, especially if your company is Atlanta-headquartered.

On the initial, screening interview, companies sometimes decline to reveal the location of their opening, in order to determine your promotability/transferability. I have even had companies describe the position as requiring a relocation, even though it was for Atlanta! Furthermore, even if (or especially if) you know the position for which you are interviewing is in Atlanta, you should state your availability for relocation, so that the company will feel you are promotable.

Consequently, unless there are absolutely no circumstances under which you will consider relocation, I urge you to state that you are totally open for relocation, now as well as later. Should you receive a job offer in a location unacceptable to you, you can simply say no. But you will never have the opportunity to evaluate the whole offer, if your restrictions stop the interview process at the beginning.

Realistically, however, I realize that you may have a logical reason for your relocation restrictions, or even simply that you prefer to remain in Atlanta; after all, that is probably why you bought *ATLANTA JOBS*, and not Cleveland Jobs! From my own personnel experiences, I know that finding applicants who will relocate is perhaps the single greatest problem in job placement, and I suggest that most corporate recruiters would concur.

So if you don't want to relocate, how do you answer these questions? That depends on your reasons and how well you present them, although any reason will be viewed with suspicion.

A few years ago, I secured employment in Atlanta for an applicant whose child was in extensive therapy at Emory University Hospital, and thus he needed to remain here for the near future. That was an understandable reason, and the company wanted him enough to accept this, at least temporarily.

On the other hand, I also have interviewed hundreds, maybe thousands, of applicants (especially recent grads) who simply liked the good lifestyle in Atlanta and would not relocate. From a corporate standpoint, that's not a good reason, and again I urge you to reconsider, or at least come up with a better, more acceptable reason.

In between these two extremes are some valid cases for remaining in Atlanta. For example, dual-career families especially can be a potential problem. In this case, tell the interviewer that relocation would be considered, assuming that your spouse could continue his/her career at that locale. In fact, with the rapid increase of two-career families, many companies now offer all sorts of job placement and assistance to relocated spouses, and it would be proper to ask the interviewer if that company has any such programs.

Financial considerations, such as owning real estate here, may seem like a plausible reason to you, but from a company's viewpoint, it is merely another roadblock to promotions and transfers. Wanting to be near aging or ailing parents could be acceptable for a short time, but the interviewer will want to know how you plan to handle this situation in the future. If you have still other reasons for wanting to stay in Atlanta, first try to view them from the company's perspective before you explain them to the interviewer.

In summary, you should be as flexible in your inflexibility as possible. Nevertheless, if there are legitimate reasons for your inability to move, explain them to the interviewer. Realize, however, that your reasons may not be viewed as adequate for spurning a solid career opportunity, and so for the last time, I again suggest you carefully consider your stance on this subject. But whatever you decide, decide it *before* the interview, and be prepared with your answer.

Salary Questions[1]

One of the hardest questions to handle during an interview is "What are your salary requirements?" It is difficult to answer for several reasons:

• You may not know the full scope of the position.

• You are afraid to over-price yourself and miss out on a good career opportunity.

• If you name a figure too low, that may be interpreted as being under qualified.

• You suspect that your past compensation is higher than they have budgeted for this position and you fear being labeled overqualified.

• You certainly do not want to name a figure that may be less than the salary they are prepared to offer.

In short, if you name a figure too high or too low, you may be eliminated from consideration.

When this question is asked on your first, exploring interview, you have good reason to avoid an answer, especially if you have not yet determined the full responsibilities and duties of the position. In this case, I suggest you say, "I have researched your company and know that you offer fair and competitive salaries. But since I do not yet

---

[1] For a thorough discussion of salary negotiating, see Chapter VII. For now, we will concern ourselves with the interview questions related to salary.

know the full scope of the position or its potential, I am hesitant to state a figure now. Can we discuss salary later?" If the interviewer persists, I suggest you give a broad salary range (but not too broad!), adding that you will be able to give a more specific figure when you learn more about the position.

However, if your interview has been arranged through a third party (*e.g.*, a personnel agency or employee of the company), you already should know their salary structure. In this case, omit the run-around and simply say what they want to hear.

After you have had one or more interviews, you should be knowledgeable enough to determine what salary to request. By then, you will know what is expected in the position and you may have been given a hint as to what salary they have in mind. Although you must be prepared to name a salary if pressed, I encourage you to allow the company to state a figure first. If the figure is what you had anticipated, say that the salary is in line with your thoughts too. If the figure is higher than you expected, don't salivate, but simply say that the figure is acceptable.

If the salary stated is less than what you feel the position should command or less than you feel you deserve, then be prepared to negotiate, using the guidelines and principles explained in "Chapter VII: Salary Negotiating."

"Why were you fired?"

Even more difficult to handle are questions concerning your dismissal from a prior job, especially your most recent. Short of an absolute lie, avoid any comment that would reveal that to be the case. Say that you left your position to pursue other opportunities (which is true) and that you have letters of recommendation, should your interviewer wish to see them.[1] However, if you were the victim of a

---

[1] Regarding letters of recommendation, you should always ask for one whenever you change jobs. On future job interviews, you may need one but not be able to locate previous supervisors, who may have changed jobs or moved. Thus, whenever

corporate reduction-in-force, state that as the cause and then indicate that your position was not refilled.

Nevertheless, if your interviewer knows you were fired or is perceptive enough to conclude that, be prepared with a counter-attack. Recognize that no excuse will be entirely adequate, but attempt to put your dismissal in the most positive light possible.

The best approach is to be open and honest, and hope for empathy. We all make mistakes in life and the important result is to learn from them. How many times have you heard, "Experience is the best teacher"? Reveal the reason for your termination, and then discuss what you have learned from the experience and have done to remedy that situation. Since it is unlikely you can convince the interviewer that you were fired without cause, you can use your understanding of the firing to show that you have grown professionally, improved your skills, and are now a more valuable employee than before. If possible, have letters of recommendation from previous supervisors that indicate you have performed well in the past.

Personality conflicts are a frequent cause for firing, but I suggest you not blame that, since there are two sides to every issue and the interviewer has no reason to believe your version. Definitely don't imply that for some reason your boss "was out to get you." Instead, consider saying that you had concluded some time ago that your position was no longer challenging and that you were not growing professionally. You had decided to look elsewhere, and your attitude may have affected your job performance. Then detail your logic in

---

you leave a job, even summer jobs or internships, obtain these letters and keep them on file for future need.

Personnel departments will never authorize a letter of recommendation, for legal reasons too involved to discuss here. However, you often can obtain one from a supervisor. If you were fired by your most recent manager, ask a former supervisor. If you cannot get anyone within your company to write one, then try clients or some other person with whom you dealt in your job. If you have documentation, such as sales quotas or other data that indicate your success, then you can use that instead of a recommendation.

deciding to change jobs. Again, have letters of recommendation to show your success.

Oftentimes, when your company learns that you are actively seeking other employment, you will be terminated immediately. If that was the case, you have a plausible excuse available, but you will need to explain why you had decided to leave your employer. If there was some other reason for your dismissal and you want to discuss it, be certain you have sufficient documentation to support your case.

If you were terminated for immorality or dishonesty, you are in deep trouble, and no excuse is acceptable. Admit your mistake and explain what you have done to overcome it or compensate for it.

Have questions of your own.

For most of the interview, you will be asked questions which will allow the interviewer to determine if you will be a good match for the company and the job vacancy. However, at some point in the interview, you must have several pertinent, well-conceived questions of your own.

Why? There are two reasons:

1) If you don't, the interviewer will think you are disinterested or unintelligent. Surely everything was not explained thoroughly.

2) Equally as important, you must evaluate the company and the position to decide if they fit into your career plans.

Some questions you can plan in advance, but you also need to have some spontaneous questions that show you have listened and comprehended what the interviewer has said. Choose some questions that reveal your research and preparation, and some others that show interest in the job, company, and career path. Although it is important to ask questions, it is more important to ask *good* questions! And make them flow logically and spontaneously, and not sound rehearsed or "canned."

Here are some suggestions, and you will want to add more:
- What are the projections for the growth of your company and its industry?
- What is a reasonable career path for me to expect?
- Why is the position open?
- What characteristics seem to be present in your most successful employees?
- Why has your company been so successful?
- What problems has the company encountered in the manufacturing process [or sales, accounting, engineering, etc.]?
- What do you want done differently by the next person to fill this job?
- What are the most challenging aspects of the job?

Unless specifically asked, here are some topics you should not discuss on your first interview:

- Salary and benefits. Again, you should seem more interested in the job and potential with the company, than you are in immediate compensation.

- Location, unless you can work it into the conversation without giving the impression that location is of primary importance.

- How soon to the first promotion or salary review. Although the interviewer undoubtedly will be evaluating your long-term potential, you must not seem overly concerned with the next step. Rather stress how well you can accomplish the job for which you are interviewing.

Preparation is undoubtedly the most important factor in interviewing, but there are other subjects you should consider. Many of these are "givens," but let's go over them anyway.

- **Proper dress**: Always dress conservatively and traditionally. Pay attention to details such as polished shoes, clean fingernails, limited cologne, etc. Do not wear anything distracting, such as tinted glasses or flashy jewelry. There is no excuse for failing an interview because you were inappropriately attired.

- **Punctuality**: Always arrive a few minutes early, but never more than ten minutes. If you are not familiar with the area where the interview is to take place, make a practice trip the day or night before. As with proper dress, there is no excuse for failing the interview because you were late.

> **ajobs.com**
> TripQuest allows you to input your address and the location of your interview, then gives detailed directions. including a map.

- **Body language**: Sit up straight in the chair and do not slouch. Gesticulate some, but don't get carried away. Be appropriately animated and seem genuinely interested. Project a positive, optimistic mien. Body language is important – I have read opinions that it accounts for up to 55% of an interview.

- **First impression**: Strive to make an excellent first impression. From my own perspective and from my discussion with other interviewers, a truism to remember is that 90% of the interview occurs in the first minute! Offer a firm, dry handshake, and do not sit until told to do so. Be poised and with an air of self-confidence. Thank the interviewer for seeing you, and then wait for the session to begin.

  Don't overlook the impression you make on the office support staff. Be polite and pleasant to the secretary/receptionist and maintain a professional stance as you wait in the lobby. Don't slouch on the furniture or make a mess.

- **Ending the interview**: When you sense the interview is over, again thank the interviewer for his/her time and consideration, and shake hands as you leave. If you have not already been informed of their selection process, now is the time to ask. How many additional interviews will be required, and with whom? Ask when you can expect to hear from them, should you be selected for the position or a follow-up interview.

- **Thank-you note**: As soon after the interview as possible, send a short note thanking the interviewer and expressing your interest. Refer to "Chapter VIII: Correspondence" for more information on this subject.

And finally, consider these few admonitions:

- Never chew gum and do not smoke, even if offered. If having a luncheon or dinner interview, do not drink alcohol.

- Never use profanity. Over the years, I have been amazed at the number of applicants who were rejected because of this. Even the mildest "four-letter word" could be offensive to the interviewer or may be interpreted as a lack of sensitivity.

- Never "bad-mouth" former employers or teachers. Present a positive attitude and avoid making any negative statements.

- Don't make excuses for failures or mistakes. Avoid even mentioning them at all, but if you must, present them as positive learning experiences from which you gained much insight and knowledge.

- Be careful not to make statements that interviewers might view as "red flags." Try to imagine yourself on the other side of the desk, listening to your answers. Are you saying things that seem to disturb the interviewer? For example, I recently spoke with a former school teacher who was telling potential employers that she resigned from teaching on the advice of her psychiatrist! Almost a year later, she couldn't understand why she hadn't found a job.

Evaluate your interview.

Immediately after each interview, sit down with pen and paper, and think through the interview and your performance. Record specific questions you were asked and what a better answer from you might have been. List things you might have done better and how. What did you do well? What did you say that the interviewer seemed to like?

Conclusion

Interviewing – and interviewing well – is a job in itself, and the more you do it, the better you will become. I mentioned earlier practicing with a friend, and I suggest it again. Although some interviewers may not appreciate this, I also suggest that you accept one or two interviews in which you have little interest, just for the interviewing experience.

During the past twenty years, I have interviewed thousands of applicants and overseen the interviews of countless others. In addition, I have discussed interviewing techniques with numerous corporate recruiters and compiled their thoughts also. Thus, the information I have relayed here is from personal knowledge and experience. I guarantee that if you follow my suggestions, you will have the best possible interview.

Interview Check List

Have you . . .

▶ Researched the company and the position?

▶ Rehearsed probable questions and your answers?

▶ Prepared your questions?

▶ Reviewed your list of accomplishments?

▶ Checked your attire?

▶ Packed your resume, business cards, etc.?

▶ Determined the location of the interview?

CHAPTER VI

STEP FIVE:

CLOSE THE DEAL!

Follow-Through

Great lines from job evaluations

Someone emailed these to me, and I don't know the origin. Some are funny – you decide! Hope none appeared on your evaluations.

1. I would not allow this employee to breed.

2. This associate is really not so much of a has-been, but more definitely a won't be.

3. Works well when under constant supervision and cornered like a rat in a trap.

4. When she opens her mouth, it seems it is only to change whichever foot was previously there.

5. He would be out of his depth in a parking lot puddle.

6. This young lady has delusions of adequacy.

7. He sets low personal standards and then consistently fails to achieve them.

8. This employee is depriving a village somewhere of an idiot.

9. This employee should go far and the sooner he starts, the better.

10. Not the sharpest knife in the drawer.

11. Got into the gene pool when the lifeguard wasn't watching.

12. A room temperature IQ.

CHAPTER VI

Step Five: Close the Deal!

Follow-through

Pat yourself on the back; you deserve it! When you reflect on all the work you have done to get to this stage, I'm sure you feel the same.

But don't let up now. There are still a few points to cover, and these are also important in obtaining a job offer.

First of all, a thank-you note is now in order. As soon after the interview as possible, send a short note to express your interest and to thank the interviewer(s) for spending time with you. If you can enclose an item relevant to your discussion, such as a newspaper or magazine article, or can mention some other recent media report, do so. If you are sending more than one note, personalize each with a comment relating to your interview with that person.

Most importantly, keep this note short. You have made a good impression; don't ruin it now with overkill. (See "Chapter VIII:

Correspondence" for instructions on writing this note, and to Appendix B for examples.)

If you are interviewing for a technical, computer-oriented position, you can email your thank-you note. For all other positions, an old-fashioned letter via USPO is best.

The Interview Process

Knowing the interviewing and hiring procedures practiced at most firms will be helpful in understanding what to expect and in planning for subsequent interviews.

Most companies do not extend job offers after the first interview, unless that interview was an all-inclusive session with several authorities. Most often, companies have a three-step interviewing process. However, I know several companies that take longer, so don't be upset if you're called for more interviews, testing, or psychological evaluations.

The first interview is a basic screening, usually conducted by a personnel representative, and this sometimes could be simply a phone interview. To help you with your planning, I suggest that at the end of this initial contact, you ask about their usual hiring procedure and when you should expect to hear from them again.

The second interview is most often with the primary decision-maker(s) or the person to whom the position will report. By the time you are invited back for a third interview, the decision has been made to offer you the job, or almost so. The final interviewer will be a higher authority, perhaps in corporate headquarters or at the location where you will be employed.

Sometimes the second or third interview will be a simulated role playing or a sort of on-the-job situation. For example, sales applicants are frequently sent to conduct sales calls with a company sales representative. This allows the applicant to better understand the nature of the job and the company's salesperson to relay his/her impressions of the applicant to the hiring authorities.

If you anticipate that you will be called for another interview, you must do additional research on the company before that next interview. The company will expect that if you are sincerely interested in the position, you will have done something more to learn more about them and/or their position. For example, if you are interviewing for a job in college textbook sales, you could call on a few college professors and ask about the company's books and reputation. If you are interviewing for a position as Plant Engineer, you could do research on the product they manufacture and the process involved, and have several relevant statements and questions ready to show for your efforts.

I WANT THIS JOB!

When you find a job that you really like and definitely are qualified, then consider this: Are there any individuals (former employers or supervisors, clients, college professors, etc.) who would attest to your abilities? If so, ask one or two of them to call the company and give you a verbal recommendation. Should that person also be regarded highly by your potential employer, this well could be the boost that takes you over the top. Of course, you cannot use this push after every interview or you will wear out your references. Save it for the special ones you truly want.

I cannot overstress the importance of this additional preparation. In practice, I have had applicants rejected after the second interview because they had not taken the time to investigate the company and position further, and thus could not display additional knowledge of the company or its products. Do this extra research; it will separate you from other applicants and impress the interviewers.

CHAPTER VII

SALARY NEGOTIATION

CHAPTER VII

Salary Negotiation[1]

How much are you worth?

You have a job offer, or expect one very soon, and you are concerned about the total compensation package – salary and benefits. Is it enough, and what is "enough"? Could you negotiate a better package?

Many job seekers have developed an attitude that salary negotiation is somehow a "dirty business" and they think that companies frown on any suggestion that you may feel that their offer is inadequate or could be enhanced. This simply is not true, and you need to orient yourself to understand that salary negotiation is just another part of the employment process.

Salary negotiation is not a true science, in that there are no hard-and-fast rules that fit every instance. All negotiating, including salary

---

[1] How to answer salary-related interview questions, such as "What are your salary requirements?" are discussed in "Chapter V: Interviewing Techniques."

negotiating, involves some "gut feeling." Even acknowledging that some guesswork and being-in-the-right-place-at-the-right-time is involved, however, the key to "naming your salary" is knowledge:

- knowledge of the company's compensation system and its flexibility,

- and knowledge of your ability to perform the job and your value to the company.

Compensation Systems

The first item you need to learn is how the company's compensation plan works. Is it a well-defined system or determined at the whim of the company's owner? During subsequent interviews, but never your first, you can ask questions such as these:

"How is your compensation package determined? Do you have a formal classification system or is it determined individually?"

"How often do you conduct performance or salary reviews?"

Or more to the point, "How are salary, benefits, and promotional opportunities determined with your company?"

Most major corporations, as well as many smaller organizations, utilize a compensation system referred to as a "point-factor system." This means that each job is classified based on several factors, including

1) The requirements needed for the job,

2) The duties and expectations of the job, and

3) The salary range assigned to the position.

These factors will remain constant, regardless of who is in the position. When you are being considered for employment, the interviewer is evaluating you with reference to those three factors, plus one more:

4) How promotable are you? What is your potential with the firm?

Even if the company does not have a formal compensation system, those four factors still will determine your starting compensation, so let's discuss each one.

Requirements: If you have the minimum requirements for the job, you can expect the minimum of the salary range. However, if you have additional talents that could be useful later, you can negotiate.

Duties and expectations: How well can you perform the job now and how much training will you need? If you have previous experience doing the same functions or training related to the position, you have a bargaining tool. If you have experience doing the same functions plus additional duties as well, you have another tool.

Salary range: Note this is a salary *range*, not a specific figure. Companies generally prefer to hire at the middle of the salary range ("mid-range") or lower, and reserve the upper range for salary raises to incumbents. However, if you can demonstrate your ability to perform the full job right away, you may be able to go above mid-range.

Long-range potential: No company is so short-sighted that it plans only for its immediate needs. In fact, I have had many applicants rejected for a position for which they were perfectly qualified, but the company determined that they were "not promotable," *i.e.*, they lacked potential for growth within the company. On the positive side, if the company views you as having the ability to thrive in their culture, they may be willing to pay more now.

Now answer the question posed earlier, "How much are you worth"? Several online sites can be very helpful, including Salary.com, DataMasters, and homestore. Most of these sites also offer a method to calculate your salary for different geographical areas, based on cost of living data for metropolitan areas, and some give information on relocating. I'm not certain how accurate they are, though, and you can obtain more reliable information with just a little effort.

ajobs.com
Links to online salary info

Since salaries often vary by geographic location, national figures do not always reflect salaries in the Atlanta area. Professional associations frequently conduct salary studies for their specific membership, and if you are a member of an association, you can obtain the information from the headquarters office. For example, the Atlanta chapter of the Society for Human Resource Management commissioned a study of local salaries, which is available to their membership only. However, if you know a personnel manager or even are willing to make a cold-call to one, you can probably obtain the information you need.

In addition, you can network for the basic information. Call someone in a similar position and ask what the usual salary range is for that position. Ask the personnel agency recruiter with whom you are working. College professors in your field are likely to know the current wage.

Learning about comparable salaries for the position is useful, but you still haven't determined *your* value for this specific situation. By the time you receive the offer, you should know all the duties of the job, as well as your potential with the company. Be as objective as possible, and determine what salary you should expect. You should conduct this self-evaluation before your final interview, if possible, so you will be in the position of knowing whether or not to accept the offer. If you are satisfied that the offer is fair, accept it, and confirm a starting date.

But if you feel you are worth more, then let's negotiate!

Your first effort should be simply to get the salary increased. Tactfully, say that you appreciate the offer and are enthusiastic at the prospects of joining their firm. However, you feel you are worth more than their offer and then explain your reasons. For example, describe the success in your previous employment, stressing your accomplishments and achievements. Or point out that you need no additional training for the position and can be a productive employee immediately.

If the company states flatly that the salary is not negotiable, consider some other possibilities:

Creating a new job classification: One method of negotiating a higher compensation is to create a new position, tailor-made for your background and thus not yet firmly classified. For example, if your previous experience included all the duties for which you are being hired, plus you have some additional experience you also can perform now, you can create a new position above the one for which you are being hired.

Indirect compensation: Another area for negotiation is in "indirect compensation," *i.e.,* benefits and other non-salary considerations. For example, the company may offer to pay for additional education and training courses or they may pay for association dues or you may be able to get another week's paid vacation. Use of a laptop computer, an increase in expense allowances, or offering the use of a company car are other examples.

Sign-on bonus or executive bonus: These bonuses are one-time cash payments, generally paid when you begin employment. They are not included in your annual salary and do not affect future compensation. Their primary use is in overcoming "internal equity," *i.e.,* paying you more than other employees in the same job classification, but they also can be used simply as an inducement to have you accept the position. This form of additional compensation was very popular during the last employment boom, as a way to hire scarce talent. Generally, however, it is reserved for upper level positions.

Performance review: During your interviewing, you should have asked how often the company conducts "performance reviews," a critique of your performance and success in the job. These reviews are generally tied to salary increases, and if the company agrees to review you earlier than usual, you can have your salary increased sooner.

If their offer is not negotiable in any way, then you must decide if you feel the job satisfaction, potential, or some other factors are worth the lesser salary. Continue to be polite and upbeat, and leave on a positive note. Thank the interviewer for the offer and then say that you want to discuss it with your spouse or other family member or friend. State that you will give them a decision by the end of the week or some other specific date; don't say "in a few days or so." Having said that you will call by a certain date with your decision, definitely do so.

Conclusion

We have dealt with the question "What are you worth?" Now I want to make a distinction between that and "What can you get?"

If you are a consummate negotiator, you might be able to receive an offer that exceeds your worth. Don't do it. You must realize that if you somehow are able to negotiate compensation higher than what you are worth, you are heading for trouble. When the company realizes your limitations, your career there will be dead. If the offer is fair, don't tamper with it. Save your negotiating skills for a later time when you really need them.

Also, to avoid later misunderstanding, always obtain a letter from your new employer outlining your full compensation agreement (including salary, incentive program, expenses, or any other monetary considerations), starting date, and job title or function. This is a reasonable and accepted request, and I require all of my placements to have this letter prior to beginning employment. Most large corporations provide such a letter as a matter of course, but if it has not been mentioned, you should ask for one. Certainly, never resign your current position without it.

CHAPTER VIII

CORRESPONDENCE

Cover Letter
Broadcast Letter
Thank-You Note
Salary History

RECRUITERS TALK
ABOUT COVER LETTERS

The two most important pieces of information recruitment professionals want to learn from a job candidate's cover letter are (1) relocation stance and (2) most recent salary, according to a survey conducted by Career Transition Solutions, an Atlanta outplacement firm.

Harvey Brickley, president of CTS, offers several explanations for the relocation question. Probably the primary reason has been increasing parity in incomes between working spouses. Relocating, even for a raise, creates the need to find a second new job in order to maintain the family's standard of living. A second reason is the continued preference for the climate and lifestyle in metro Atlanta. Once people move here, most want to stay. A third reason is the desire to have high school age children complete their education with their current peers.

Less frequently mentioned in the recruiters' preferences was a statement as to why the person seeks a new position and a concise statement of their job objective, suggesting these are still important. All recruiters indicated a disdain for "fanciful statements" and "meaningless rhetoric."

One recruiter summed up his feelings this way: "Let the resume tell about your past. Use the cover letter to indicate where you want to go in the future."

CHAPTER VIII

Correspondence

In a simpler era (barely a decade ago!), job seekers had one resume, which was mailed with a standard cover letter via US Postal Service (USPS). No more – in the past few years, many changes, developments, and advances have increased the options tremendously. Now you must choose between a standard cover letter, T-letter, broadcast letter, fax transmittal form, and/or some other cover sheet, and you can send your information by USPS, fax, or email.

Each cover sheet has distinct purposes, and after you finish this chapter you will better understand when to use each one. (Examples are included in Appendices A and B.) Following these rules will help you decide which to apply.

- Whenever you send your resume, you should include a cover page of some sort.
- When replying to a classified ad, either from the newspaper or the internet, use either a standard cover letter or preferably a T-letter when applicable. If additional information is requested (e.g., salary information) include that in your letter if possible, although a separate salary history page is acceptable.
- When mass mailing your resume to Human Resources Departments, send your resume with cover letter.
- When mass mailing to other department managers or hiring authorities, use the broadcast letter only (no cover letter).

Whichever options you choose, keep in mind that recruiters will receive many, many resumes. Anything you do that makes their job easier will be appreciated and rewarded. Thus, *Rule #1* in writing a cover page is this: Keep it brief and to the point, with the most important information easy to see.

You will note that all the advice here stresses simplicity, as well as providing ready information to make a positive impression of you. In my discussions with other personnel managers, I find total agreement in that short, concise information is more effective than long, detailed cover letters. Recruiters often feel that a long, wordy letter indicates an excessively verbose person. Don't trap yourself by trying to include too much information.

Should I use USPO, Fax, or Email?

In my most recent survey, most companies prefer you either fax or email your resume, although you can use USPO when expedient. Each mode has its own advantages and disadvantages, as this chart illustrates.

	Advantages	Disadvantages
USPS	Hard copy arrives in office, addresses easy to find, can be addressed to specific department or title	Slow, costly, labor intensive, envelope must be opened
Fax	Inexpensive, copy in office, instantaneous, easy	May not be clear copy, fax numbers difficult to find
Email	No cost, instantaneous, easy to use	Must be downloaded and opened, difficult to determine addresses, everyone using email now

You see that no method is without its drawbacks, but most recruiters, myself included, prefer to receive resumes through email BUT with the provisos stated below. I like having it stored in my computer database so that I can retrieve it whenever I want and make

202

as many copies as I wish, all of which will look better than a photocopy. Also, before I send it to my clients, I can make changes to emphasize specific data.

Sending Your Resume Via E-Mail

Sending your information through email is easy (assuming you have the email address) and free, so most job seekers also prefer this medium. That is the biggest drawback; it is so simple and free that companies are being flooded with resumes.

Remember I stated earlier that anything you do to help the recruiter is important. Unfortunately, too many resumes I receive are titled simply "Resume." I have no idea what the applicant's experience is or what he/she is looking for. Like an unfocused resume, I tend to pass over those resumes in favor of those that indicate what the applicant's specialty is. Of course, I tell myself I will come back to those unopened files later, but truthfully, I often don't and in time, they simply drop off into cyberspace.

Thus, follow these rules in sending your resume by email and review the examples in Appendix B:

(1)   In the space on your email form called "Subject," indicate your general background (e.g., Accountant or Engineer, Electrical) or the specific job for which you are applying (e.g., Programmer C++ or Marketing Development Manager; or the "job number" if responding to a classified ad) followed by a dash, your last name, comma, first name (e.g., Manufacturing Management – Nelson, Jim). This allows the company to understand why you are sending your resume and for what you are applying, as well as your name.

(2)   Attach your resume in MS Word, unless instructed to use ASCII (plain text). Absolutely do not title your attachment "Resume" or some other generic name, but use the same title you have in your "Subject" space. Thus when it downloads, the recruiter can easily identify it and save it in the appropriate file.

(3)   Use the message space wisely. You only want to include important information, especially that which will encourage the reader to download and open your resume.   Do not include so much information that the reader will need to scroll down to see it all. If you plan to attach a cover sheet to your resume download, don't include the same information here. If you are responding to a classified ad, mention that here, along with a few career highlights. Do mention that your resume is attached in MS Word format.

I have noticed lately that many companies require you to paste your resume in plain text or ASCII format in the message space, rather than including an attachment. This saves the recruiter the time of downloading and reopening, and prevents virus infections from downloading. If you are so instructed, you may still wish to include a few significant qualifications before your resume.

(4)   Attach a cover letter or T-letter to your download, just as you would if replying by fax or USPS.

STANDARD COVER LETTER

Think back to our discussion of resume preparation. Remember that the purpose of a resume is to obtain an interview and that it must be perfect since it is to be the first impression that the company will have of you. The same is true of cover letters, and more:

- It will be read before your resume, and thus it establishes an even earlier impression of you than does your resume.

- Companies realize that you may have had your resume professionally prepared, and thus the cover letter could be a more accurate reflection of you than your resume.

- It serves as an introduction to your resume, an enticement to the reader to peruse your resume.

- It includes information not on your resume, but requested by the company, such as salary history, restrictions, and availability.

- It can zero in on specific experience you have that fits the needs of the company.

- It allows you to emphasize the accomplishments and achievements that illustrate your general qualifications.

It can also highlight information contained in your resume that is important and germane to the job for which you are applying. However, the purpose of the cover letter is *not* to repeat the same information in your resume. Rather, you should emphasize factors you feel will be important to the reader and will encourage him/her to read your resume and invite you for an interview. Appendix B contains many examples.

Strive to make your cover letter appear to be a personal, original response. Your resume is somewhat generic in nature, and the cover letter is your opportunity to make it seem relevant to the company and their needs. Thus, do not adopt an obvious form letter, never use a fill-in-the-blanks form, and do not copy verbatim a cover letter you have read somewhere, not even the ones illustrated here.

Another strong suggestion is to find out the name of the individual with whom you are corresponding, and include it on your correspondence. I realize that this is not always possible, but personnel managers really notice which applicants took the extra time to learn their name. It may seem like a minor detail to you, but some recruiters feel it is an indication of thoroughness and attention to detail. If you cannot obtain the name, then direct your correspondence to "Attn: Engineering Recruiter," or whatever corporate function you are writing.

Type your cover letter on the same paper as your resume, and proofread it carefully for accuracy and neatness. This is the company's initial impression of you, so make it good.

Format

All cover letters have the same basic format, with some variations to suit a specific purpose. The three sections of a cover letter are

Purpose, Qualifications, and Closing. Usually these sections are incorporated into three paragraphs, each representing a section. Refer to Appendix B for examples.

1) *Purpose*: The Purpose section explains why you are contacting the company and for what position(s) you would like to be considered. For example, you are responding to a classified ad, you were referred by someone, or you are making a direct inquiry. One or two sentences should be enough for this.

2) *Qualifications*: Although the Qualifications section will be the longest section, it should highlight only the best of your qualifications, not explain in detail. Stress your accomplishments and achievements, and the specific experience or background that qualifies you for your job objective. This section may be one or two paragraphs, depending on your layout, but it should never be more than eight or ten sentences, preferably less. You are trying to make a strong first impression by emphasizing a few hard-hitting facts. If you dilute this with a lengthy description, you will lose the impact.

3) *Closing*: End your cover letter with a standard closing paragraph of two or three sentences. First, thank the reader for his/her time and consideration. Then state your availability for an interview and indicate that you plan to call in a few days. Do not say you will call to arrange an interview. Although you want your cover letter to be aggressive and upbeat, that is too aggressive and presumptuous, and some recruiters find it offensive.

Now let's address some specific situations:

Responding to Classified Advertising

In this case, your opening Purpose sentence is simply, "I am enclosing my resume in response to your ___(date)___ classified ad for a _____."

Since you have read the ad, you have some knowledge of what the company is seeking. Thus, the objective of your Qualifications section is to show how closely you fit that job description. Refer to the ad, and using your highlighting pen, mark the key factors sought by the company. Then tailor your letter to fit those requirements, using specific references to that ad. You may even use the same words from the ad. One method is to use three or four "bullet sentences" or phrases to emphasize your qualifications that closely match their description.

If the ad has thoroughly detailed the job requirements, the "T-letter" format is very effective. Instead of the usual second paragraph, substitute two columns, one titled "Your Requirements" and the other "My Qualifications." Thus, you graphically and concisely show how closely you match their needs. See "Appendix B" for an example.

I very much like T-letters, since they quickly reveal an applicant's fit for the position. Anything you do that saves a recruiter's time will reflect well on you also.

In addition to the standard information in your closing paragraph, include data not in your resume but requested by the company, such as compensation or availability.

Making a Direct Contact

In the above example, you were responding to a specific opening you knew existed. In making a Direct Contact, you do not have that information, and thus your cover letter will be more open and general. If you are writing to a company official not in human resources, consider using the Broadcast Letter, discussed later in this section.

The Purpose paragraph states that you are writing to inquire about opportunities in your field or job objective. Mention why you chose to contact them (_e.g._, you read a magazine article about them or you know of their reputation), which makes your letter seem more personal.

The Qualifications section will emphasize a few of your career honors and/or accomplishments. Since you don't know what their needs might be, use this section to show your general patterns of achievement, and don't get too specific.

Close your letter with a standard Closing paragraph.

Referral Letters

In between the response to an ad and a blind Direct Contact letter is this situation. Here, a source you developed through networking has referred you to the company.

In your opening paragraph, mention the person or organization that referred you, and for what position(s). This assumes, of course, that you have permission to use that name and that it will be known to the reader.

The content of the Qualifications section will be dictated by the quantity and quality of information you were given, using a variation of the above two formats. For example, if you were told of a specific opening, use the former; if all you know is that there might be some position, use the latter.

Again, use a standard Closing paragraph.

BROADCAST LETTER

Broadcast letters were discussed in Chapter IV as "Tool #1: Mass Mailings" and examples are in Appendix A.

This correspondence is a one-page information letter, combining the best of the cover letter and resume, and is used in place of a resume with cover letter when you are trying to blanket a large number of companies. It is most useful when contacting department managers or other corporate executives not in human resources.

Your purpose is to present a few hard-hitting facts about your background that will encourage the reader to call you for more information or a complete resume. Remembering that all companies are very "bottom-line"-oriented, you want to direct your appeal to what you can offer the reader and the company. What have you accomplished with your previous employers that contributed ultimately to increased profitability? For example, if you have been in manufacturing management did you increase productivity or decrease rejects? If your background is in human resources, did you find new ways to contain benefit costs or reduce employee turnover? Salespersons should emphasize sales increases or new clients.

Broadcast letter format

The most important section of your broadcast letter is the first paragraph, which should be only one or two strongly worded sentences that will gain the reader's attention and serve as an enticement to read further. Use this paragraph to emphasize your most outstanding quality, skill, or achievement, and to state your job objective, either explicitly or implicitly.

Your next paragraph will be a short narrative on your last two positions and/or employers. Do not digress into too much detail, but only hit the highlights that will reinforce the overall positive tone of this letter.

Either at the end of your second paragraph or in a separate one, list a few of your top accomplishments, no more than six or eight. Precede these statements with a "bullet" for emphasis, and start each with an action verb such as "achieved," "increased," etc.

Next, if you have an advanced degree, special training, and/or other outstanding skills, mention them in a short, separate paragraph. If you don't have advanced education, omit this paragraph. Remember, you are trying to impress the reader with your accomplishments and abilities, not your academics.

Conclude your letter with a vigorous statement such as, "Should you be looking for someone who can bring this expertise to your organization, please call me," or "Should your company be in need of a results-oriented, bottom-line manager, please call me."

In writing your broadcast letter, also follow these guidelines:

- Do not include dates, unless these events happened in the past year.

- Do not specify company names, unless they are recognized as industry leaders.

- Bullet statements are more emphatic than ordinary sentences, but don't overuse them or they will lose their effectiveness.

- This letter must _never_ be more than one page and do not include so much information that the reader loses interest.

The broadcast letter has become very popular as a tool to make direct contact with company managers and hiring authorities. When contacting human resources you should continue to use the resume and cover letter format. Those personnel professionals are trained to work with full resumes and will want to see all your information rather than the abbreviated information in the broadcast letter. The opposite is generally true of busy executives who are more interested in what you can offer their specific department, which is why you emphasize your revenue increasing and cost cutting accomplishments.

THANK-YOU NOTE

What are employers and interviewers _really_ looking for?

Obviously, you must have the skills and experience required, but beyond that, what can you do to show you are the best applicant for the job?

One item often overlooked is thoroughness and attention to detail, showing you are willing to do more than may be required in order to assure success. For example, you should research the name of the hiring authority or interviewer, so you can address your cover page to "Dear Somebody" instead of the impersonal "Dear Sirs." Another excellent example is sending a "thank-you note" after each interview.

You may wonder if this correspondence is really necessary. Frankly, I have spoken with many interviewers who said that they attach little or no significance to these notes, and that the notes will not affect their decision. On the other hand, I have spoken with others who feel that this extra detail is indicative of a more thorough person, one who is willing to go the extra mile. Even those former interviewers usually admit that a good thank-you note could be the feather that tips the scales, when two applicants are so identically qualified. Since you have nothing to lose and much to gain by sending a short note, I recommend you do so. Several examples are included in Appendix B.

Your reasons for sending a thank-you note are

- to thank the interviewer for time and consideration,

- to express your interest in the position, and

- to reinforce the positive impression you created during your interview.

Remember this is a note, not a letter. It should be only a very few sentences, so do not digress into details. Assuming you had a good interview, don't ruin it now with verbosity and overkill. If your interview did not convince the interviewer that you are a likely candidate for the position, now is too late. You should, however, re-emphasize in one or two sentences why you fit the position.

Make your note more personal by referring to a topic you discussed during the interview. Better still, enclose a news article you think might be of interest to the interviewer, or at least refer to a related item you recently read or heard.

Your note can be typed or handwritten, depending on the quality of your handwriting, and sent via the USPO. For technical IT positions, you may email your note.

You also should send a note or email to individuals who have been helpful during your job search. For example, thank a networking contact who provided you with information that led to an interview. Someone who allowed you an "information interview" definitely deserves a thank-you note. Everyone enjoys receiving a short correspondence, and a thank-you note will create a very positive impression of yourself and may lead to more help in the future.

SALARY HISTORY

I recently surveyed *The Atlanta Journal-Constitution* Sunday want ads, and observed that at least 90% of the professional-level, company-sponsored ads requested either a salary history, current salary, or salary required. In addition, numerous search firms also have begun asking that information. Most companies even stated that those resumes accompanied by salary histories would be considered first, or that resumes without a salary history would not be considered at all.

An often asked question at my seminars is whether or not to include a salary history when one is requested. Would a corporate recruiter really toss a qualified applicant's resume just because the salary history was not included? You bet they would! You were told to send your salary history, and if you don't, then you are not following instructions. Moreover, I have spoken with many recruiters who said they won't even review the non-conforming resumes at all, so they won't know if you are qualified or not.

For many reasons, you often would rather not reveal your salary information prior to the interview. If your salary or salary requirements are too high or too low, you may be excluded from a job for which you are qualified and that you really want. Perhaps you are willing to accept a salary cut in order to remain in Atlanta, to gain valuable experience, to associate with a more dynamic company or industry, or to change career directions. But for whatever reason, you would like not to include this requested information – but you must. How?

If you are being asked only for current salary or salary required, you can include that in your cover letter, either in the final paragraph or in a separate paragraph. If salary is not your main motivation, you can add that you are more interested in other factors than compensation. Here are some examples, and others are included in Appendix B.

Thank you for your time and consideration, and I will call you next week to confirm that you have received my resume. My current salary is $65,000, and although I am seeking a comparable salary, I am more interested in long-range potential and opportunity with your company.

As I am seeking to make a career change from sales into manufacturing management, I do not expect to maintain my current salary of $65,000. Rather, I am more interested in developing my new career, using my product knowledge and experience, and thus the career opportunity with your company is my priority.

However, if salary is a primary consideration, make that clear:

Thank you for your time and consideration, and I will call you in a few days to confirm that you have received my resume. My current salary is $65,000, and I am seeking compensation in the $75,000 range.

Salary histories can be handled in one of two ways. If you have been employed for only a few years with the same company and have had no major promotions or salary increases, a simple addition to your cover letter is sufficient:

During my five-year employment with ABC Corporation, I have progressed from a trainee salary of $33,000 to my current base salary of $46,000. In addition, I receive a quarterly incentive bonus, up to 10% of base salary, and a car and expense account are furnished.

If you have had more than one employer or have received several promotions, you may wish to include a separate "Salary History" page. Examples are given in Appendix B.

Whether you include this information in your cover letter or on a separate sheet, keep in mind why companies want this information. The most obvious reason is to ascertain if your salary requirements are within the salary range they are offering, but there are other, more subtle reasons as well.

You may remember in our interviewing discussion that interviewers evaluate your life patterns – that is, demonstrated patterns of success, accomplishment, over-achievement, etc., and the opposites. If your salary history reflects a steady increase in salary, it suggests success with your company(s). If your salary has been decreasing or vacillating, that suggests problems. Also, if your salary is far below your peer group, it will be viewed negatively. Consequently, if you have some oddity in your salary history, you should explain it in one or two positively-worded sentences.

Conclusion

You may have noticed a recurrent theme running throughout this chapter – and for that matter, throughout the entire book. That theme is to keep all of your correspondence concise, to the point, and relevant to your objective. Trust me on this one: company interviewers and other readers really respect the applicant who can sift out the chaff from the wheat.

I am not suggesting that you exclude important information in the name of brevity, but that you learn to discern the important from the unimportant, and the most important from the less important. You need only to include the information necessary for the reader to get an accurate, positive assessment of your skills and abilities. Beyond that, you are wasting your words and the reader's time.

CHAPTER IX

"WHAT MORE CAN I DO?"

Evaluating your job search.

The Job Seekers'

Seven Deadly Sins

1) Failure to recognize the need for job search information and help

2) Poor organization

3) Uncertain career focus

4) Not using your time wisely

5) Inadequate preparation

6) Conducting a "passive" job search

7) Fear of new technology

CHAPTER IX

"What more can I do?"

If you are following my suggestions so far, you should have all the interviews you can handle. Take care not to tire yourself by planning too many interviews in a short period. Interviews can be stressful, and you should plan to have no more than two on one day. Plus, you need time to research each company before the interview.

If you think you are following my plan but still not finding enough interviews, then you need to conduct some serious evaluations of your job search techniques. This objective evaluation of yourself may be difficult, and you may need to ask others for help. What you see in the mirror could be entirely different from what someone else may see.

Evaluate your organization. Are your materials organized so that you can refer to them quickly? Are you keeping complete records of your activities and are you following through on all you have learned?

Evaluate your time management. Are you spending enough time on your job search and is your time well planned? Are you following the time schedule I outlined in Chapter II? Are you spending too much time on the Internet? Are you spending enough time developing your job network? Try this test: for five consecutive days, record how you spend every minute from 8am – 5pm; I'll bet you will be surprised to discover what you really do with your time.

Evaluate your resume. Have you discussed your resume with anyone, especially a corporate recruiter? Does your resume emphasize accomplishments and achievements? Would a topical resume format be more effective?

From my experiences, the most common resume mistake is having a resume that is too long or detailed. A two-page resume is the most you need, and one page is definitely preferable. If you have reduced the margins or the size of the type to squeeze your information onto two pages, then you have too much.

Lately I have spoken with a number of job seekers who blamed their resume for a lack of interviews. In some cases they were at least partially correct, but generally speaking, the problem was more in their marketing approach than with the resume. Don't waste time nit-picking your resume, when that time would be better spent on your marketing efforts.

Evaluate your marketing approach. First, reread Chapter IV, and I'll bet you have overlooked some of the tools I have described. You may even need to read this text a third or fourth time, in order to catch every suggestion mentioned.

• Are you taking advantage of all the free material and links on www.ajobs.com?

• Are you attending job network groups? • Have you used the free services described in the Public Agencies section?

• Have you sought out privately funded organizations that offer job assistance to specific constituencies (*e.g.*, blacks, women, Hispanics, Jews, older employees, etc.)? I have included many of these services in Chapter IV and links on ajobs.com.

- Are you attending professional association meetings?
- Have you conducted at least one "information interview" each week?
- How effective is your "30-second resume"?
- Are you spending enough time cultivating a job network? Recognizing that more job seekers find employment through some form of job networking than all other methods combined, constantly strive to add new contacts to your networking resources.
- Have you been to a Georgia Career Center, especially the office in Toco Hills Shopping Center on North Druid Hills Road? They offer many new services, including computer banks with internet access, networking groups, etc.

Evaluate your interviewing techniques. Have you practiced your interview with a friend? Have you listed potential questions and your answers, and discussed them with someone who will know how to interview correctly? Do you objectively evaluate your interview after each one? Have you asked the recruiter at a personnel agency where you are registered to critique your interview? Have you recontacted a company with whom you interviewed to ask their human resources representative for a critique of your interview there? When asking for opinions, stress that you really need an honest, objective answer, and don't become defensive to what you hear.

Videotaping a mock interview could be very helpful in graphically revealing your mistakes, but if that is not possible, you should at least audio-tape your interview for evaluation. Have a friend conduct the interview and test you with questions that you are not expecting.

Evaluate your product – yourself. Back in Chapter IV, I made the analogy that you are now in a sales/marketing position, with yourself as the product. Just as every company periodically evaluates its product line, you too must objectively appraise your career potential to include the future trends in your industry and your ability to remain competitive in it. In today's rapidly changing world, your industry or specialty may be going the way of the dinosaurs. For example, is your industry growing? Do you have the advanced training or education needed to keep ahead of your peers? Now could be the time to consider a career change or to study the advancements in your field. Also, in choosing which companies to target, lean toward the ones considered to be industry leaders, not the "has-beens."

Evaluate your personal appearance. Individuals often have difficulty judging their own appearance, and family and friends may find this too personal to discuss objectively. I encourage you to ask a non-interested acquaintance or business associate for an unbiased, blunt critique of your over-all appearance, not just your attire. If you have the time and money, there are several listings in the Yellow Pages for "image consultants," but for free advice, you can ask your personnel agent or outplacement counselor. Believe me, companies are very aware of the image you would project as their employee.

Evaluate your attitude. I recently read an article suggesting that half of your job search success depends on your attitude and behavior. Maintaining a positive attitude in light of mounting bills is difficult, and casting blame on the economy, yourself, or some other factor will not help either. Are you really trying or have you decided, "What's the use?" Are you projecting an air of desperation? Has your prolonged job search tinged your interviews with bitterness or sarcasm? Keep your interviews upbeat and strive to maintain your self-confidence, even in the face of repeated disappointment.

When your job search has begun to run out of steam, don't panic. Calmly sit down and assess what you have done so far: What has worked best? What has been less successful? Don't be afraid to try new approaches and ideas, especially various forms of job networking.

Energizing Your Marketing Approach

I am often asked what is the most common mistake made by job seekers. Although there are many, probably the worst is a poor marketing approach. Too many applicants conduct a "passive" job search when they should be more "aggressive." Let me illustrate.

Applicants frequently tell me that this is the first time they have had to look for a job themselves, that in the past they received unsolicited calls from companies offering them a job. The implication here is that a job search is somehow beneath them and that they are afraid to get their hands dirty looking for one. I personally don't care if this is their first or tenth job search, but they are embarrassed and uncomfortable with their relative position. This psychological discomfort encourages and allows the easy way out, attempting a "passive job search":

• They call personnel agencies, hoping that these firms will do all the work for them;

• They buy a book with hundreds or thousands of company names and addresses, and then blindly send out as many resumes as they have stamps; or

• They read the want ads and respond to every one that sounds even vaguely close to their background.

? They post their resume on a few web sites, expecting recruiters to call.

And then they sit at home, waiting for the phone to ring with their next glorious job offer. Or they go play tennis, occasionally checking for messages on their voice mail.

True, personnel agencies do find jobs for their applicants; your "resume blizzard" occasionally might locate an opening; companies obviously will hire from their classified advertising; and many companies and agencies surf the web for qualified applicants. Nevertheless, remember that fewer than 25% of all job seekers will find their jobs through the total of these four sources combined. If you passively sit waiting by the phone, you still may be sitting there long after your unemployment benefits have expired!

My sarcasm is not meant to further irritate sensitive nerves, but to point out the folly of the "passive job search." You need to be conducting an "aggressive job search," using as many approaches as possible and remaining in control over all the segments in your search:

• Instead of calling all the personnel agencies listed in the Yellow Pages, research which ones will be most helpful to you, using the criteria described in Chapter IV. Then establish a strong working relationship with those few agencies.

• Prudently select the companies to which you send your resume, contacting only those you have reason to think will have recurring needs for your background. Included in Appendix C are the active hiring companies in Atlanta and the types of individuals they generally seek. You may need to do additional research as well. Limiting your resume blizzard to those companies will save time and money by not sending your resume to companies who will have no interest. Plus, you will receive fewer rejection letters!

• In responding to classified ads, follow the procedure outlined in Chapter IV, phoning the companies first when possible and then following up on your resume.

? Do post your resume with web sites, but don't let that be your primary job search tool.

Those steps will cover your bases with the "visible job market," but if you stop there you will be eliminating the other 75% of available job openings. Now you should add these to your job search:

• Remembering that more job seekers find employment through some form of job networking than through all other sources combined, establish a job networking campaign. Use professional associations, job network groups, "information interviews," and other sources that you develop. These tools are discussed fully in "Chapter IV: Get That Interview!"

• Volunteer your time to help at associations, not just your professional group, but other non-profit or charity organizations. Volunteering will allow you to display your abilities to a new set of contacts, many of whom may be executives with useful connections. In addition, you will keep your skills current and have a positive outlet for your frustrations.

• Search out your college alumni association, speak with the president, and plan to attend their meetings. You likely will find alumni with backgrounds and degrees similar to yours, and their experiences can be very helpful in your job search. Also, many alumni associations have a job search coordinator to help members and some conduct annual job fairs.

• Use public agencies to locate government jobs, as well as some private sector jobs. List with public job banks, newsletters, and free computer job matching systems.

• Locate privately funded organizations that offer employment assistance for specific minority groups, as well as other special-need groups. Many of these organizations are mentioned in Chapter IV, and you may find others as well.

• Add helpful publications to your data base, to be used for your marketing campaign and for interview preparation. Visit your public library and review the publications in their career help section.

• Use personnel agencies for more than just company contacts. A knowledgeable personnel recruiter can make valuable suggestions regarding your resume, interviewing techniques, appearance, and more.

No company can exist for long if it passively relies on the whims of others. On the contrary, companies are actively reviewing their marketing techniques at all times and using as many approaches as possible. You too must aggressively market your product – yourself – as much and in as many ways as possible.

Interviewing Faux Pas

During the past twenty years, I have interviewed thousands of applicants and overseen many of their interviews with companies. Here are the major interviewing mistakes I have observed.

• *Failure to prepare.* You must never attempt an interview without prior research and preparation. If you're nervous before an interview, that could be a sign you are not adequately prepared. Being prepared not only settles the stomach, it impresses the interviewer as well!

Your preparation will include three factors:

1) Research the company (and the interviewer, if possible). Call the company and request an annual report, information brochure, or recruiting information to be mailed to you. Visit a local library or the placement department of a local college and review their company information. Network, by asking friends and business associates what they know of the company.

ajobs.com
Much info is on the company's home page or other online service.

2) Anticipate certain questions from the interviewer. Write down in advance as many probable questions as you can and decide your answers. Start with the most popular interview question of all, "Tell me about yourself."

3) Plan questions of your own. There are some questions you can plan in advance to ask, but you also need to have some spontaneous questions that show you have listened and comprehended what the interviewer has said. Choose questions that show interest in the job, company, and career path.

- *Lack of focus.* This is especially true of recent grads, but older applicants suffer from this also. If I had a dime for every applicant who has expressed a desire for "personnel" or "public relations," I could retire tomorrow! When I then ask why they want a career in personnel, they all answer, "Because I like people." Believe me, simply "liking people" is no logic for pursuing a career in personnel – which incidentally in now called Human Resources anyway – and no interviewer will accept that answer. Worse still is the reply, "I enjoy entertaining," as a reason for a career in public relations.[1]

If you really do want a career in Human Resources, your answer should be more like this: "I have spoken with a number of human resources professionals to learn more about the field. I think that the

---

[1] In all fairness, I must confess that when I decided to leave teaching and moved to Atlanta to seek a new career, I listed my two career objectives as "personnel" and "public relations." I have learned a lot since then!

skills I possess closely match those that seem to be necessary for success in human resources, and I especially feel that my ability to listen carefully and then analyze what I have heard could be developed as a recruiter. In addition, I am interested in learning more about government regulations concerning compensation and benefit programs, and I have recently attended a seminar sponsored by the International Foundation of Employee Benefit Plans." That answer shows a seriousness and commitment, not just a frivolous afterthought, and your interviewer will be impressed.

In short, your reasons for pursuing a specific career objective must be well-defined and expressed with a clear knowledge of why you expect to be successful in that capacity. In other words, you must show job focus.

• *Unwillingness to relocate.* Unless you are interviewing with a company that has only one location, you must accept the possibility of relocating to another city at some time in your career with them. In fact, unless you say otherwise, companies will expect you to be available for transfers, especially for a promotion. And if you do indicate your unwillingness to relocate, your interview will be dead at that moment!

I strongly urge you to say that you are open for relocation, even if you would rather not, in order to continue the interviewing process. The offer may be so tempting that you will forget your reluctance to move, or the initial assignment could be just where you want to be. Even if the offer is not what you want, you will never have the chance to evaluate it if you cut off the possibility of an offer early in the interviewing process by saying "no" to relocation.

• *Verbosity.* This is my own personal "pet peeve," and I have seen many applicants flunk an interview because they didn't know when to stop talking. If this is a well-developed character trait of yours, there may be little you can do to curb it now. Try objectively to listen to yourself, and if you are taking more than three or four minutes to answer a simple question, you probably are talking too much.

Interviewers are much more impressed with a concise answer than a long, detailed one.

- *Profanity.* I am constantly amazed at the number of applicants who use profanity during an interview, and I have had dozens of applicants rejected for this reason. Even the mildest four-letter expletive may be offensive to your interviewer, and it will be viewed as insensitive and immature.

- *Blaming others for your problems at work, especially a supervisor.* Why should the interviewer accept your version of the situation? Never denigrate an employer or supervisor, or complain that you were mistreated. When asked why you are changing jobs, the best answer is that you are seeking a greater challenge and more opportunity for career advancement.

If you were fired, acknowledge your mistake and explain what you have done to overcome the problem. If your termination was the result of a reduction-in-force, stress that your position has not been refilled.

- *Too much emphasis on salary and benefits.* Never bring up the subject of compensation on your first interview with a company, unless you have firmly established your ability to perform the job and have shown strong interest in the company and position. Generally speaking, wait for the interviewer to broach the subject first.

- *Being overly concerned with promotions*, especially the first promotion. Similar to the problem above, don't give the impression that you are more concerned with your first promotion and/or salary review than you are in performing the position for which you are interviewing. This will be interpreted as a concern that you may become bored with the initial assignment or that you feel over-qualified for the job.

The company indeed will be evaluating you as a career employee, including promotions, and that will be a major factor in their decision to hire you or not. Nevertheless, you want to impress on them your ability to perform the job at hand. During the interviewing process, you may ask what their career path usually entails, but avoid asking directly, "How long to the first promotion?"

• *Not showing enthusiasm for the job.* Always appear enthusiastic about the job and the company, until you have decided the position is not right for you. Unless you demonstrate your enthusiasm, the interviewer will assume you are not interested and may offer the position to some other candidate. And if you do want the job, don't hesitate to say so, clearly and emphatically!

• *"Applicants say and do the dumbest things."* This catch-all category includes blunders such as these:

• The school teacher who told the company interviewer she was changing careers on the advice of her psychiatrist;

• The young man who freely acknowledged that he was fired for having an affair with his boss's wife (in fact, he seemed pleased!);

• The applicant who supplied a potential employer with personal references who gave him terrible recommendations;

• The recent grad who told interviewers he wanted a job for only a year or two, until he decided to begin graduate school.

Every personnel recruiter has a list of these jewels, and we often enjoy sitting around and exchanging laughs over them. Maybe one day I will write a book about them, and also include some of the funniest resumes I have received. You wouldn't believe some of the resumes job applicants send out – ah, but that must wait for another day!

ajobs.com
Direct links to the Atlanta job listings of many companies and commercial web sites.

You too may be saying something absurd without realizing it. When evaluating your interviewing techniques, try to imagine yourself on the other side of the desk, listening to your answers. In your analysis of each interview, observe which answers seemed to disturb the interviewer.

Adding New Technology to Your Job Search

If you are not using the internet as one of your resources, you are living in the dark ages - but I suspect you already know that. Several large web sites are devoted to listing classified job listings, just as in the newspaper, but with a bonus: oftentimes you can apply directly to the company on-line or fax your resume directly. Other web sites will give you directions to an interview location, help you research companies, give job search advice, and much more. The most helpful of these sites are linked on **ajobs.com**.

If you don't have a computer with internet access at home, you can find many free or low cost sources. Public libraries, college career placement departments, the state Career Centers, and even friends with computers are all possible outlets. All of the local Kinko Copy Centers in Atlanta provide inexpensive computer time rental.

Conclusion

This covers most of the mistakes you may be committing, but now it is up to you to make corrections. In your planning, allot time for frequent evaluations and analyses of your job search methods, and how you can improve on them. Use as many approaches as you can, and be open to suggestions for still more.

You probably have heard the truism, "Finding a job is a job in itself." Now you understand what that means.

CHAPTER X

CONCLUSION

Tips for

CLIMBING THE CORPORATE LADDER

- <u>Make a career plan.</u> Know where you expect to be in one, five, and ten years, and don't be sidetracked. Set your goals and work towards them.

- <u>Stay in the mainstream.</u> The "glamour" jobs are often the first to go in a recession. Top executives traditionally come from the sales and/or finance ranks.

- <u>Education is a constant.</u> Stay current on technology, especially computers and software pertaining to your career; work towards certification, if applicable to your field; and read the latest business books. Attend seminars offered by your professional association.

- <u>Remember the basics.</u> Be on time, dress appropriately, pay attention to details, and always project a professional image. Your superiors know that your appearance is how outsiders will perceive the company.

- <u>Make your boss look good.</u> Never go over your boss' head, and don't try to outshine him or her. Your boss' good fortune often will be yours as well.

CHAPTER X

CONCLUSION

I am frequently asked for a final word of advice to job seekers, and I often reply _persistence_. Persistence takes many forms:

• If you have decided that after much thought and logical reasoning, you want a specific job or a specific company and you think you are qualified, don't take "no" for a final answer. Keep trying, using as many techniques as you can for gaining an interview and evaluation, and you may have your wish. I have witnessed many surprises over the years, so be persistent.

• Probably the hardest part of conducting a job search is keeping your spirits high, especially when you have just received a mail box full of rejection letters. Remember "Persistence," say it aloud several times, put the letters away, and then immediately start back to work on your job search.

- As I have said many, many times, networking may be the most time consuming marketing tool, but it also yields the best results. Even though you may be tired of all the networking meetings, continue to attend them. When you would rather do anything than speak with another potential source, call anyway. You never know when the next encounter may be **the** one.

Accepting New Employment

YES! All the organization, preparation, and work has paid off. But before accepting a job offer, evaluate it thoroughly.

If you already have decided to accept or reject the offer, you certainly can say so when the offer is extended. If you have not, however, don't feel pressured into making a decision on the spot. Rather, you should thank the person for the offer, express how highly you value the company and position, and then state that you will give them your decision on a specific date, usually less than a week. Do not say "in a few days," but specify exactly when.

Through your research, you should have determined what salary to expect. If the salary offered is not up to what you anticipated, the best time to negotiate a better compensation package is when you receive the offer. Refer back to "Chapter VI: Salary Negotiation" for strategies to raise your offer.

Don't be frightened into accepting the first offer you receive, but don't reject it just because it is the first offer and you wonder what else is available. Sit down with pen and paper and objectively decide if it is best for you. Draw a line down the center of the paper and label one side "pro's" and the other, "con's." Here are some factors to consider, and you may have other priorities as well:

- Salary
- Location
- Job responsibilities

- Potential with the company
- Experience to be gained
- Company reputation

- Most importantly, how does this fit in with your career plans, immediate and long-term? How will it look on your next resume?

Dealing with rejection

Life indeed would be nice if you received an interview from every company you contact and a job offer from every interview. Unfortunately, that is just not reality.

In my discussions with job seekers, I have found that dealing with rejection is a very common problem. Although I am not a psychologist, I do have some observations on the matter, and I can offer some suggestions on coping with it, and even using it to your advantage.

Let's say that you contacted 25 companies, received 23 "no interests," and two interviews. (Actually that's really good; don't be surprised if you need 100 calls for even one interview.) The first interview was so-so, but you felt that the second interview went extremely well, and thus you excitedly are planning to do more research. Then you receive a rejection letter in the mail. Or worse yet, you never hear from them again, and they refuse to return your phone calls. How do you handle this downturn of events?

All those personalized cover letters, all those phone calls, all that research – none of it paid off. But did it?

Well, for one thing, there are 25 fewer companies for you to contact. Your research taught you where to find company information, and you gained knowledge on an industry.

Better still, there is one more item you may be overlooking: feedback from the interviewer. Once you know you didn't get the job, call the interviewer and very politely inquire why. Were you not qualified or did you present yourself poorly? Does he/she have any suggestions for you? If the interviewer will be honest with you, this information alone is worth all of your efforts.

Occasionally applicants call me back and want to know why I will not refer them to a certain job opening or why they were turned down for a position for which they had interviewed. When I try to explain, they become defensive and argumentative, and so instead of giving them good feedback and advice, I just shut down and try to end the conversation as quickly as possible.

Those applicants missed out on excellent constructive criticism that could have been very helpful in future interviews. Thus, when asking for this constructive criticism, do not be argumentative, but leave with a positive impression. Stress your need for good critiques and advice. Also, another job may become available later that you will fit.

Nevertheless, you must accept the fact that you will hear "No" far more often than you will "Yes." That's life, and we simply learn to expect it and deal with it. During your career search, you will speak with many people – companies, agencies, network sources, *et al.* – but unfortunately, only a few will be able to assist you. Surely they would if they could, and they harbor no personal ill will toward you.

Anticipate the problems and rejections you will undoubtedly encounter, and learn to face them with a positive attitude. When needed, call on your emotional support system for a lift. In addition, allot time to work on developing and maintaining your self-confidence and a strong self-image. Then begin each day with the enthusiasm needed to start over at Step One, if necessary.

Beyond rejection

If you have correctly followed the steps in the CAREER SEARCH SYSTEM, you should be receiving interviews and offers. If you are not, then I suggest that you may not have assessed realistically your wants or abilities, and you are interviewing for positions that are not available or that are beyond your grasp. Perhaps you should consult an industrial psychologist or career counselor to gain insight into your capabilities. Consider taking courses or re-training for one of the "hot" fields of the millennium, such as the environment, health care, or computer science.

The System works! I know it does, because I have seen it in action countless times. Follow it through and you will have a most successful job search.

Best wishes!

APPENDIX

APPENDIX A:

SAMPLE RESUMES, REFERENCE PAGES, and BUSINESS CARDS

The following resumes all conform to the CAREER SEARCH SYSTEM principles of the "Power Resume":
- All emphasize accomplishments and achievements when possible.
- They are all very positive in tone and include no negative factors.
- They are neat, accurate and to the point.
- Most are one page, or two pages maximum.
- All were typed with at least an electronic typewriter and letter-quality printer. Most were formatted using a word processor and printed with a laser printer.

I have included examples of several different backgrounds (accountant, engineer, sales rep, etc.), formats (functional/chronological and topical) and various lay-outs. There are also resumes for a career change (named "Tanner" and "Lindsey"), re-entering the workforce ("Rose"), and one illustrating combining jobs ("Smith"). In addition, you will find good examples of the use of "Objective" and/or "Summary" (or sometimes "Qualifications"), the inclusion and omission of "Personal," and various methods of describing your education.

The sample business cards are neat, informative and uncluttered. They do not attempt to be a condensed resume.

LLANA S. FRANCO

348 Bulldog Drive
Athens, GA 30601
(404) 353-7621
lsf@aol.com

Permanent Address:
1234 Azalea Road NW
Atlanta, GA 30327
(404) 262-7890
lsf@aol.com

Recent college graduate majoring in **International Business and Spanish**. Career objective is employment with a multi-national corporation, preferably with operations in Latin America. Areas of interest include marketing, international banking and finance, and import/export operations.

Education

UNIVERSITY OF GEORGIA, Bachelor of Business Administration, graduation planned for June, 2001. Relevant curriculum has included the following:
- Macro and Micro Economics
- Principles of Accounting I & II
- International Marketing
- Statistics
- Commercial Spanish
- Business Law I & II

Employment

IBM Corporation (Summer Internship, 2000):
Diverse duties giving exposure to the operations of a major multi-national corporation. Worked in both Marketing and Personnel departments, under minimal supervision. Operated IBM 5520 Word Processor.

Elson's Gift Shops, Atlanta International Airport (Summers 1997 - 1999):
Sales Clerk, serving international passengers and using Spanish and Portuguese languages daily.

U S Army Hospital, Fort Benning, GA (Summer 1996):
Medical Clerk, working with wounded Salvadoran military personnel.

Personal

Born January 23, 1980 . . . . . Single, excellent health . . . . . Open for travel and relocation, including international . . . . . Fluent in Spanish and Portuguese . . . . . Interests include international events, reading and art.

References available on request.

239

EDMOND R. SMITH

1200 Franklin Road, Apt. F-1
Charlotte, NC 28754
(704) 847-1234 • esmith44@earthlink.net

Summary

Accounting Professional with more than fifteen years financial experience. Consistently promoted as a result of dependable performance culminating in accurate accomplishments. Seeking position as **Internal Auditor** or **Financial Control Supervisor**. Open for travel and relocation.

Experience

AUDITING:

Western Union Telegraph Co. (12/89 - present) As **_Senior Internal Auditor_** and **_Supervisor Financial Control_**, conducted autonomous audits of all accounting and money order processing functions. Detected and corrected error in audit procedure, resulting in a revenue increase of $272,000 per year. As **_Internal Audit Supervisor_**, reviewed work papers, prepared audit reports and supervised up to eight staff auditors in performance of all internal audit assignments.

PRIVATE ACCOUNTING:

Convenient Systems, Inc. and E. L. Lowie & Co. (9/84 - 11/89) As **_Assistant Controller_**, supervised eight accountants in the preparation and adjustment of monthly financial statements. Designed and implemented new profit and loss statement format for retail and manufacturing locations. As **_Accounting Manager_**, supervised accounting staff of six, and insured proper and accurate recording of all daily accounting transactions.

PUBLIC ACCOUNTING:

A. M. Pullen & Co. (6/81 - 9/84) As **_Senior Accountant_**, planned and conducted audit engagements; drafted audit programs; prepared time budgets, financial statements and accountants' reports; and filed federal, state and city tax returns.

Education

University of North Carolina at Greensboro
Accounting major, 1981
Maintained GPA 3.0/4.0

University of North Carolina at Chapel Hill
Bachelor of Arts in English Education, 1978
Financed education through summer employment, student loans and part-time employment during school year.

SUSAN B. SWIFT
3829 Helen Lane
Durham, NC 27702
(919) 282-4837
swift919@aol.com

PROFESSIONAL EXPERIENCE

Professional Sales background selling food products to the grocery industry, including 12 years experience as food manufacturer's representative. Worked with two national manufacturers calling on grocery chains, wholesalers and drug chain accounts, covering the states of Georgia and Florida. Extensive experience with food brokers, headquarters presentations, new item introductions, business reviews, and SAMI and Nelson data.

EMPLOYMENT HISTORY

1997 to present

Wyeth-Ayerst Laboratories, Philadelphia, PA
Sales Manager, Atlanta District
Manage sales, promotions, pricing and plan-o-grams. Full sales responsibility for grocery chains, wholesalers and drug accounts for the sales of infant formula in Georgia and Florida. Sell and coordinate distribution with 51 major accounts with total sales of $9.7M in 1995. Performed under an MBO system for bonuses and pay raises.
Accomplishments:
• 45% sales increase (1999 over 1998)
• 42 new item placements in 1997
• Manage Eckerd Drug Company account
• Manage major food brokerage companies in Georgia and Florida

1995 - 1997

Common Communications, Atlanta, GA
Sales Representative
Calling on large and small business owners, sold communications equipment and systems. Developed clientele through referrals and cold calling.

1987 - 1995

Sunshine Biscuit Company, Atlanta, GA
Account Manager
Supervised and coordinated merchandising activities of two major retail chain accounts. Full sales responsibilities, including promotions, business reviews, credits and new item presentations. Also maintained 55 other retail accounts.
Accomplishments:
• 30% sales increase per year for three consecutive years with Kroger account
• 1985 received Salesman of the Year Award for highest division sales

EDUCATION

B. B. A., Georgia State University, Atlanta, GA, 1987
Self-financed all personal and tuition expenses.

241

FRANK N. CHRISTOPHER

398 Colony Court
Smyrna, GA 30020
(404) 435-0876

OBJECTIVE

Marketing and sales position with a product- or service-oriented firm, where experience and qualifications can be effectively used.

QUALIFICATIONS

Background and Scope of Development: Currently employed as Marketing Representative with Xerox Corporation. Prior experience with IBM Corporation and Wachovia Bank. Master's Degree and Bachelor's Degree in Business Administration.

Capabilities: Three years of corporate sales experience has involved such areas as cold calling, prospecting, territory management and extensive sales training. Consistently exceeded quotas.

EXPERIENCE

XEROX CORPORATION
June 1995 - present
Marketing Representative
• Market entire office product line of computers, typewriters, copiers, facsimile and systems. Activities include developing new accounts and managing established accounts.
Accomplishments: Consistently surpass sales quotas and performance goals.

IBM CORPORATION
February 1994 - May 1995
Marketing Support Intern
• Responsibilities included cold calls, sales and training of IBM equipment for the general sales force.
Accomplishments: Achieved highest sales ranking of the year during internship.

Wachovia BANK
September 1991 - January 1994
Financial and Budget Analyst
• Prepared detailed financial data including the assets and liabilities of First Atlanta Bank and holding companies, and presented monthly to senior management.

EDUCATION

Samford University, Birmingham, AL
MASTER OF BUSINESS ADMINISTRATION, June 1994
BACHELOR OF SCIENCE in Marketing, June 1991

Activities: Served as President of Alpha Kappa Psi, business fraternity; Vice-President, Pi Kappa Phi, social fraternity; President, Intrafraternal Council.

LOUIS C. CARTWELL

1234 Apple Lane NW, Columbia, SC 29202
(803) 250-0215
lctanner@mindspring.com

Summary

MBA graduate with five years management experience in United States Army as commissioned officer. Seeking Management Development Program with a major corporation, utilizing well-developed supervisory skills.

Experience

UNITED STATES ARMY
(June 1998 - present)

CAPTAIN, eligible for promotion. Consistently promoted ahead of peer group. Available for employment October 2003. Summary of duties and responsibilities follows:

Maintenance Management: As Company Maintenance Officer, coordinated all scheduled and unscheduled maintenance for organic vehicles, engineer and support equipment from 1999 to date. Managed training of all maintenance personnel and equipment operators to insure cost effective utilization of manpower and material.

General Management: Managed safety program for the 8th Aviation Company in 2000 - 2001. As Safety Officer, identified areas of high accident potential, suggested corrective actions and educated unit personnel in accident proofing techniques. Managed Unit Postal Facility serving eighty men. While Platoon Leader in an aviation unit, motivated and trained up to 25 men in the accomplishment of a wide variety of activities. Served six months as Financial Custodian over funds for 1,000 dependent children.

Aviation: Received private pilot's license in 1998. Completed Army Aviation helicopter training with honors in 1990 and received FAA commercial helicopter certification. Have flown 850 accident-free hours to date flying VIP missions in support of the Division Commanding General and his staff.

Education

MASTER OF SCIENCE in Business Administration with honors, Boston University, 2001. Completed program while working full-time in the Army.

BACHELOR OF BUSINESS ADMINISTRATION in Management, North Georgia College, 1998. Served as President, Student Government Association. Active in Sigma Nu fraternity, distinguished Military Graduate.

References

Outstanding Officer Efficiency Reports available on request.

CHARLES G. PULLER
244 Mecklenburg Avenue
Greensboro, NC 28664
(919) 954-1042
cgp123@earthlink.com

Objective
Manufacturing Management, either in production, operations or administration, where education, abilities and experience can be best utilized.

Experience
JOHN H. HARLAND COMPANY, printer of bank stationery and other commercial printing. (1987 - Present)

PRODUCTION MANAGER, Greensboro, NC (1997 - present):
Have profit center responsibility for subsidiary involved in technical printing (forms, stationery, cards and mail order checks) and related direct mail operations. Direct the activities of four Supervisors managing a staff of 40 persons. Oversee inventory/quality control, efficiency, personnel, audit preparation and purchasing. Extensive involvement in overall company efficiency planning.

Accomplishments: Reduced labor costs by 5% per month. Boosted profit margin by 4% (from minus 2% to plus 2% level). Won "Best Quality Division" awards (1997 and 1998). Reduced turnover from more than 50% to under 20%.

ASSISTANT PLANT MANAGER, Orlando, FL (1993 - 1996):
Supervised staff of 15 administrative employees in a check printing facility. Directed all daily operations in such areas as personnel management, accounting, safety, audit preparation, billing, customer service, purchasing, security, attitude surveys, customer relations and P&L statements. Served as Sales/Plant Coordinator for 13 Sales Representatives in Colorado, Wyoming, Utah and Montana.

Accomplishments: Heavily involved in planning and implementation of move into new printing facility. Received three "A's" on periodic plant audits. Developed new Employee Training Manual later utilized in three plants. Established procedure that reduced weekly billing errors by over 40%.

PLANT SUPERINTENDENT, Orlando, FL (1991 - 1993):
Directed activities of 50 production employees and five supervisors in a check printing facility. Managed production planning, scheduling, maintenance, quality control, inventory control and cost containment.

Accomplishments: Increased operational efficiency by 12% per year. Improved delivery time from 79% to 93%. Established quality standards for employees, reducing rerun rate from 3.4% to 2.6%.

Education
MASTER OF BUSINESS ADMINISTRATION, concentration in accounting, University of North Carolina at Greensboro, 1999. GPA 3.8/4.0.

BACHELOR OF SCIENCE in Industrial Management, North Carolina State University, 1990. GPA 3.7/4.0.

(Sample ASCII format of previous resume)

CHARLES G. PULLER
244 Mecklenburg Avenue
Greensboro, NC 28664
(919) 954-1042
cgp123@earthlink.com

Objective
Manufacturing Management, either in production, operations or administration, where education, abilities and experience can be best utilized.

Experience
JOHN H. HARLAND COMPANY, printer of bank stationery and other commercial printing. (1987 - Present)
PRODUCTION MANAGER, Greensboro, NC (1997 - present):
Have profit center responsibility for subsidiary involved in technical printing (forms, stationery, cards and mail order checks) and related direct mail operations. Direct the activities of four Supervisors managing a staff of 40 persons. Oversee inventory/quality control, efficiency, personnel, audit preparation and purchasing. Extensive involvement in overall company efficiency planning.
- Accomplishments: Reduced labor costs by 5% per month. Boosted profit margin by 4% (from minus 2% to plus 2% level). Won "Best Quality Division" awards (1997 and 1998). Reduced turnover from more than 50% to under 20%.

ASSISTANT PLANT MANAGER, Orlando, FL (1993 - 1996):
Supervised staff of 15 administrative employees in a check printing facility. Directed all daily operations in such areas as personnel management, accounting, safety, audit preparation, billing, customer service, purchasing, security, attitude surveys, customer relations and P&L statements. Served as Sales/Plant Coordinator for 13 Sales Representatives in Colorado, Wyoming, Utah and Montana.
- Accomplishments: Heavily involved in planning and implementation of move into new printing facility. Received three "A's" on periodic plant audits. Developed new Employee Training Manual later utilized in three plants. Established procedure that reduced weekly billing errors by over 40%.

PLANT SUPERINTENDENT, Orlando, FL (1991 - 1993):
Directed activities of 50 production employees and five supervisors in a check printing facility. Managed production planning, scheduling, maintenance, quality control, inventory control and cost containment.
- Accomplishments: Increased operational efficiency by 12% per year. Improved delivery time from 79% to 93%. Established quality standards for employees, reducing rerun rate from 3.4% to 2.6%.

Education
MASTER OF BUSINESS ADMINISTRATION, concentration in accounting, University of North Carolina at Greensboro, 1999. GPA 3.8/4.0.

BACHELOR OF SCIENCE in Industrial Management, North Carolina State University, 1990. GPA 3.7/4.0.

Sandra Kendman
5849 Bacchus Way
St. Louis, MO 55002
(217) 355-0912

A results-oriented manager, with more than seven years of achievement in training, communications, and administration. Proficient in German and French. Available for travel and relocation. Seeking position in Human Resources, especially in employee training and development.

PROFESSIONAL ABILITIES

TRAINING:
- Received special recognition for superior technical training of co-workers in specialized instructional strategies.
- Trained and supervised more than 150 workers in basic skills competence, providing effective corrective and positive feedback.
- Documented detailed policies and procedures to enhance delivery of organizational objectives.
- Effectively analyzed causes of worker performance problems; recommended, implemented and monitored the alternatives.
- Conducted ongoing performance appraisals at regular intervals.
- Motivated and coached workers to improve productivity and to achieve successful performance.

PROGRAM DESIGN:
- Organized, developed, implemented courseware and systems for work management, basics instruction and training development.
- Analyzed job tasks, established measurable objectives, tracked performance and successful completion of assignments.
- Created successful performance feedback systems and established system to monitor and record results.
- Planned and produced audio-visual courseware.
- Organized, planned and conducted educational tours, related to increasing job knowledge and performance.

COMMUNICATION SKILLS:
- Developed and delivered presentations to groups of up to 100 people.
- Counseled, interviewed and negotiated with co-workers, management, public officials and the general public to enhance inter-communication and working relationships.
- Edited reports, researched, composed and distributed written information and materials.

EMPLOYMENT HISTORY

1997 - 2002 Educator, Stuttgart, West Germany
Department of Defense Dependent Schools
1992 - 1997 Educator, Richmond City Public School System

EDUCATION

BOSTON COLLEGE, Chestnut Hill, Massachusetts, 1992
BACHELOR OF ARTS in Education, *magna cum laude*
Dean's List, all semesters
Most Valuable Player, Water Polo, Fall 1983. Varsity Letter in Swimming.

246

BARBARA B. ROSE

1899 Flagstone Road
Providence, RI 02906
(401) 874-7892
bbr60@earthlink.com

CAREER OBJECTIVE

Operations Management position utilizing proven skills in organization and management.

SUMMARY OF QUALIFICATIONS

Strengths: More than ten years experience in planning, financing and administering business activities and fund raising events for several non-profit organizations. Have well-developed skills in
- organizing and streamlining projects,
- managing personnel and delegating responsibility, and
- working within budgets and resources.

Education: University of Florida, Gainesville, FL
Bachelor of Arts in English, 1979
Graduated *cum laude*, GPA 3.63/4.0
Active in student government, sorority (Rush Chairperson and Treasurer) and volunteer civic projects.

EXPERIENCE HISTORY

ATLANTA HUMANE SOCIETY AUXILIARY
Elected as Board Member (1985 - 1995), Assistant Treasurer (1986) and Director (1992 - 1994). Organized and chaired three highly successful fund raisers.
- Originated and implemented new fund raiser ("County Fair") which has become an annual event.
- Was first chairperson to successfully operate Gift Shop at a profit.
- Operated "Casino Party" fund raiser within budget restrictions and exceeded all previous years in gross profits.

ATLANTA CHILDREN'S THEATRE GUILD
Served as Board Member (1984 - 1987), Events chairperson (1984) and Vice-President and Fund Raising Chairperson (1991).
- Investigated and negotiated sites for meetings and luncheons, and was responsible for artwork, printing and mailing invitations.
- Supervised five committees and thirty persons, who were responsible for catering, administration, decorations, transportation and gift shop for Christmas House Fund Raiser. Achieved highest profit to date.
- Established policies and procedures for gift shop, resulting in 50% increase in profit.

ALL SAINTS' EPISCOPAL CHURCH
As Chairman of Christmas Pageant (1995), recruited volunteers, organized and directed participants, and initiated inclusion of other church classes.

REFERENCES AVAILABLE ON REQUEST.

LIBBY C. DOUGLAS
231 South Street
Greenwood, SC 29661
(803) 684-2716

OBJECTIVE

Project/Process engineering

EXPERIENCE

ELMHURST CHEMICALS, Spartanburg, SC

Process Engineer (January 1991 - present):
Responsible for directing and controlling a number of distinct chemical processes, including blends and specialty chemicals for the plastics, automotive, and textile industries.

Achievements:
- Implemented a quality program that allows the middle 30% of a product's specifications to be obtained consistently.
- Implemented a statistical process control program on 25 products that has improved quality 15%.
- Aided in research and development of five new fiber finish products.
- Assisted in the design and start-up of a $400,000 capacity expansion for a polyolefin clarifier.
- Implemented a cost reduction program which cut total variable conversion costs by 9.6% for an annual savings of $75,000, with zero capital investment.
- Have completed 400 hours of continuing education in such areas as public speaking; computer training in Autocad, Lotus, and Word-perfect; statistics; Managerial Grid; Organic Chemistry; and CPR.

DEPENDABLE ENVIRONMENTAL SERVICES, INC., Atlanta, GA

Field Analytical Technician (Summers of 1989 and 1990):
Responsible for observation, documentation, and all sampling techniques on asbestos abatement projects, including project leader on major asbestos abatement projects in Memphis, TN and Charleston, SC.

EDUCATION

Bachelor of Science, Chemical Engineering, December, 1990
Georgia Institute of Technology, Atlanta, GA
Earned 75% of education expenses.

Activities and honors:
- American Institute of Chemical Engineers, 1988 - 90
- Elected Board Member of Student Center, 1987 - 90
- Alpha Sigma Delta Phi Honor Society, 1986 - 87

248

MARGARET H. MARSHALL

77 Smom Court
Kansas City, MO 64114
(816) 395-3790
mhoy@aol.com

Objective   Senior manufacturing/engineering management position

Summary   Seven years senior management experience in manufacturing extending from factory operations to multi-facility responsibilities. Achievement in factory modernizations, tightly timed new product introductions and significant capacity increases. Expertise in cost reduction, quality improvement, materials, control, employee relations and strategic planning. Results oriented. MBA from the University of Chicago.

Experience   **SCHWINN BICYCLE COMPANY**, Chicago, Illinois, since 1991

Director of Manufacturing
Responsible for all domestic manufacturing for this leading bicycle manufacturer with plants in Wisconsin and Mississippi. Management responsibilities include materials requirements planning (MRP), capacity planning, staffing and industrial relations, quality assurance (QA), facility maintenance, automation planning, and cost management. Manage a staff of 200 through four direct reports and a budget of approximately $19 million. Report to the Chief Financial Officer.

Results:
• Assessed existing staff, reorganized where necessary and upgraded the professional factory staff.

• Upgraded the manufacturing process, virtually eliminating frame alignment defects, saving $228,000 annually.

• Doubled on-time delivery performance while increasing production volume by 45%.

• Developed a program to use temporary labor to offset cyclical market demands, saving the company $150,000 in labor costs.

• Managed the successful implementation of the manufacturing process for an all new state-of-the-art aluminum bike, the first entirely new (non-steel) bike in Schwinn's history.

• Installed cost control system enabling the organization to better measure factory expenses.

WILSON SPORTING GOODS COMPANY, River Grove, Illinois, 1985 - 1991

Director of Engineering Services
Managed a staff of 28 through four direct reports. Responsible for process automation, facilities engineering, industrial engineering, and operations planning in 13 domestic and foreign factories and four distribution centers. Reported to Senior Vice President, Operations.

Results:
• Established a manufacturing cost reduction program which saved more than $21 million during a five-year period (approximately 3% of the annual manufacturing costs).

• Accomplished a critical $3.7 million tennis ball capacity expansion in concert with the introduction of a blow molded tennis ball "can" and a new specialty product.

• Built a composite tennis racket factory in Kingstown, St. Vincent, and transferred the manufacturing equipment from the US in time to meet demanding production requirements.

• Responsible for $1.7 million of new process equipment and facilities which produced two new golf ball products against a tightly timed introductory schedule.

PROCTER & GAMBLE COMPANY, Cincinnati, Ohio and Jackson, Tennessee, 1976 - 1985

Engineering Manager, Jackson facility, 1983 - 1985

Results:
• Provided design services for automated cookie mix production.

• Accomplished energy conservation projects, reducing utility costs by 11%.

Operations Manager, Jackson facility, 1980 - 1982
Packaging Department Manager, Cincinnati, 1978 - 1980
Deodorizer Department Manager, Cincinnati, 1976 - 1979

Education   MBA, Executive Program, University of Chicago, 1990
BSIE, Georgia Institute of Technology, 1975
Honors: Tau Beta Pi - Engineering Honor Society
Alpha Pi Mu - Industrial Engineering Honor Society

K. W. TANNER
5547 Roswell Road NE, Apt S-5
Atlanta, GA 30342
(404) 843-5678

Objective

To apply skills gained in management, physical therapy, and training to a corporate environment. Open for travel and relocation.

Experience

MANAGEMENT: More than seven years supervisory experience of up to ten employees. Interview and hire office and support staff. Handle accounting and bookkeeping functions, client liaison and sales/marketing strategies.

TRAINING: Train all clerical and administrative employees. Write and develop training programs for individual and client needs. Conduct lectures, seminars and platform training classes for up to fifty persons, including managers and other trainers. Highly skilled in one-on-one patient care and education.

GENERAL: Past employment has all involved extensive public contact and has required exceptional communicative skills, oral and written, on a variety of levels. Have developed excellent research skills.

Employment

Operations Manager, Goodhealth Fitness Center, Inc. (1993 - present): Hire, train, and supervise office and professional staff for Physical Therapy facility, which combines the benefits of medical expertise with an exercise center. Responsible for clinical aspects of patient care, education, class development, and progress evaluation. Also handle communications with physicians and other consulting professionals.

Prior employment has been as ***Physical Therapist*** for two major health centers, Dekalb General Hospital and Sinecure Health Center, conducting both in-patient and out-patient treatment.

Education

BACHELOR OF SCIENCE in Biology, University of South Carolina, 1986
Graduated *Phi Beta Kappa*

Certificate in Physical Therapy, University of Oklahoma, 1985.

Additional graduate-level courses taken at Georgia State University and Southern Technical Institute in Physical Therapy and Technical Writing.

Shaun H. McDonough
3580 Northside Drive NW
Atlanta, GA 30305
(404) 231-0988
mcdon@ugs.edu

Objective

Seeking career in Insurance and Risk Management. Long range career plans include training in several facets of the insurance industry, including Underwriting, Claims Adjusting, Loss Prevention, Risk Management, and other related fields. Immediate employment objective is a trainee position with a major insurance company.

Education

BACHELOR OF BUSINESS ADMINISTRATION in Risk Management and Insurance, University of Georgia, graduation planned for December, 2001.

Will graduate in the top 10% of the Business School.

Honors/activities: Dean's List several times, GPA 3.4/4.0, elected to membership in Beta Gamma Sigma (business honor society), recipient of academic scholarship for excellence in insurance curriculum, member of Collegiate Insurance Society.

Experience

Several years of *__retail sales__* in family-owned clothing store during high school and college. Employed full-time during first year of college and during summers. Also assisted with formal *__bookkeeping__* functions, including general ledger entries, accounts payable and receivable, payroll, and financial statements.

Most recently have been employed part-time at local distribution warehouse, in a shipping and receiving position.

Personal

Born November 17, 1979 . . . . . Married, no children . . . . . 5'10", 165 lb., excellent health . . . . . Open for travel and relocation . . . . . Interests and hobbies include physical fitness, reading, and personal investments.

References available on request.

(Sample references page)

SUSAN B. SWIFT
3829 Helen Lane
Durham, NC   27702
(919) 282-4837

REFERENCES

HENRY C. ROBIN (client)
Purchasing Manager
North Carolina Food and Drug Distributors, Inc.
2173 Coventry Lane
Charlotte, NC   28760
(704) 822-9273
robin@ncfaddi.com

HAROLD T. HILL (former employer)
Southeast Region Sales Manager
Sunshine Foods, Inc.
7893 Chattahoochee Avenue SW
Atlanta, GA   30325
(404) 522-9754
hill@sunfoods.com

BETTY W. REICHTER, CPA (personal)
Eastland, Wright and Morris, CPA's
8384 Holcombe Bridge Road
Chapel Hill, NC   28876
(919) 777-1829 - office
(919) 929-9293 – home
bettyr@aol.com

LLANA S. FRANCO

Temporary address:
348 Bulldog Drive
Athens, GA 30601
(404) 353-7621
lsf@aol.com

Permanent Address:
1234 Azalea Road NW
Atlanta, GA 30327
(404) 262-7890
;sf@aol.com

REFERENCES

Steve R. Smithe (summer internship supervisor)
Director of Marketing
IBM Corporation
1 Atlantic Center, Suite 3890
Atlanta, GA 30309
(404) 888-6255

Dr. Nancy M. Ethyl
Associate Professor of Business
University of Georgia
Athens, GA 30601
(404) 567-8238

Nancy T. Chapman (personal)
Director of Human Resources
ABC Corporation
872 Fourth Street
Atlanta, GA 30308
(404) 876-7725 - office
(404) 252-9872 - home

SAMPLE BUSINESS CARDS

GEOFFREY WILLIAMS
BBA, University of Georgia, 1995
Marketing major, 3.4 GPA
Dean's List, Intramural Sports, Fraternity President
Sales experience

3445 Piedmont Road NE, #R-3
Atlanta, GA 30342
(404) 278-7873
gwms@mindspring.com

Human Resources Generalist

LINDA B. ANALTO
Recruiting • Benefits • Employee Relations
12 years experience

3890 Little Tongue Road, San Antonio, TX 78204
(512) 898-5241 • analto@att.com

BS/MS, Mechanical Engineering
Seven years manufacturing experience

BRICKLEY H. MARIST
Pepsico (1992 - 1995)
Proctor & Gamble (1989 - 1992)

248 Dover Road, Milwaukee, WI 78906
(888) 111-1111 • bhmarist@cts.com

SUZANNE HOYETTE, C.P.A.
Accounting and Financial Management
10 years experience
Seeking position as Corporate Controller

231 E. Atlantic Street, South Hill, VA 23970
(804) 447-8746

Communications Specialist
Spanish Bilingual

JOY K. BAER
345 Cloverhill Lane
Decatur, GA 30303
(404) 377-0987
jkb215@earthlink.net

B.A. Journalism
M.A. Communications

MARY W. SMILEY
B.B.A., Management, 1992
First Lieutenant, US Army, 1992 - 1996
Materials Management

8943 Roswell Road NE, Roswell, GA 30076
(404) 789-3333 • smiley@newleaf.com

APPENDIX B: CORRESPONDENCE

All job-related correspondence should conform to these two rules:

(1) Keep it brief, relevant, and to the point.

(2) Make it as personal as possible.

The following cover letters and thank-you notes illustrate those principles. In addition, observe that they are very positive in tone, with an emphasis on achievements and accomplishments.

Finally, remember your purpose in writing these correspondences:

- Including a cover letter with your resume is to create a good, strong first impression and thus get your resume read.

- If you include a separate salary history page, your purpose is not only to relay information requested, but also to continue on the positive track created through your cover letter and resume.

- A thank-you note should express your interest in the position and reinforce the positive impression you made during your interview.

Keeping those objectives in mind will help you compose your documents.

(Sample "T-Letter")

HARRY M. FOREMAN
2937 Woodland Brook
Dallas, TX 75219
(214) 770-8409
hmf@mindspring.com

April 14, 1999

Suburban Hotel Corporation
342 Mockingbird Lane
Dallas, TX 75200

RE: Job #C-34

Dear Sir or Madam:

As a professional with more than twenty years experience in the hospitality industry, I read with interest in the April 11, 2003, issue of *The Dallas Morning News* your advertisement for a Food and Beverage Marketing Manager. Please consider the following:

YOUR REQUIREMENTS:	MY QUALIFICATIONS:
Experience developing event marketing	Extensive experience developing marketing plans from concept to implementation to evaluation
Ability to conduct and control research	Several years of market research working directly in a supervisory and analytical capacity.
Coordinate promotional and advertising campaigns	Developed the concepts, slogans, and graphics, and oversaw implementation of the advertising and promotional campaigns for two major hotels in the Dallas market.
Extensive knowledge of the food and beverage industry	Possess keen understanding of the food and beverage industry through employment with three international hospitality leaders.

As requested, I have enclosed my resume with further details of my background, qualifications, and accomplishments. I look forward to meeting with you to discuss how I may fit into the Suburban Hotel Corporation, add to your professional staff, and lead your marketing functions.

Sincerely yours,

Harry Foreman

258

(Cover Letter Sample 1)

STEVE JARVIS
876 Sprayberry Lane
Charlotte, NC 28241
jarvis321@aol.com

November 17, 2003

Mr. Dick Brookson
Human Resources Manager
Union Camp Corporation
4341 Paper Bag Lane
Savannah, GA 31404

Dear Mr. Brookson:

I am enclosing my resume and salary history in response to your recent advertisement for a Marketing Development Manager. I am additionally familiar with Union Camp through Bill Smith, one of your Sales Managers in Savannah, and a former business associate. We worked together on a quality control problem at our company's Miami facility, and he has offered to be one of my references.

I have eight years of highly successful sales and promotion experience in the wood products industry. I have exceeded my weekly sales quotas by 40%, resulting in a total sales increase of 18%. I attribute this success to my strong problem-solving and interpersonal skills, and my ability to develop a close and creditable relationship with my customers.

Thank you for your time and consideration, and I will call you in a few days to confirm that you have received my resume. As your advertisement requested, I have enclosed my salary history. I am available for an interview at your convenience.

Sincerely yours,

Steve Jarvis
(704) 237-8724

(Cover E-mail Sample)

E-Mail – New Message

TO: recruiter@xyzcorp.com
cc:

Subject: Programmer C++ -- DeHoff, Anna

Message:

I am responding to the job vacancy listed on your web site for a C++ Programmer, and my resume is attached in MS Word format and titled "Programmer C++."

My degree is in computer science and I have three years experience as a C++ Programmer. Each year with my company, I received an evaluation of "5," which is the highest rating possible.

Thank you for your time and consideration. I am available for an interview at your convenience.

Anna DeHoff
adehoff@earthlink.com

Attachment

(Cover Letter Sample 1)

Lynn K. Parsons
879 Ridge Point Drive
Smyrna, GA 30339

April 7, 2003

Mr. John Thompson, Director of Personnel
Chicken Little Company
456 Corn Street
College Park, GA 30365

Dear Mr. Thompson:

Thank you for your time on the phone today and for the information regarding your current need for an Industrial Engineer. As you requested, I am enclosing my resume for your review.

During my three years with ABC Textiles, I have been responsible for implementing and managing projects very similar to the ones you described to me. A few of my recent assignments include these:
    -- Organized and conducted a study to determine and document causes of dye department downtime.
    -- Designed, estimated cost and proposed layout for relocation of maintenance shop, resulting in a 20% increase in efficiency.
    -- Assisted Safety Department in training employees on the proper use of new machinery, resulting in a decrease of 25% in time lost due to accidents.

Thank you again, and I look forward to hearing from you soon. My current salary is $37,000 annually, and I am available for relocation.

Sincerely yours,

Lynn K. Parsons
(404) 433-4898
lkp@kpl.com

(Cover Letter Sample 4)
4011 Roswell Rd NE, #F-6
Atlanta, GA 30342
November 18, 2003

Cartwell Chemical Company
7890 Riviera Parkway
Jacksonville, FL 32306

Dear Sirs:

Under my direction, production planning has been optimized at multiple facilities, including contract manufacturers and overseas facilities.

As you are advertising for an experienced Department Manager, you may be interested in my qualifications:

- As Inventory Control Manager, I reduced inventories from $50M to $42M, while improving product availability.
- I designed and implemented a material recovery program that saved more than $175,000 annually.
- Working with the MIS Department, I installed a database and operating program, substantially reducing inventory loss.

In addition, I have a Master's degree in management and a Bachelor's degree in chemistry.

Thank you for your time and consideration, and I will call you soon to confirm that you have received my resume. My enclosed salary history reflects consistent salary promotions in all positions held. I am available for interviews at your convenience.

Sincerely yours,

Celia Mosier
(404) 250-1234
ccm@aol.com

(Cover Letter Sample 5)

ANITA C. ST. JOHN

4488 Springdale Lane
Charlottesville, VA 23932
acsj4@msn.com
(704) 896-3748

January 22, 2003

Ms. Shiela DelRag, Region Sales Manager
ABC Laboratories, Inc.
3333 Interstate Parkway
Marietta, GA 30367

Dear Ms DelRag:

I am contacting you at the suggestion of Mike Douglas, the ABC Laboratories Sales Representative who handles our account. I am seeking to make a career change, out of purchasing and into a medical sales position. My resume is enclosed for your perusal.

My five years of experience as a hospital purchasing agent has given me valuable insight into the problems encountered by both your sales force and their clients, and I believe that knowledge will be most helpful in my new career. In addition, I have recently received my Bachelor's degree in marketing, while employed full-time at Carolinas' Medical Center.

I realize that my current salary of $32,000 may be higher than the salary generally offered to entry-level sales representatives, and thus I am flexible in my compensation requirements. My primary concern now is to establish a career in medical sales.

I trust my experience and initiative will be desirable attributes for ABC Laboratories, and I will call you next week to answer any questions you may have. I am available for an interview at your convenience.

Sincerely yours,

Anita St. John

(Sample Broadcast Letter)

ANNA Z. ELKIN
640 Westchester Square NE
Atlanta, GA 30309
(404) 881-8433
azelkin@bellsouth.net

April 18, 1998

Mr. Clyde Nann
Flight Simulations, Inc.
246 Park View Ave.
Oswego, NY 60634

Dear Mr. Nann,

As Manager of Marketing, I initiated a fundamental change in product development strategy which led to a 31% increase in market share.

I am writing you because I am certain I would have similar results working in your organization. A few of my other achievements follow:

- Developed and executed marketing plans which led to a 175% increase in international sales in two years.
- Positioned and launched three new product lines which account for more than 90% of sales volume.
- Lowered the cost per unit of advertising and sales support material by 50% while maintaining quality and effectiveness.
- Lowered the cost of market research by 80% through more efficient use of internal resources.
- Increased inventory turnover 15% through use of refined forecasting techniques.

I have an MBA and fifteen years of professional experience.

I would welcome the opportunity to discuss my background further. Please call at your earliest convenience.

Sincerely,

Anna Elkin
(404) 881-8433

(Sample Broadcast letter 2)

ISABELLE S. MINAFROW

104 Westwynn Court NE
Atlanta, GA 30309
(404) 892-8121 home
(404) 261-3169 office

March 28, 2003

Mr. Tom A. Perrin
WorldFaze, Inc.
3344 Kathleen Drive
San Mateo, CA 64545

Dear Mr. Perrin,

In these "Leaner and Meaner" times, when every dollar must do the work of two, perhaps your company could use the services of a senior-level manager who is bottom-line, profit-driven, and with an outstanding reputation for building value in products and services.

As a Senior Manager for the past 12 years, I have developed and implemented several strategies that resulted in a favorable impact on net profits. Some of my achievements include these:

- Increased sales volume 14% in the "Top Five" major accounts over the previous year, through product line penetration, merchandising techniques, and promotional programs.
- Achieved an 11.1% reduction in distribution, sales, and administrative costs from the prior year by implementing organizational modifications.
- Delivered a $1.7 million dollar improvement to net profits in a single year.
- Enhanced sales staff effectiveness through teambuilding and motivational training.

I excel at my work because I enjoy it. Increasing sales and teaching individuals to be more effective in their work is the greatest satisfaction I derive from my daily activities. I realize that efficient employees, exceeding customer expectations, and driving volume, but while containing operating costs, means more profit dollars for the company.

I am confident that I can deliver this level of success to your organization, and I would welcome the opportunity to speak with you. Thank you for your consideration.

Sincerely,

Isabelle S. Minafrow
Meina@aol.com

LAURIE T. MACON

3345 Winestain Road NE
Atlanta, GA 30326
(404) 262-7331
ltmisslob@msn.com

SALARY HISTORY

Bruce D. Morgan & Associates, Importers (1997 - Present):

National Sales Manager (2002 - present)
$97,500 salary + commission + bonus

Region Sales Manager (1999 - 2002)
$58,000 salary + commission

Sales Representative (1997 - 1999)
$29,000 salary + commission

All positions included company car and expense account.

Seeking initial total compensation of $100,000+. Long range advancement and income incentives are paramount. Will consider lower salary/draw with high commission potential.

(Salary History Sample 2)

KIM R. SCULLY

342 Moldy Fox Road, Detroit, MI 28803
(313) 274-4578 • scull@ajobs.com

Salary History

Western Union Telegraph Company (December 1998 - present)

Senior Internal Auditor (4/01 - present)	$ 81,150
Supervisor Financial Control (4/00 - 4/02)	72,600
Regional Staff Manager (12/98 - 4/00)	67,150

E. L. Lowie & Company (December 1994 - November 1998)

Assistant Controller	$60,500

Convenient Systems, Inc. (October 1992 - November 1994)

Divisional Controller (8/93 - 11/94)	$55,000
Accounting Manager (10/92 - 8/93)	44,600

A. M. Pullen & Company (June 1989 - September 1992) $30,000

LURLINE C. HARRIS

231 E. Rock Springs Rd NE
Atlanta, GA 30324
(404) 876-2388
lch1029@aol.com

SALARY HISTORY

Synergism Systems (March 1992 - present)

Director of Compensation and Benefits	$65,000

Citizens and Southern National Bank (May 1989 - March 1992)

Senior Compensation Analyst	$50,000
Compensation Analyst	45,000
Exempt Recruiter	39,000

(Note: Income reduction accepted in order to enter corporate Human Resources.)

Blinders Personnel Service (July 1986 - May 1989)

Accounting Division Manager	$49,000
Senior Recruiter	40,000
Staff Recruiter	18,000

(Thank-you Note Sample 1)

LURLINE C. HARRIS
231 E. Rock Springs Rd NE
Atlanta, GA 30324
(404) 876-2388
lch1029@aol.com

November 18, 2002

Mr. Thomas C. Browder
Hillside Energy and Automation
235 Peachtree St NE
Suite 2330
Atlanta, GA 30303

Dear Mr. Browder,

Thank you and your staff for the time you spent with me today. I very much enjoyed learning more about Hillside Energy and Automation and the new compensation program you are developing. With my five years of compensation and benefits experience, I am certain I can give excellent direction to your program and would greatly enjoy the challenge.

I am enclosing an article from the recent edition of <u>Compensation Today</u>, which describes a compensation program similar to the one we discussed. I thought it might be of interest to you.

Thank you again, and I look forward to hearing from you soon.

Sincerely yours,

Lurline C. Harris

(Thank-you Note Sample 2)

LLANA S. FRANCO

Temporary address:
348 Bulldog Drive
Athens, GA 30601
(404) 353-7621
lsf@aol.com

Permanent Address:
1234 Azalea Road NW
Atlanta, GA 30327
(404) 262-7890
lsf@aol.com

April 21, 2001

Mr. Wynn Patterholm
Wachovia Bank of Georgia
191Peachtree St NE
Suite 1234
Atlanta, GA 30303

Dear Mr. Patterholm,

As a recent college graduate, I realize that although my business experience is indeed limited, my potential is vast! My achievements and accomplishments to date illustrate the pattern of success I am certain I will continue.

Thank you for your interview time today at the University of Georgia's Career Day. I am very interested in Wachovia's Management Development Program, and I feel that I have much to contribute. I look forward to hearing from you soon. After graduation on May 21, I can be contacted at the permanent address above.

Sincerely yours,

Llana S. Franco

(Thank-you Note Sample 3)

JAN COTTON

789 Park Drive NW, Snellville, GA 30098
(404) 928-5673
jcotton@earthlink.net

September 8, 2002

Mr. Alan Lewinsky
Mobil Chemical Company
P O Box 78
Covington, GA 30302

Dear Mr. Lewinsky,

Thank you for your time and information yesterday, and especially for the tour of your facility. With your state-of-the-art equipment, I can easily understand why Mobil Chemical has been so successful, and I would like the opportunity to contribute to that success.

As I stated during our interview, I have been the top sales representative in my district with Scott Paper Company for the past three years. That achievement illustrates the abilities I also could bring to Mobil.

Thank you for your consideration. I am available for further interviews at your convenience.

Sincerely yours,

Jan Cotton

APPENDIX C:

Detailed Profiles of Selected Companies

NEW in 2004
Continuous updates available through
www.ajobs.com.
We update all the companies here plus new companies when
information is available.

The following employers are among the largest hiring companies in
Atlanta. These companies were selected primarily based on the large
number of salaried (versus hourly) and professional-level employees
hired annually, and also for diversity and variety. In developing a
direct contact marketing strategy, these are the ones you should
contact on your own, following the principles explained in Chapter IV.

EXPLANATION OF TERMINOLOGY

I have frequently made use of the terms "**exempt**" and "**non-
exempt**" in describing positions. These terms relate to the federal
wage and salary laws, and to avoid boring
you with a lengthy explanation of a
complex system, just remember that
generally speaking, most on-going career
positions with executive potential are
called "<u>exempt</u>" (that is, they are exempt
from the federal wage and salary laws),

> **ajobs.com**
> Provides links to most of the
> companies listed here, and newer
> ones when available.
> - Company home page
> - Company's Atlanta job
>   vacancies

although there are numerous exceptions.
For example, banks frequently hire individuals into non-exempt Teller
positions, and then promote into exempt positions when one occurs.
Other companies like to hire recent college grads in non-exempt
positions, in order to learn their business "from the bottom up."

This explanation may seem irrelevant to you now, but since it does affect your time and income, I have noted it in my company descriptions. Also knowing the number of exempt employees at a specific company will yield a general idea of the career potential there.

Another term you may not understand is "**IT**," an abbreviation for Information Technology, a "catch-all" acronym for general data processing and computer positions.

DISCLAIMER

The information contained herein was obtained from company officials and/or published sources, and is believed to be accurate. However, the author and publisher assume no liability for errors or the consequences thereof. Employment figures are generally approximate and can fluctuate.

The statement "Unable to determine employment projections" in a company's profile generally means that the company would not disclose these figures or did not return repeated phone calls. In some cases, I have been able to learn their employment process from other sources. Please send any corrections or additions to PO Box 52291, Atlanta 30355.

Suggestion

Scan through the companies here, highlighting those in which you have an interest and the ones who often have job vacancies for your specialty. Then go to ajobs.com, to the "Atlanta Companies" page, then click the "Job Vacancies" button. Go to each company you have highlighted to check for current openings to which you then can apply on-line.

A.D.A.M., INC. (www.adam.com)

Profile: Atlanta-based developer and publisher of innovative, high quality multimedia products that provide anatomical, medical and health realted information for the consumer, education, and professional markets worldwide. Employs 37, 35 exempt. Most hires are for software engineers and telesales reps. Uses Macintosh computers.

Procedure: Job site updated as needed. Send or email resume to Human Resources Manager
1600 RiverEdge Parkway, Suite 800, Atlanta GA 30328
(770) 980-0888; Fax (770) 989-4977
email resume to: careers@adam.com

A T & T COMPANY (www.att.com)

Profile: Southern Region Headquarters, covering 11-state territory. Employs 12,000 in Atlanta with 40% exempt. Opportunities for both recent college graduates and experienced professionals in sales/marketing; engineering; information management; MIS;and MBA. Also has clerical, admin, customer service, and technical positions.

Procedure: Employment is conducted thru web site. Go to
http://att.hire.com/joblist.html
1200 Peachtree St NE, Promenade I, Room 7075, Atlanta GA 30309
(800) 505-2162 Job line; Fax 810-2933

AARON RENTS (www.aaronrents.com)

Profile: Atlanta-based, largest furniture rental and sales company in US. Corporate office numbers 100± (50 exempt), plus store managers and staff. Seeks recent grads for manager trainees and experienced personnel for corporate offices.

Procedure: Lists jobs on Monster, HotJobs, and CareerBuilder. Also apply directly to store, or send or email resume to Recruiting Manger
309 E. Paces Ferry Road, Atlanta GA 30305
(404) 231-0011; Fax (404) 240-6593
email resume to: aaronbvb@atl.mindspring.com

ACE USA (www.acelimited.com)

Profile: Atlanta-based, commercial specialty insurance company. Employs 200 with 120 exempt. Seldom hires recent grads, but has needs for experienced underwriting, claims, and accounting/finance.

Procedure: Send resume to personnel
6 Concourse Pkwy, Suite 2500, Atlanta GA 30328-5346
(770) 393-9955; Fax (770) 441-5075

ACUITY BRANDS (www.acuitybrands.com)

Profile: Atlanta-based parent of several companies, including Lithonia Lighting and Zep Manufacturing (see listing for each), each of which conducts own hiring. Small Hq staff, occasional for accounting/finance and auditing.
Procedure: Jobs not online. Send resume to
1170 Peachtree Street, NE, Ste 2400, Atlanta GA 30309
(404) 853-1400; Fax (404)

AETNA U.S.HEALTHCARE (www.aetnaushc.com)
Profile: SE Region Headquarters for HMO, employing 500 here in sales, underwriting, finance, marketing, PR, medical delivery, nurses, quality, and MIS. Recent grads need some prior business experience. Experienced exempt are hired in the above areas.
Procedure: Send resume to Human Resources
11675 Great Oaks Way, Alpharetta GA 30022
(770) 346-4300; Fax (404) not accepted

AFC ENTERPRISES (www.afc-online.com)
Profile: Parent company of Churchs and Popeyes fried chicken and Chesapeake Bagle Bakery chains, with 2500+ restaurants nationwide. Employs 350 on corporate staff, 90% exempt. Headquarters seldom hires recent grads without experience; experienced exempt needs are in finance, marketing, legal, human resources, and restaurant development. Accounting department in Texas, not Atlanta, and MIS is out-sourced.
Procedure: For corporate positions, send resume to Recruiting Coordinator
6 Concourse Pkwy, Suite 1700, Atlanta GA 30328
(770) 391-9500; Fax (770) 353-3058
email resume to: afcrecruiting@afce.com

AGCO (www.agcocorp.com)
Profile: Atlanta-based manufacturer of farm machinery and equipment, employing 300 at headquarters, 250 exempt. Exempt openings in distribution.
Procedure: Send resume to Human Resources
4205 River Green Pkwy, Duluth GA 30096
(770) 813-9200; Fax (770) 813-6140
email resume to: HR.Duluth@agcocorp.com

AGENCY FOR TOXIC SUBSTANCES AND DISEASE REGISTRY (ATSDR)
(www.atsdr.gov)
Profile: Employing 400 here, ATSDR is an Atlanta-headquartered public health service agency that works closely with both the Environmental Protection Agency (EPA) and with state and local health officials to ensure public safety from hazardous materials. Hires MIS and scientific

specialists including toxicologists, environmental health scientists and engineers, etc.

Procedure: Hiring is handled by the Centers for Disease Control and Prevention, and thus the procedure is the same. Call the Job Line and apply as instructed, or call the CDC Job Information Center and request a copy of announced positions and an application form.
4770 Buford Hwy, Atlanta GA 30341
(770) 488-1725; (888) 232-4473 Job Line; Fax (770) 488-1979
email resume to: only fax and USPO

AGL RESOURCES, INC (www.aglr.com)

Profile: Atlanta-based regional energy holding company with operations throughout the Southeast. (see listing) Employs 1750 with 550 exempt (2200 companywide). Hires mostly recent grads in engineering (ME, CE, IE), MIS and accounting. Has co-ops in engineering.

Procedure: Send resume to Personnel Manager
P O Box 4569, Atlanta GA 30302
(404) 584-9470; 584-4705 Job Info Line; Fax (404) 584-4676
email resume to: pgnann@mindspring.com

AKZO COATINGS, INC. (www.sikkens.com)

Profile: Manufacturer and distributor of technical paint and coatings for auto aftermarket. Employs 250 in Atlanta, 175 exempt. Does not hire recent grads, but seeks experienced exempt in accounting/finance, auto aftermarket sales, manufacturing and distribution, engineering (ChE), and MIS (AS 400; netware/pansophic).

Procedure: Send resume to Human Resources
5555 Spalding Drive, Norcross GA 30092
(770) 662-8464; Fax (770) 662-8620
email resume to: resumes.ancrna@akzonobel.com

ALLIED HOLDINGS, INC. (www.alliedholdings.com)

Profile: Atlanta-based, second largest car hauler in US. Employs 375 in Atlanta with 240 exempt level. Hires recent grads in accounting/finance and experienced exempt in operations management. No MIS needs.

Procedure: Send resume to personnel
160 Clairmont Ave, Suite 600, Decatur GA 30030
(404) 371-0379; Fax (404) 370-4298

ALLSTATE INSURANCE (www.allstate.com)

Profile: SE regional office for largest US property and casualty insurance company, employing 1200 in Atlanta. Seeks experienced agents and personal financial representatives, plus claims, finance, HR, mktg, risk mgt, and support staff.

Procedure: Send resume to Human Resources

3100 Interstate North Circle, Atlanta GA 30339
(678) 589-5500; (678) 589-6168 Job line; Fax (678) 589-6139
email resume to: careers@allstate.com

ALLTEL TELECOMUNICATIONS (www.alltel.com)
Profile: Telecommunications company with more than 800 employees in
             Atlanta. Mostly hires experienced exempt for account/finance,
             management, engineering, and MIS; some recent graduates are hired for
             MIS.
Procedure: Fax resumes to Director of Human Resources
             615 South Thornton Ave, Dalton GA 30720
             (706) 279-7600; Fax (706) 279-7004

AMEC (www.amec.com)
Profile: (Formerly Simons Consulting Engineers) Atlanta-based, multi-
             discipline design and consulting firm, specializing in the design of
             industrial manufacturing facilities. Employs 370 with 240 exempt.
             Most personnel needs are for engineers and designers (CE, ChE, ME,
             EE and Pulp and Paper), some recent grads but mostly experienced.
             Also hires some experienced exempt in accounting/finance, MIS (DEC
             VAX) and personnel. Has co-op program for engineering students. Job
             openings at web site and accepts resumes via email.
Procedure: Send resume to Personnel
             P O Box 1286, Atlanta GA 30301
             (404) 370-3200; Fax (770) 370-7707

AMERICAN CANCER SOCIETY (www.cancer.org)
Profile: National home office of the nationwide community-based voluntary
             health organization; also has state and local offices in Atlanta. Employs
             600+ at home office (400 exempt), plus state and local offices not hired
             at this office. Rarely hires for entry-level, but recruits experienced
             personnel in administration, accounting/finance, health education, fund
             raising, information systems, communications (marketing, public
             relations, creative services) and scientific and medical fields.
Procedure: Job site updated weekly. Email resume from web site to Human
             Resources
             1599 Clifton Rd NE, Atlanta 30329
             (404) 320-3333; Fax 636-2317

AMERICAN MEGATRENDS (www.ami.com)
Profile: Atlanta-based designer and manufacturer of IBM AND PC compatible
             Motherboards, BIOS, and utility products, employing 145. Most hires
             are for engineers (EE), both entry-level and experienced, Master's degree
             preferred.
Procedure: Send resume to personnel

6145-F Northbelt Pkwy, Norcross GA 30071-2976
(770) 263-8181; Fax (770) 263-9381

AMERICAN RED CROSS (www.redcross.org)
Profile: Non-profit emergency assistance and blood bank, employing 550 in Atlanta, including 120 exempt. Seeks entry-level and experienced accountants, nurses, medical technologists and lab technicians (ASCP or NCA certification required). Also seeks about 20 marketing/sales grads each year for community relations positions in donor resources and experienced MIS (HP 3000 and AS 400). Lists all jobs with GA Dept. of Labor.
Procedure: Send resume to Human Resources
1955 Monroe Drive NE, Atlanta GA 30324
(404) 876-3302; Fax (404) 575-3086
email resume to: cmaynard@arcatl.org

AMERICAN SECURITY GROUP (www.americansecurity.com)
Profile: Dutch-owned credit insurance company, US headquarters in Atlanta, employing 775 here with 300 exempt. Hires recent grads and experienced exempt in all areas, including accounting/finance, sales, management, MIS and insurance specialties.
Procedure: Send resume to Human Resources, Employment Specialist
P O Box 50355, Atlanta GA 30302
(770) 763-1000; Fax (770) 859-4605

AMERICAN SOCIETY OF HEATING, REFRIGERATING, AND AIR-CONDITIONING ENGINEERS, INC. (ASHRAE) (www.ashrae.org)
Profile: Atlanta-based engineering membership society, employing 104 in headquarters, 68 exempt. Most exempt are in communications, and they hire only experienced. This office does not hire engineers. (See listing in Appendix E for engineering assistance) Their web site has many job listings for ASHRAE members only.
Procedure: Send reusmes via US mail, fax or e-mail.
1791 Tullie Circle NE, Atlanta GA 30329
(404) 636-8400; Fax (404) 321-5478
email resume to: personnel@ashrae.org

AMERICAN SOFTWARE USA, INC. (www.amsoftware.com)
Profile: Atlanta-based corporation that develops, manufactures and markets software for business applications. Employs 600 in Atlanta, 575 exempt. Very rarely hires recent grads, but will hire 100+ experienced exempt, nearly all in MIS, including programmer analysts and systems analysts, or sales-related. MIS applicants must have 2+ years experience in software development for multi-platform environments; sales applicants should have 5+ years software sales experience.

Procedure: Send resume to Corporate Recruiting
470 East Paces Ferry Rd NE, Atlanta GA 30305
(404) 261-4381; Fax (404) 238-8499
email resume to: amsoft@provenmethod.com

AMREP, INC (www.amrep.com)
Profile: Atlanta-based manufacturer of specialty chemicals, lubricants, and grease products, employing 135 with 15 exempt. Seeks technical personnel (IE, and chemistry, aerosol and liquids experience good) and hourly machine operators and manufacturing workers.
Procedure: Send resume to Director of Human Resources
990 Industrial Park Drive, Marietta GA 30062
(770) 422-2071; Fax (770) 422-1737
email resume to: stacey.halyard@amrep.com

ANHEUSER-BUSCH (www.anheuserbusch.com)
Profile: Brewery employing 575, 100+ exempt. Hires mostly experienced exempt in accounting and production management or for specialty backgrounds. Has several coop positions.
Procedure: Does not maintain a resume file, so sending a resume may not be productive. Advertises all exempt openings in the Sunday classifieds of The Atlanta Journal and Constitution.
P O Box 200248, Cartersville GA 30120
(770) 386-2000; Fax (770) 606-3018

ARRIS GRP (www.arrisi.com)
Profile: Atlanta-based manufacturer and distributor of high- and low-tech equipment for cable and telephone industries. Employs 450 total, 75% exempt, and growing rapidly. Hires recent grads and experienced exempt in all technical areas. Jobs and applications at web site.
Procedure: Send resume to Human Resources
11450 Technology Circle, Duluth GA 30097
(678) 473-2000; Fax (678) 473-8454
email resume to: hr@arrisi.com

ARTHRITIS FOUNDATION (www.arthritis.org)
Profile: Atlanta-based, non-profit organization, providing education and fund raising activities relative to arthritis disease. Employs 140 with 50% exempt. Hires no recent grads, but experienced exempt positions may become available in accounting, MIS (DEC VAX), fund raising, program coordination , writing and other editorial staff.
Procedure: Send resume to Employment
1330 West Peachtree NW, Atlanta GA 30309
(404) 872-7100; Fax (404) 872-0457

ASSEMBLEON AMERICA (www.assembleon.com)
Profile: Division of Philips Electronics, sales and service of high speed
            component placement machines for electronic manufacturing,
            employing 110 with 80 exempt. Hires in all areas (accounting/finance,
            sales, and operations), although more needs for engineers (applications,
            IE), entry-level and experienced, and customer support.
Procedure: Job site updated as needed. Send or email resume to Human Resources
            5110 McGinnis Ferry Road, Alpharetta GA 30202
            (770) 751-4420 ; Fax (770) 751-4450
            email resume to: assembleon.resumes@philips.com

AT&T WIRELESS ()
Profile: Wireless telecommunications provider, employing 250 in Atlanta.
            Openings in accounting/finance, sales, telesales and customer service.
Procedure: Apply online or send resume to
            1420 Oakbrook Drive, Norcross GA 30093
            (800) 462-4463; Fax (404)

ATHLETE'S FOOT, THE (www.theathletesfoot.com)
Profile: Corporate headquarters for this specialty retailer in athletic footwear.
            Has 700+ stores worldwide in 40 countries, including 176 company-
            owned (others franchised). Employs 140 at headquarters with 40
            exempt. Most recent grads hired are for Retail Management and
            accounting. Hires experienced personnel annually in many areas,
            including accounting/finance, MIS (AS 400 and PC's), retail operations,
            human resources, merchandising, distribution, buying, franchise
            coordination, etc.
Procedure: Jobs updated weekly. Send or fax resume to Corporate Recruiter
            1950 Vaughn Road, Kennesaw GA 30144
            (770) 514-4500; Fax (770) 514-4829
            email resume to: taf@rpc.webhire.com

ATLANTA BRAVES (www.atlantabraves.com)
Profile: Major league baseball team. Has several programs: Trainee Program
            for recent grads (3.0 required) interested in career in professional sports
            administration; training runs from January - Novemeber, with
            applications accepted in October prior year. Has 11-week internships
            for college juniors and seniors with 3.0 GPA. Sponsors annual job fair
            in January for seasonal non-exempt employees.
Procedure: Jobs available listed at www.turnerjobs.com. For application process
            and info, contact Human Resources
            P.O. Box 4064, Atlanta GA 30302-4064
            (404) 522-7630; 614-1506 job line; Fax (404)

ATLANTA COCA-COLA BOTTLING COMPANY (www.cokecce.com)

Profile: Also functions as Atlanta Region of Coca-Cola Enterprises. Bottles and distributes Coca-Cola brands of soft drinks, and a division of Coca-Cola Enterprises. Employs 1800+, including 300 exempt. Hires mainly experienced personnel (but recent grads) into sales, accounting, and manufacturing operations.

Procedure: Send resume to Human Resources Manager
P O Box 723040, Atlanta GA 31139-0040
(770) 989-3100; job line 989-3500; Fax (770) 989-3533

ATLANTA CONVENTION AND VISITORS BUREAU (www.atlanta.net)

Profile: Private, non-profit organization created to market Atlanta and GA regionally, domestically, and internationally to both groups and individuals. Employs 75 with 50 exempt. Most recurring needs are in admnistrative support and sales (hotel or corporate experience best).

Procedure: Send resume to Human Resources
233 Peachtree St NE, Suite 100, Atlanta GA 30303
(404) 521-6600; Fax (404) 577-3293
email resume to: jclaxton@acvb.com

ATLANTA FALCONS (www.atlantafalcons.com)

Profile: Atlanta football franchise. Has occasional exempt needs in many corporate areas, including admin, finance, media, PR, IT, and sales. Offers internships.

Procedure: Apply online for open positions or create a "future notification" profile to be called when positions arise.
4340 Falcon Pkwy, Flowery Branch GA
(770) 965-3115; Fax (404)

ATLANTA JOURNAL-CONSTITUTION (www.cox.com)

Profile: Largest daily newspaper in the Southeast, employing 7300 (many of whom are part-time) with 1000 exempt. Recent grads are hired in accounting, customer service, and advertising as Account Executives or Sales Support; recent journalism grads need some work experience with a smaller newspaper or internship. Will also seek experienced exempt, in all areas including journalism. In addition, they offer internships, mostly in news journalism.

Procedure: Journalists, reporters, and interns in newsroom, send resume to Managing Editor. For other positions, do not send resume, as Human Resources Dept. no longer accepts unsolicited resumes or walk-in applicants. All available positions are advertised in the Sunday edition of the A J-C and you must respond to a specific opening then.
72 Marietta St NW, Atlanta GA 30303
(404) 526-5151; Job Information Line 526-5092; Fax (404) 526-2607

ATLANTA MARRIOTT MARQUIS (www.marriott.com)

Profile: Atanta's largest hotel with 1671 rooms and 69 suites, employing 1,250, 100 exempt.
Procedure: Send resume to personnel
            265 Peachtree Center Ave, Atlanta GA 30303
            (404) 521-0000; job line 586-6240 (International job line 1-800/4marriott); Fax (404) 586-6265

ATLANTIC AMERICAN CORP. (www.atlam.com)
Profile: Atlanta-based life, health, and casualty insurance company, employing 140 with 65 exempt. Has no training program, and most exempt needs are for experienced insurance backgrounds and occasional staff accountant.
Procedure: Send resume to Human Resources
            4370 Peachtree Rd NE, Atlanta GA 30319
            (404) 266-5500; Fax (404) 239-0207

ATLANTIC SOUTHEAST AIRLINES (www.flyasa.com)
Profile: Atlanta-based feeder airline for Delta Airlines, employing 2200 nationwide and growing. Like Delta's career policy, all employees pass through the same entry-level training program, and there are openings for all types – accounting/finance, sales, management, MIS, etc., plus flight attendants.
Procedure: They receive thousands of resumes and applications, and thus do not respond to all. If in Atlanta, you can complete an application form at their offices on Wednesday from 8 - 5 pm; out of Atlanta, send stamped, self-addressed evelope requesting an application. They will notify you if you are being considered for an opening. Do not mail your resume
            100 Hartsfield Centre Pkwy, Suite 800, Atlanta GA 30354
            (404) 766-1400; Fax (404) 209-0162

AUTOMATIC DATA PROCESSING (www.adp.com)
Profile: Nation's largest independent data services company, providing computerized transaction processing, recordkeeping, data communications, and information services. Employs 350 with 150 exempt, and growing. Hires numerous business grads with majors in accounting/finance, marketing, and management, plus experienced exempt in those disciplines. Also seeks MIS (IBM 3090), entry and experienced.
Procedure: Send resume to Dirctor of Human Resources
            5680 New Northside Drive, Atlanta GA 30328
            (770) 955-3600; Fax (770) 980-6897

AUTOMATIC DATA PROCESSING - NATIONAL ACCOUNTS (www.adp.com)

Profile: Handles large accounts for nation's largest independent data services company. Employs 500 here with 375 exempt. Seeks business degrees, especially accounting/finance, and experienced personnel in payroll accounting.

Procedure: Send resume to personnel
5800 Windward Parkway, Alpharetta GA 30005
(770) 360-2000; Job line (888) 611-3177; Fax (770) 360-4275

AUTOMATIIC DATA PROCESSING (www.adp.com)

Profile: Electronic Services Division, consisting of seven companies in software and applications development for service and financial industries. Employs 700 here, 50% exempt. Hires a few recent grads in accounting and computer science, and many experienced exempt in many areas including accounting, sales, marketing, tech wirters, software development, applications, etc.

Procedure: Send resume to Human Resources
1505 Pavilion Place, Norcross GA 30093
(770) 492-7200; Fax (770) 931-7418
email resume to: humanresources@peachtree.com

AVADO BRANDS (www.avado.com)

Profile: Restaurant chain (McCormick & Schmick, Don Pablo's, Hops, Canyon Cafe) employing 100 at headquarters with 70 exempt, plus store personnel. Headquarters needs are for experienced exempt, mostly accounting/finance and also human resources, marketing, real estate/site selection, and construction management. Also seeks restaurant managers, experienced and trainee.

Procedure: Send resume to Human Resources
Hancock at Washington Streets, Madison GA 30650
(706) 342-4552 ; Fax 706-342-9283

AVAYA, INC. (www.avaya.com)

Profile: Atlanta-bsed communications networks including secure and reliable internet protocol telephony systems, software, applications and services. Employs 400. Hires recent grads and experienced exempt, plus interns (all levels).

Procedure: Complete online applications or mail resume to
420 Technology Pkwy, Ste 100, Norcross GA 30092
(770) 421-5000; Fax (404)

B B D O ATLANTA (www.bbdoatl.com)

Profile: Largest advertising agency in the Southeast. Employs 270 in Atlanta, mostly exempt. Hires a few recent grads, mostly for entry-level, non-exempt positions, but with good opportunity for advancement. Hires experienced advertising personnel and accountants. Also offers advertising internships.

Procedure: Send resume to Director of Human Resources
3500 Lenox Rd, Ste 1900, Atlanta GA 30326
(404) 231-1700; Fax (404) 841-1893
email resume to: jobs@bbdoatl.com

BANK OF AMERICA (www.bankofamerica.com)

Profile: Largest US bank, headquartered in Charlotte, NC. Atlanta is headquarters for General Bank division. Employs 5000+ with about 30% exempt. Seeks recent grads, mostly accounting/finance, management, and MBA's, plus experienced personnel (prefers financial services backgrounds) in accounting/finance and management.

Procedure: Recent grads, direct resume to Manager of College Relations; experienced personnel, direct resume to Management Recruiting. Both at
100 N. Tryon St, Charlotte NC 28255
(404) 607-6157; job line: (800) 587-5627; Fax (404) 607-6186

BANKER'S BANK (www.bankersbank.com)

Profile: Atlanta-based correspondence bank serving smaller, community banks, employing 220. Hires recent grads in non-exempt positions, then promotes as needs arise. Hires experienced exempt as needs arise, mostly in banking, investments, operations, and marketing.

Procedure: Fax or email resume to personnel
2410 Paces Ferry Rd, Suie 600, Atlanta GA 30339
(404) 848-2900; Fax (770) 805-2166
email resume to: resumes@bankersbank.com

BARCO PROJECTION SYSTEMS (www.barco.com)

Profile: Atlanta-based distributor of visualization equipment, including monitors, displays, projection systems, and cable and satellite equipment. Employs 85 with 60 exempt. Most hires here are for technicians in repair and sales support, and entry-level customer service/support.

Procedure: Send resume to Human Resources Manager
3240 Town Point Drive, Kennesaw GA 30144
(770) 218-3200; Fax (770) 218-3357

BARCOVIEW (www.barco.com)

Profile: Atlanta-based developer and manufacturer of high performance color graphic work stations, employing 100 with 80 exempt. Most needs are for engineers (EE and CS generally), entry and experienced. Seldom has openings for IS or accounting.

Procedure: Send resume to human resources
3059 Premiere Parkway, Duluth GA 30097

(678) 475-8000; Fax (678) 475-8160

BARD, C. R. INC. — UROLOGICAL AND MEDICAL (www.crbard.com)
Profile: Division headquarters facility that manufactures and markets medical devices. Employs 550 with 200 exempt. Seeks both recent grads and experienced exempt for accounting/finance, engineering (ME mostly, especially with plastics background), bioscience, sales, and materials management.
Procedure: Job site updated weekly. Apply online or send resume to Human Resources Department
8195 Industrial Blvd, Covington GA 30014
(770) 784-6100 or (800) 526-4455 x6749; Fax (770) 784-6731

BEAZER HOMES USA (www.beazer.com)
Profile: Atlanta-based national homebuilder wtih operations in 30 mkts. Also provides mortgage and insurance services. Has needs for accounting/finance, mortgage and construction backgrounds, and sales.
Procedure: Send resume to human resources
5775 Peachtree-Dunwoody Rd, B200, Atlanta GA 30342
(404) 250-3420; Fax (404)

BELLSOUTH ADVERTISING AND PUBLISHING CORP. (www.realpages.com)
Profile: Responsible for sales and information included in BellSouth Yellow Pages. Employs approximately 1100, with 30% exempt. Hires recent grads and experienced personnel (40+) annually in sales and graphic arts.
Procedure: Send resume to Employment Manager
2247 Northlake Pkwy, Tucker GA 3084
(770) 908-6200; Job Information Line: (800) 992-8840; Fax (404) 491-5054

BELLSOUTH — GENERAL EMPLOYMENT OFFICE (www.bellsouth.com)
Profile: Hires non-exempt employment for BellSouth/Georgia's regulated companies, approximately 12,000 total employees. Most needs are for marketing graduates to be in customer service/telemarketing and for two- and four-year technical graduates to be technicians. Reduction-in-force is anticipated. Hires also in temporary positions.
Procedure: Send resume to Human Resources
1760 Century Circle, Suite 6, Atlanta GA 30346
(770) 329-9455, but first call job info line @ (404) 249-2246; Fax

BELLSOUTH TELECOMMUNICATIONS - MANAGEMENT EMPLOYMENT CENTER (www.bellsouth.com)
Profile: Hires all exempt employees for BellSouth's regulated companies. Hires recent grads and experienced specialists, as well as college co-op

positions. Primary needs currently are for management, sales, marketing and engineering (EE, IE). Hires 500± annually. [Note: Sales/marketing personnel are hired through BellSouth Business Systems in Birmingham, AL; (800) 368-3395 job line]

Procedure: Best to first check web site jobs listing thru ajobs.com, then email resume thru web site. Located at
2310 Parklake Drive, Suite 400, Atlanta 30345
(770) 492-4400; (800) 992-8840Job Line; Fax

BIOLAB, INC (no web site)

Profile: Atlanta based manufacturer of water treatment products. Seeks entry and experienced exempt in IT, accounting/finance, HR, sales, and bio-chem R&D. Moving HQ to 1735 N. Brown Rd, Lawrenceville, GA 30043 in 2003.

Procedure: Fax or email resume to Staffing Specialist
PO Box 1489, Decatur GA 30031
(404) 378-1753; Job line x1960; Fax (404)
email resume to: jobs@biolabinc.com

BLOCKBUSTER ENTERTAINMENT (www.blockbuster.com)

Profile: Nation's largest retailer of video rentals and supplies, with 100+ stores in Atlanta. Most store managers are hired as either Ass't Store Managers or as entry-level hourly positions, then promoted up. Promotes heavily from within.

Procedure: Send resume via US mailto Regional Human Resources Manager
2900 S. Cobb Drive, Smyrna GA 30080
(770) 431-0132; Fax (770) 431-0720

BLUE CIRCLE AMERICA (www.bluecircle.com)

Profile: Atlanta HQ for British manufacturer of aggregates, cement, ready-mix concrete and block, employing 300 here. Most needs are for accounting/finance, MIS, and human resources.

Procedure: Send resume to human resources
1800 Parkway Place, Marietta GA 30067
(770) 423-4700; Fax (404)

BLUE CROSS/BLUE SHIELD OF GEORGIA (bcorpening.bcbs-ga.com)

Profile: BC/BS is the nation's largest health care insurer, although each member company operates autonomously. Employs 1500 here with 900 exempt. Recent grads with some related experience are usually hired into non-exempt positions, then promoted when an exempt position occurs; many are hired annually into accounting and insurance specialties. Experienced exempt are needed in accounting/finance, sales, management, insurance specialties (managed care, risk management, underwriting, etc.), and IS (IBM with Cobol, LAN, WAN, client server). Has interns in underwriting and actuarial.

Procedure: Only accepts resumes for current positions. Call job line and follow prompts, then send or email resume to Employment Representative, 3350 Peachtree Rd NE, Atlanta GA 30326
(404) 842-8001; 842-8060 job line; Fax (404) 842-8803
email resume to: hr_corp@bcbs-ga.com

BOWNE OF ATLANTA, INC. (www.bowne.com)

Profile: World's largest financial printer, furnishing multi-lingual and multi-media document building solutions. Employs 190 with 25 exempt. Hires recent grads in liberal arts and business, and a few MIS and accounting. Seeks experienced exempt with financial printing backgrounds.

Procedure: Send resume to Human Resources
1570 Northside Drive NE, Atlanta GA 30318
(404) 350-2000; Fax (404) 350-2004

BOYS & GIRLS CLUBS OF AMERICA (www.bgca.org)

Profile: Corporate headquarters in Atlanta with 220 employees here, 140 exempt. Hires backgrounds in marketing/communications, office services, human resources, resource development, accounting, administrative support, and youth development programs. Prefers to hire experienced, or promote from within or from local clubs.

Procedure: Call job line and reply for specific vacancy to address specified. Or send or email resume to corporate Human Resources
1230 West Peachtree St. NW, Atlanta GA 30309
(404) 815-5700; job line (404) 815-5828; Fax (404) 487-5788
email resume to: cwagner@bgca.org

BWAY CORP (www.bwaycorp.com)

Profile: Atlanta-based manufacturer of steel containers. Needs in operations, finance, sales, marketing, systems and administration.

Procedure: Email or send resume to HR,
8607 Roberts Dr, Ste 250, Atlanta GA 30350
(404) 645-4800; Fax (404)
email resume to: hr@bwaycorp.com

BYERS ENGINEERING CO. (www.byers.com)

Profile: Atlanta-based consulting firm that provides engineering and computer graphic services for major utilities; employs 1000+. Two divisions, each conducting their own recruitment: Information Systems hires experienced MIS (Windows and/or OS/2 object oriented C++ programmers); engineering division requires telephony experience.

Procedure: Send resume to Human Resources Manager at the appropriate division (MIS can be emailed to walter.stovall@byers.com); both located at 6285 Barfield Rd, Atlanta GA 30328
(404) 843-1000 x 235 for MIS; x 402 for engineering; Fax (404) 843-2116

C V S PHARMACY (www.cvs.com)
Profile: Largest pharmacy chain in Atlanta, with 100 stores here and 400 in Georgia. This office hires only for store managers, recent grads and experienced.
Procedure: Send or email resume to Recruiter
821 Atlanta Street, Roswell GA 30075
(678) 461-3041; Fax (770) 844-2168
email resume to: michael.pagano@internetmci.com

CAGLES, INC. (www.cagles.net)
Profile: Atlanta-based poultry processor.
Procedure: Send resume to personnel
2000 Hills Ave NW, Atlanta GA 30318
(404) 355-2820; Fax (404)

CANADA LIFE ASSURANCE COMPANY (www.canadalife.com)
Profile: US Division headquarters for international life insurance company. Employs 425 here, 100 exempt. Hires experienced specialists in pension, actuarial, individual life, group life and health.
Procedure: Send or email resume to personnel
6201 Powers Ferry Road NE, Atlanta GA 30339
(770) 953-1959; Job Line (770) 953-1959 x2335; Fax (770) 952-9252
email resume to: jobs@canadalife.com

CANON USA (www.usa.cannon.com)
Profile: SE region sales and distribution center for office equipment and consumer photographic products, employing 125 with 100 exempt. Most needs are for experienced sales reps and technical sales support.
Procedure: Job site updated monthly. Fax or e-mail resume to Human Resources Dept.
5625 Oakbrook Pkwy, Norcross GA 30093
(770) 849-7800; Fax (770) 849-7809
email resume to: hratlanta@cusa.cannon.com

CARAUSTAR INDUSTRIES (www.caraustar.com)
Profile: Atlanta-based manufacturer and converter of paperboard products, employing 100 in Hq w/ 50 exempt, pluss 350 in mfg. Hires mostly technical and engineering backgrounds, including pulp and paper, both

recent grads and experienced exempt. Good source for Junior Military Officers.

Procedure: Send resume to Human Resources
3100 Joe Jenkins Blvd, Austell GA 30106
(770) 948-3100; Fax (770) 732-3433

CARE (www.care.com)

Profile: World's largest private international relief and development organization. Employs 225 here with 120 exempt. Hires recent grads and experienced exempt in all areas as needed.

Procedure: Send resume with cover letter expressing areas of expertise to Human Resources
151 Ellis Street NE, Atlanta GA 30303-2439
(404) 681-2552; Fax (404) 577-9418

CARTER, WILLIAM COMPANY (www.carters.com)

Profile: Atlanta-based, children's clothing manufacturer (newborn to age 6) employing 2000 in Georgia, including 4 warehouses. Hires exempt in accounting/finance, IT, design, and sales support, plus distribution positions at facilities.

Procedure: Send resume to personnel
1170 Peachtree St, Ste. 900, Atlanta GA 30309
(404) 745-2700; Fax (404) 892-0968

CENDIANCORP. (www.cendian.com)

Profile: Atlanta-based chemical and plastics lead logistics provider. Seeks exempt personnel in all corporate functions, including accounting/finance, HR, IT, web design, sales/mktg, etc., plus numerous non-exempt support areas.

Procedure: Review vacancies online and apply as instructed to
6 Concourse Pkwy NE, #2800, Atlanta GA 30328
(678) 459-3000; Fax (678) 459-3030

CENTERS FOR DISEASE CONTROL AND PREVENTION (CDC) (www.cdc.gov)

Profile: Atlanta-based federal agency that provides national leadership for public health efforts to prevent disease and disability and to promote health. Employs 6500 in Atlanta, and hires several hundred scientific and medical research specialists annually, both recent grads and experienced, including advanced degree and experienced epidemiologists, statisticians, mathematical statisticians, health scientists, medical officers, microbiologists, toxicologists, etc. Seeks MIS experience in LAN and IBM mainframe; knowledge of C language, SPSS, SAS.

Procedure: Maintains a recorded list of vacancies, which can be faxed to you through the Job Information Line listed below. Printed copies of an

announced position and application forms may be obtained by
contacting CDC Job Information Center at
4770 Buford Hwy, Atlanta GA 30341
(770) 488-1725; (404) 232-4473 Job Line; Fax (770) 488-1979
email resume to: USPO or fax only

CERTEGY (www.certegy.com)
Profile: Atlanta-based, provides credit and debit card processing, e-banking services, check risk management, check cashing and merchant card processing services to financial institutions and merchants. Most needs are for sales/marketing and accounting (all levels).
Procedure: Send resume to personnel
11720 Amber Park Dr, Ste 600, Alpharetta GA 30004
(678) 867-8000; Fax (404)

CH2M HILL (www.ch2m.com)
Profile: Environmental, consulting engineering firm with 140 employees in Atlanta, 120 exempt. Hires both recent grads and experienced engineers (environmental-related, ChE, CE), preferably at the Master's level. No needs for accounting or MIS here.
Procedure: Send resume to
115 Perimeter Center Place NE, Suite 700, Atlanta GA 30346
(770) 604-9095; Fax (770) 604-9183

CHECKFREE CORP. (www.checkfree.com)
Profile: Atlanta-based developer of software for the financial services industry, employing 330. Rarely hires recent grads, but will seek experienced exempt in accounting/finance, sales, engineering (software-related) and MIS.
Procedure: Send resume to Human Resources
4411 East Jones Bridge Road, Norcross GA 30092
(678) 375-3000; Fax (678) 375-1332

CHICK-FIL-A (www.chick-fil-a.com)
Profile: Corporate headquarters for 750-unit quick-service restaurant chain. Headquarters staff numbers 275 with 130 exempt. Most openings will be for entry-level corporate positions requiring college degree, plus opportunites to sublease restaurants.
Procedure: Send resume to Personnel Administrator
5200 Buffington Road, Atlanta GA 30349
(404) 765-8127; Fax (404) 765-8942
email resume to: melissa.todd@chick-fil-a.com

CHOICE POINT (www.choicepointinc.com)

Profile: Insurance services company, employing 600 at this location. Most hires are IT; occasional need for accountant.
Procedure: Send resume to Human Resources, indicating adminstrative or technical, 1000 Alderman Drive, Alpharetta GA 30005
(770) 752-6000; Fax (404)

CIBA VISION CORPORATION (www.cibavision.com)
Profile: Worldwide headquarters for the eye care unit of Swiss-based Novartis AG. Research, development, and manufacturing of optical and ophthalmic products and services, including contact lenses, lens care products, ophthalmic pharmaceuticals, and ophthalmic surgical products. Total employment in Atlanta is 1800, with 700 exempt. Currently hires few recent grads. Seeks experienced exempt in numerous specialties, including manufacturing managers, product managers, accountants, sales reps, R&D scientists (polymers, micro-biologists, etc.) and IT.
Procedure: E-mail resume to Staffing Specialist
11460 Johns Creek Pkwy, Duluth GA 30155-1518
(678) 415-5555; job line (678) 415-5959; Fax (770) 418-3036
email resume to: outside.posting2@cibavision.novartis.com

CIGNA HEALTHCARE OF GEORGIA (www.cigna.com)
Profile: Atlanta's second largest health maintenance organization. No central personnel office; each department conducts own hiring.
Procedure: Call Job Information Line and respond to specific need. Send resume to 100 Peachtree St NE, Atlanta GA 30303
(404) 681-7000; x2, then 4 for Job Information Line ; Fax (404)

CLARUS CORPORATION (www.claruscorp.com)
Profile: Atlanta-based developer of financial/accounting and human resources software, employing 200, nearly all exempt. Most hires are for computer science backgrounds, recent grads and experienced, and some experienced accounting/finance.
Procedure: Send or email resume to Human Resources
3970 Johns Creek Court, Suwanee GA 30024
(770) 291-3900; Fax (770) 291-8590

CNN — CABLE NEWS NETWORK (www.cnn.com; www.turnerjobs.com)
Profile: Operates a 24-hour cable news gathering organization, which includes CNN, CNN Headline News, CNN International, CNN Airport Network, and CNN radio, and employs 1600 in Atlanta. Hires many recent grads annually for entry level positions as Video Journalist, but requires broadcast and/or internship experience. Applicants seeking on-air or correspondent positions need 5-7 years experience in television. Posts jobs at www.turnerjobs.com; the day I checked, there were 200+ jobs available in Atlanta!

Procedure: All Turner subsidiaries conduct hiring through a central staffing department. Best to check job web site and follow directions. Located at

100 International Blvd, CNN Center, Atlanta GA 30303
(404) 827-1500; Fax (404) 681-3578

COCA-COLA COMPANY, THE (www.cocacola.com)
Profile: Fortune 500 corporation headquartered in Atlanta, 5000 employees here. Hires experienced exempt personnel in a number of functional areas, such as accounting/finance, MIS, marketing, and R&D (chemists and engineers--all types). Coca-Cola does not maintain a public list of job vacancies, either on-line or phone job line.
Procedure: Send resume (fax, USPO, or email) and cover letter to Staffing Department. When it is received, you will be notified, along with their hiring procedure.
P O Drawer 1734, Atlanta GA 30301

(404) 676-2665 - recording; in-house temp agcy (404) 515-5255; Fax (404) 676-2662
email resume to: careers@na.ko.com

COCA-COLA ENTERPRISES (www.cokecce.com)
Profile: Corporate hq for world's largest bottler of Coca-cola products (see also Atlanta Coca-Cola Bottling Company). Employs 120, 60% exempt, and seeks administrative, accounting/finance, and uper-level management.
Procedure: Send resume to Human Resources Dept (no faxes)
P O Box 723040, Atlanta GA 31139-0040
(770) 989-3000; Fax (770) 989-3089
email resume to: humanresources@na.cokecce.com

COCA-COLA ENTERPRISES -- ATLANTA COMPUTER FACILITY
(www.cokecce.com)
Profile: Processes all computer functions for Coca-Cola Enterprises and hires only IS backgrounds.
Procedure: send resume to human resources
3715 Northside Pkwy, Suite 500, Bldg 300, Atlanta GA 30327
(404) 231-9553; Fax (404) 239-7439

COMCAST (www.comcast.com)
Profile: Atlanta's largest cable TV provider, employing 1300, 260 exempt. Most needs are for non-exempt service technicians, installers, and customer service reps, but has occasional need for engineers (EE, communications) and sales reps.
Procedure: Job site updated weekly. Send resume to Human Resources
2925 Courtyards Drive, Norcross GA 30071

(770) 559-2424; job line (770) 613-2498; Fax (770) 557-7620
email resume to: atl-jobpostings@cable.comcast.com

COMPAQ CORPORATION (www.compaq.com)
Profile: World's second largest manufacturer of computer systems, with 1100 employees in Atlanta, including 800 exempt. Hires liberal arts and technical recent grads, as well as experienced personnel, into all disciplines--sales, engineering, MIS, accounting/finance, marketing analysis, management, network integration, etc.
Procedure: Send resume to Employment
5555 Windward Pkwy West, Alpharetta GA 30201-7407
(770) 343-0000; Fax (770) 343-0354

COMPTROLLER OF THE CURRENCY (www.occ.treas.gov)
Profile: Government agency responsible for the safety and soundness of national banks, employing 300 here with 275 exempt. Hires recent grads in accounting/finance, management, and banking backgrounds.
Procedure: Send resume to personnel
Marquis Tower, 245 Peachtree Center Ave NE, Suite 600, Atlanta GA 30303
(404) 659-8855; Fax (404) 588-4594

COMPUTONE (www.computone.com)
Profile: Atlanta-based computer hardware and software company that designs and manufactures products for remote computer access. Employs 70 with 50 exempt. Seeks recent grads in accounting/finance and sales, and experienced exempt in engineering (software and hardware), accounting/finance, and sales.
Procedure: Send or email resume to
1060 Windward Ridge Pkwy, Suite 100, Alpharetta GA 30005
(770) 625-0000; Fax (770) 625-0010
email resume to: joellep@computone.com

CONCORD EFS (www.concordefs.com)
Profile: Data center for provider of cashless commerce and transaction processing for key retail and financial services markets. Hires recent grads for accounting/finance and customer support, and experienced exempt in technical, management, and sales positions.
Procedure: Send resume to Human Resources
2240 New Market Pkwy, Marietta GA 30367
(770) 953-2664; Fax (770) 618-6109

CONSTAR INTERNATIONAL (www.constar.com)
Profile: (Formerly Sewell Plastics.) Division of Crown Cork & Seal that manufactures plastics, especially packaging and bottles. Employs 500

here, 115 exempt. Seldom hires recent grads. Experienced exempt are needed for accounting/finance, manufacturing management, and engineering (various types); sales reps must have packaging experience. No MIS needs.

Procedure: Send resume to Human Resources
5375 Drake Drive SW, Atlanta GA 30336
(404) 691-4256; Fax (404) 691-5489

COTTON STATES INSURANCE (www.cottonstatesinsurance.com)

Profile: Atlanta-based property/casualty and life insurance company. Employs 325 total, 160 exempt. Hires experienced personnel, mostly in property and casualty claims and MIS (IBM ES 9000 MVS/XA).

Procedure: Send resume to Human Resources Specialist
P O Box 105303, Atlanta GA 30348
(770) 391-8600; job line 770/391-8989; Fax (770) 391-8986
email resume to: careers1@cottonstates.com

COUSINS PROPERTIES (http://www.cousinsproperties.com)

Profile: Atlanta-based real estate developer and manager, employing 100 with 75 exempt. Hires recent accounting grads.

Procedure: Send resume to Personnel
2500 Windy Ridge Parkway, Suite 1600, Marietta GA 30339
(770) 955-2200; Fax (770) 857-2361

COX COMMUNICATIONS (www.cox.com)

Profile: Atlanta-based, fourth largest cable provider in the nation. Hires entry-level and experienced exempt in numerous corporate areas, including accounting/finance, marketing, legal, IT, HR, and administrative.

Procedure: Reveiw openings and apply online, or send resume to Staffing
1400 Lake Herne Dr NE, Atlanta GA 30319
(404) 843-5000; Fax (404)

COX ENTERPRISES (www.coxenterprises.com)

Profile: Atlanta-based parent of newspapers, radio/TV, and auto auctions. Headquarters employs 570, with 400 exempt. Hires experienced exempt with backgrounds in IT, accounting/finance Subsidiaries conduct own hiring (see listing for Cox Communications and Atlanta Journal-Constitution).

Procedure: Jobs site updated daily. Review openings and apply online, or send resume to
5205 Peachtree-Dunwoody Rd, Atlanta GA 30328
(678) 645-0000; Fax (404) 843-5775

COX RADIO (www.coxradio.com)

Profile: Atlanta-based, third largest radio broadcasting company in the US with 79 stations. Opening in all corporate areas, plus radio.
Procedure: Apply online or send resume to Human Resources
6205 Peachtree Dunwoody Rd, Atlanta GA 30328
(678) 645-0000; Fax (404)

CRAWFORD AND COMPANY (www.crawfordandcompany.com)
Profile: International provider of full spectrum of services, primarily claims-related, to insurance industry and risk management industry. Corporate headquarters in Atlanta employs 800 (400 exempt). Hires 100+ recent grads each year, mostly in casualty claims adjusting (BBA best, but others ok). Has summer internship program in Risk Management. Experienced personnel are hired for accounting/finance, MIS, and managed care. Also seeks Spanish bilingual.
Procedure: (Note: Headquarters also operates in-house temporary agency, offering temp-to-perm positions; call for openings.) For claims adjustors (including trainees); and managed care personnel, send resume to Personnel Manager, SE Region Office, 5780 Peachtree Dunwoody Rd, Atlanta, GA 30342. Accountants and MIS personnel, send resume to Personnel Manager at headquarters
P O Box 5047, Atlanta GA 30302
(404) 256-0830 - SE Region Office; (404) 847-4080 - headquarters; Fax (404) 847-4584
email resume to: employment@us.crawco.com

CREDITOR RESOURCES, INC. (www.creditorresources.com)
Profile: Atlanta-based credit life and disability insurance administrator, employing 250 with 75 exempt. Hires recent grads (all types) and experienced exempt with insurance or credit banking experience.
Procedure: Send resume to Personnel Coordinator
1100 Johnson Ferry Road, Suite 300, Atlanta GA 30342
(404) 257-8200; Fax (404) 257-2932

CURTIS 1000 (www.curtis1000.com)
Profile: Subsidiary of Atlanta-based American Business Products, employing 100 in Atlanta, 67 exempt. Prints all types of commercial stationery and business forms. Seeks recent grads for management training program and then promotes up; thus, occasionally needs experienced exempt and sales representatives.
Procedure: Send resume to Director of Human Resources
1725 Breckinridge Pkwy, Suite 500, Duluth GA 30096-7566
(678) 380-9095; Fax (770) 717-5163

CYTRX CORPORATION (www.cytrx.com)

Profile: Atlanta-based pharmaceutical research and development company (not manufacturing). Employs 85, 70 exempt and expects an increase. Seeks recent grads and experienced exempt for R&D scientist positions (chemistry, quality control, etc.)

Procedure: Send resume to Human Resources
            154 Technology Pkwy, Norcross GA 30092
            (770) 368-9500; Fax (770) 453-0105

DELOITTE CONSULTING GROUP (www.dc.com)

Profile: Southeast headquarters for DTT consulting division, employing 400 here in three offices, most exempt. Seeks MBA's with specific industry experience (e.g., finance, manufacturing, health care, retail, utilities, information systems, et al.), and will hire 80 annually.

Procedure: Send or email resume to Recruiting
            285 Peachtree Center Ave, Suite 2000, Atlanta GA 30303-1234
            (404) 631-2000; Fax (404) 631-1300
            email resume to: adminresumesatl@deloitte.com

DELOITTE & TOUCHE (www.us.deloitte.com)

Profile: Big 5 international professional services firm employing 550 in Atlanta, 475 exempt. Has four divisions: assurance, tax services, management consulting services and human capital consulting. Hires mostly recent accounting/finance grads.

Procedure: E-mail resume to Recruiting Manager
            191Peachtree St , Suite 1500, Atlanta GA 30303
            (404) 220-1500; Fax (404) 220-1583
            email resume to: dtcareers@deloitte.com

DELTA AIRLINES (www.delta.com)

Profile: Headquartered in Atlanta and the largest airline serving Atlanta, Delta is also Atlanta's largest corporate employer with approx. 25,000 personnel. Delta hires into entry-level positions (agents, analysts, clerical, flight attendants, mechanics, pilots) and practices promotion from within for most supervisory or administrative positions. Job and application info at web site.

Procedure: Obtain an Expressions of Interest card, complete and send it to Delta's employment office. Delta only distributes applications when hiring among individuals who have previously returned the card. Cards may be obtained from any Delta ticket office, the airport ticket counter, by calling (404) 715-2501, or writing Delta Employment Office
            P O Box 20530, Hartsfield International Airport, Atlanta GA 30320
            (404) 765-2501; 404/715-2501 job line; Fax

DELTA TECHNOLOGY INC. (www.deltadt.com)

Profile: Data techonolgy company that arranges freight transportatioon. Headquarters are in Atlanta. Over 1,800 employees in Atlanta. Hires recent grads and experienced in engineering, IS, and accounting/finance.

Procedure: Send resume to Human Resources
1001 International Blvd., Hapeville GA 30354-1801
(404) 714-1500; (888) 874-4473.; Fax (404) 773-9003

DEPARTMENT OF THE ARMY CIVILIAN PERSONNEL OFFICE (www.cpol.army.mil)

Profile: This office employs 2000, 75% exempt, and handles all recruiting for civilian positions at Atlanta's Fort McPherson and Fort Gillem. Most civilian positions require that you already be in the government merit system, although there are exceptions, especially for medical personnel and engineers. There are usually 5 current openings, approximately one-half professional level (GS 9 and above).

Procedure: Call, visit or write them and request a copy of their list of current vacancies, which is updated and published the 1st and 15th of every month. The address is
Civilian Personnel Advisory Center, Attn: J. I. C. (stands for Job Information Center), 1718 Savers St., Fort McPherson GA 30330-1045
(404) 464-2502; Fax

DIGITAL INSIGHT (www.digitalinsight.com)

Profile: Provider of services to allow small and midsize banks to offer online banking to customers. Employs 160 in Atlanta (mostly exempt) and expects to double. S3eks mostly exempt with banking backgrounds, MIS (visual basic, MSTS, UNIX, IIS, Sequel, NT, HTML, ASP) and accounting/finance.

Procedure: Send or email resume
5720 Peachtree Pkwy, Norcross GA 30092
(770) 349-1200; Fax (770) 349-1527
email resume to: employment@banking.com

DIVINE (www.eshare.com)

Profile: (formerly eShare Communications) Provider of customer interactions and call management systems that enable businesses to automate call center activities and enhance telephony-based and internet-based customer interaction. Employs 260 in Atlanta, 200 exempt. Hires recent engineering grads (EE, CS) and experienced exempt in all areas.

Procedure: Email resume to Human Resources
5051 Peachtree Corners Circle, Norcross GA 30092
(770) 239-4000; Fax (770) 239-4721
email resume to: resumes@eshare.com

DUKE REALTY CORP. (www.dukerealty.com)

Profile: REIT that owns a diversified portfolio of primarily industrial, office and retail properties in 13 major U.S. cities, employing 1000.
Procedure: Send resume to personnel
3950 Shackleford Rd, Ste 300, Atlanta GA 30096
(770) 717-3200; Fax (404)
email resume to: hr@dukerealty.com

EARTHLINK (http://www.earthlink.com)
Profile: Atlanta-based, third largest internet access provider, employing 1150+. Many openings in accounting/finance, operations, administration, IS, and engineering.
Procedure: Send resume to human resources or apply online
1375 Peachtree St. NE, Atlanta GA 30309
(404) 815-0770; Fax (404) 815-8805

ECKERD DRUGS (www.eckerd.com)
Profile: Operates 130 retail stores in Atlanta, employing 2000 total with 520 exempt. This office hires almost entirely for store management and will hire 200 recent grads as manager trainees and 100 experienced retail managers for Atlanta positions.
Procedure: Send resume to Regional Recruiter
36 Herring Road, Newnan GA 30265
(770) 254-4440; job line (888) 352-6383; Fax (404) 257-1190
email resume to: storeops@eckerd.com

ECLIPSYS (www.eclipsys.com)
Profile: Supplier of information technology software and services to help healthcare providers. Employs 200 in Atlanta with 90% exempt. Seeks experienced professionals within areas of healthcare desciplines, information technology, software applications, customer support, sales/mktg, and general administation.
Procedure: Send resume to Human Resources
200 Ashford Center North, Atlanta GA 30338
(404) 847-5000; Fax (404) 847-5415
email resume to: human.resources@eclipsys.com

ELECTRONIC DATA SYSTEMS (www.eds.com)
Profile: Global information technology services company providing a range of services including management consulting and business process mgt, employing 1850 in Atlanta.
Procedure: Complete online profile or mail resume to
3715 Northside Pkwy, Ste 800, Atlanta GA 30327
(404) 297-3700; Fax (404)

EMC2 (www.emc.com)

Profile: Southeast Area Sales Office, US Professional Services HQ, and Worldwide Customer Support Center for Fortune 300 company that manufactures and sells computers, storage, servers, and provides full complement of professional services. Employs 350 here with 325 exempt. Hires no recent grads, but seeks experienced sales and technical professionals with open systems experience, plus sales support, technical support, and marketing personnel. No accounting/finance in Atlanta. Has 3 co-ops in systems engineering. Lists jobs on web page.

Procedure: Send resume to Human Resources
2850 Premiere Pkwy, Duluth GA 30097
(770) 923-0496; fax 814-3359; Fax 770/814-3359

EMORY UNIVERSITY/EMORY UNIVERSITY HOSPITAL (www.emory.edu)

Profile: Private, Methodist-affiliated university with 9000 students. Emory is composed of 17,400 employees, faculty and staff from five organizations: Emory University, Emory University Hospital, Crawford Long Hospital, The Emory Clinic, Inc, Wesley Woods Center and the Emory Children's Center. Recent grads hired in scientific research or for non-exempt positions, although some experience is preferred for most positions. Hires experienced personnel in accounting/finance, administration, MIS (IBM) and research; prior academic experience is not required for most positions. Hospital has 600+ beds and is also a teaching and research insititute. Hospital hires recent grads in medical specialties, such as nursing, pharmacy, respiratory/physical therapy, etc.

Procedure: Posts available jobs weekly on Job Board outside Human Resources bldg, and you can peruse the board at any time. For hospital and university positions, apply in person Monday - Thursday 9:00 - 4:00, if possible. Otherwise, send resume to Emory University Human Resources Department
1762 Clifton Road NE, Atlanta GA 30322
(404) 727-7611 - info line; Fax (404) 727-7108

EMS TECHNOLOGIES (www.ems-t.com; www.lxe.com)

Profile: Expanding Atlanta-based company that designs, manufactures and sells microwave components, microwave sub-systems and radio-link terminals. This office also handles staffing for their LXE subsidiary, which manufactures radio-link data terminal products, and EMS Wireless, which manufactures base station antennas. Employment for both is 1000 with 600 exempt, and they anticipate hiring more than 200 new employees annually. Hires a few recent grads in engineering (mostly ME and EE) and computer science, and hires 25+ experienced personnel in sales, engineering, and computer science. Has six co-ops in engineering.

Procedure: E-mail resume to Human Resources Manager
P O Box 7700, Norcross GA 30091

(770) 263-9200; Fax (770) 263-8130
email resume to: price_h@elmg.com

EQUANT CORP. (www.equant.com)
Profile: Atlanta-based, manages the largest private telecommunications network in the world, employing 700 here.
Procedure: Jobs not online. Email resume to human resources
400 Galleria Pkwy SE, Atlanta GA 30339
(678) 346-3000; Fax (678) 346-4882
email resume to: careers@equant.com

EQUIFAX CUSTOMER SERVICE CENTER (www.equifax.com)
Profile: Customer service center, employing 650 with 100 exempt. Most needs will be for entry-level and experienced customer service personnel (most work is done by phone).
Procedure: Send resume to Human Resources Manager
P O Box 740256, Atlanta GA 30374
(800) 851-1761; (770) 375-2558 job information line; Fax (770) 375-1196
email resume to: justinakelly@equifax.com

EQUIFAX, INC. (www.equifax.com)
Profile: Headquartered in Atlanta, Equifax is the nation's largest supplier of computer-based information gathering company, with offices throughout the the world. Employs 3000 in Atlanta, 1000 exempt. Seeks recent grads in accounting/finance, operations management, and MIS (IBM and DEC VAX); liberal arts grads often hired for customer service, and marketing grads for research and analysis positions. Experienced exempt are hired for the same areas, and insurance or banking background is helpful. Also seeks recent MBA grads in accounting/finance and experienced MBA's in marketing.
Procedure: Send resume to Human Resources
1600 Peachtree Street, Atlanta GA 30309
(404) 885-8000; Fax (678) 587-3310
email resume to: susiemitchell@equifax.com

EQUIFAX —TECHNOLOGY CENTER (www.equifax.com)
Profile: One of the largest data centers in Atlanta, employing 600 with 300 exempt. At least 90% of their hiring is for MIS personnel, recent grads and experienced, and they have IBM, PC's, Amdahl, and DEC VAX hardware, UNIX, VMS environments; uses Cobol, Assembler, C and Natural.
Procedure: Send resume to Human Resources, HRD
1525 Windward Concourse, Alpharetta GA 30005
(770) 740-6857; job line 740-4635; Fax 885-8055

ERNST & YOUNG (www.ey.com)

Profile: World's largest CPA and consulting firm, employing 700 in Atlanta with 630 exempt. Atlanta office for Tax, Audit, and Entrepreneurial Services divisions of E&Y, each with their own recruiter. Hires mostly recent accounting/finance grads and MBA's, plus a limited number of experienced exempt for Health Care Consulting; Management Consulting; Special Services Group; Acturial, Benefits and Compensations Group.

Procedure: Send resume to Director of Recruiting —[specify division]
600 Peachtree St NE, Atlanta GA 30308
(404) 892-9451; Fax 817-4301
email resume to: russell.weaver@ey.com

EZGOV (www.wzgov.com)

Profile: Atlanta-based developer of software for needs of federal, state and local governments. Recruits for backgrounds in business development, accounting/finance, IT, HTML, and epecially sales/marketing (software background preferred).

Procedure: Identify opening and requirements at site, then email resume.
1375 Peachtree St NE, Atlanta GA 30309
(404) 888-9801; Fax (404)
email resume to: jobs@ezgov.com

FANNIE MAE (www.fanniemae.com)

Profile: Secondary mortgage company, employing 170 in Atlanta, 150 exempt. Hires few recent grads and prefers backgrounds in mortgage lending and real estate sales. Uses IBM PC's.

Procedure: Prefers that you first call the job info line or refer to the on-line postings, and then respond to a specific opening. Uses Resumix database. Send resume to Human Resources
950 East Paces Ferry Rd, Suite 1900, Atlanta GA 30326-1161
(404) 398-6000; 398-6242 job info line; Fax 398-6619

FEDERAL DEPOSIT INSURANCE CORP (www.fdic.gov)

Profile: Region office covering seven states, employing 80 in Atlanta, 40 in Norcross, and 200+ in region. Approx. 40 new hires in '97, mostly entry-level bank examiners: must have 24 semester hrs of business-related subjects, including six hours in accounting. High GPA important.

Procedure: Send resume to Examinations Specialist - TC
1201 West Peachtree St NE, 1 Atlantic Center, Suite 1800, Atlanta GA 30309-3415
(404) 817-1300; (800) 695-8052 Job Line; Fax (404) 817-8808

FEDERAL HOME LOAN BANK OF ATLANTA (www.fhlbatl.com)

Profile: The Federal Home Loan Bank of Atlanta, one of 12 districts Banks in the Federal Home Loan Bank System, is an $90B reserve credit bank that provides low-cost financing and other banking services to more than 1100 member financial institutions that offer housing finance to consumers in seven SE states and DC. Employs 275 here with 150 exempt. Backgrounds in finance, accounting, and banking are given most consideration.

Procedure: E-mail resumes to staffing@fhlbatl.com
1475 Peachtree St NE, Atlanta GA 30309
(404) 888-8000; 888-5331 Job Line; Fax 888-5645
email resume to: staffing@fhlbatl.com

FEDERAL RESERVE BANK OF ATLANTA (www.frbatlanta.org)

Profile: Head office for the Sixth District of the Federal Reserve System, employing 1240 here with 500 exempt. Regulates commercial banks, conducts economic research used to impact monetary policy made by the Federal Reserve Board in DC, and provides financial services such as check clearing services, cash distribution, ACH, electronic payments and wire transfers. Will hire recent grads in accounting/finance/business, including MBA's. Will hire experienced personnel in accounting/finance, operations management, audit, regulation, data-base analysis and MIS (IBM mainframe; programmers in C++ and Java, MS SDL, object oriented programming).

Procedure: Send resume to Employment Specialist, or send your resume on-line at http://www.frbatlanta.org/cgi-shell/resume/resume.pl
1000 Peachtree St NE, Atlanta GA 30309-4470
(404) 498-8500; Fax 498-8142

FEDERATED DEPARTMENT STORES (www.federated-fds.com)

Profile: Division headquarters for Rich's-Macy's, Goldsmith's, and Lazarus department stores, operating 75 stores in nine SE and MW states. Employs 5600 in Atlanta (including 15 Rich's-Macy's), 1200 exempt. Most recent grads are needed for their Executive Training Program, which encompasses all facets of the corporation. Experienced exempt hired are retail professionals and MBA's for sales support group. Most MIS functions are handled by Federated Systems Group (see listing). Accounting/finance at Cincinnati headquarters only.

Procedure: Send resume to Executive Recruitment Staff
223 Perimeter Center Parkway, Atlanta GA 30346
(770) 913-5176; Fax (770) 913-5114

FEDERATED SYSTEMS GROUP (www.federated-fds.com/support)

Profile: Atlanta-based, serves as technology hub of Federated department stores, parent of Atlanta-based Rich's-Macy's department stores and others.

Creates and supports integrated line of high-performance systems for retail transactions and support. Employs 1250 with 900 exempt. Nearly all recruitment is for MIS (IBM 3090; client server, oracle, window NT, C++, visual basic, Java, and HTML), recent grads and experienced.

Procedure: Job site updated daily. Send or apply on-line to
5985 State Bridge Rodad, Duluth GA 300097
(678) 474-2000; Fax (678) 474-3015

FIRST DATA POS (www.firstdatacorp.com)

Profile: Provides asset and terminal management, PC software and information delivery systems to credit-related industries. Corporate office employs 150 with 125 exempt, and seeks experienced accounting/finance and MIS (Unisys).

Procedure: Prefers you not call. Send resume to Human Resources
2155 Barrett Park Drive, Suite 215, Kennesaw GA 30144
(770) 218-5000; (770) 857-7238 job line; Fax 770/428-5448

FIRST NORTH AMERICAN NATIONAL BANK (www.fnanb.com)

Profile: Operates as the credit card bank for Richmond, VA-based Circuit City, a national retailer of electronics and home appliances. Issues Circuit City, Mastercard, and Visa cards. This office also houses First North American Credit Corporation, which operates as loan officials for Carmax, an auto store that sells used cars. Employs 900, 150 exempt. Hires both entry-level and experienced exempt in several areas, including credit.

Procedure: Send or fax resume to Human Resources
225 Chastain Meadows Court, Kennesaw GA 30156
(770) 423-7900; job line 1-800/job-plug; Fax (770) 423-4353

FIRSTWAVE TECHNOLOGIES (www.firstwave.net)

Profile: Atlanta-based company in customer information systems software, employing 125 here, 75 exempt. Most openings for MIS backgrounds and VB development.

Procedure: Send resume to Corporate Recruiter
2859 Paces Ferry Road, Suite 1000, Atlanta GA 30339
(770) 431-1200; 431-1238 Job Line; Fax (770) 431-1201
email resume to: judiv@firstwave.net

FISERV SOLUTIONS (www.fiserv.com)

Profile: Provides data processing services to financial institutions. Employs 235 with 90 exempt. Seeks experienced exempt in accounting/finance, management (banking and loan application backgrounds ideal), and MIS – programmers, operators. Always needing candidates with ITI background.

Procedure: Send resume to Human Resources

1475 Peachtree St NE, Suite 600, Atlanta GA 30309
(404) 873-2851, HR at ext. 5; Fax (404) 897-3876

FORD MOTOR COMPANY—ATLANTA ASSEMBLY PLANT 340 (www.ford.com)

Profile: This facility assembles Ford Taurus and Mercury Sable cars, employing 2450 hourly and 210 salaried exempt. Most exempt hiring here is for supervisors and electrical engineers (trainee and experienced) in manufacturing management, plus some needs in Human Resources (MBA best). Accounting/finance is centralized in Detroit.

Procedure: Send resume to Salaried Personnel Office
340 Henry Ford II Avenue, Hapeville GA 30354
(404) 669-1547; Fax 669-1400

FORTIS FAMILY (www.fortisfamily.com)

Profile: Life insurance company, employing 170 with 85 exempt at headquarters. Primary hiring is for eentry-level positions, and thus frequently hires recent grads in service support (claims, customer service, etc.) and management. MIS requires Wordperfect and Excel.

Procedure: Send resume to Human Resources Department
10 Glen Lake Pkwy, Suite 500, Atlanta GA 30328
(770) 206-6400; Fax (770) 206-6383

G E CAPITAL COMPUTER AND TELECOMMUNICATIONS SERVICES
(www.gecits.ge.com)

Profile: Computer support organization of GE Capital. Currently employs 160, mostly exempt. Hires recent computer science grads for Help Desk (customer service) and experienced software programmers (IBM systems).

Procedure: Send resume to Human Resources Representative
1001 Windward Concourse, Alpharetta GA 30202
(770) 446-6733; Fax (770) 442-6500

GATE GOURMET (www,gategourmet.com)

Profile: Provides airline catering service at Atlanta airport. Employs 1400 in Atlanta, 100 exempt. Hires mostly entry-level production-oriented and aircraft loaders (called customer service assistants) for their 85-truck fleet.

Procedure: Send resume to Personnel Services Manager
P O Box 45485, Atlanta GA 30320
(404) 530-6300; Job line (404) 530-6320; Fax (404) 530-6323

GE POWER SYSTEMS (www.gepower.com)

Profile: Atlanta-based GE subsidiary in power generation technology and services, providing technology-based product and service solutions for the energy industry.

Procedure: Send resume to human resources
4200 Wildwood Pkwy, Atlanta GA 30339
(770) 859-6000; Fax (404)

GEAC ENTERPRISE SOLUTIONS (www.geac.com)
Profile: Designs and manufactures client server & mainframe business software systems in accounting/finance, human resources, and manufacturing. Employs 800 in Atlanta with 600 exempt. Expects to hire up to 300 exempt (not all for Atlanta) in accounting/finance, MIS (IBM) and sales (no trainees).
Procedure: Send resume to Director of Recruiting
66 Perimeter Center East, Atlanta GA 30346
(404) 239-2000; Fax (404) 239-3282
email resume to: latanya.kelly@geac.com

GENERAL MOTORS (www.gm.com)
Profile: The Doraville manufacturing facility operates two shifts, employing 3800 with 270 exempt. Most non-manufacturing functions are in Detroit headquarters. Most exempt hires here are for engineering co-ops and interns (ME,EE), then promoted into management positions.
Procedure: Interns and co-ops can send resume here. Other exempt needs are handled through GM's Central Staffing Center in Detroit. Or review their job site online www.gm.com/careers.
3900 Motors Industrial Way, Doraville GA 30360
(770) 455-5100 - hourly recording; Fax (770) 455-5190

GENUINE PARTS CO. (www.genpt.com)
Profile: Atlanta-based automotive parts distributor/wholesaler, employing 200 at headquarters, 135 exempt. (See also NAPA Auto Parts.) Hires mostly exempt personnel for management trainee positions which will involve assignments throughout the US. Promotes heavily from within and thus seldom needs experienced personnel.
Procedure: Send resume to Human Resources
2999 Circle 75 Parkway, Atlanta GA 30339
(770) 953-1700; Fax (770) 956-2375

GEORGIA INSTITUTE OF TECHNOLOGY (www.gatech.edu)
Profile: State university with 14,000 students, ranking among the top 50 best in the nation. GA Tech is the South's largest industrial and engineering research agency. Research is conducted for industry and government by the academic units and departmetns, the GA Tech Research Institute (see listing), and more than 55 inter disciplinary units on and off campus. Has 5700 employees (including faculty), with approximately 4100 exempt. This office hires for technical and profesional, enginering, administration, and skilled labor.

Procedure: Job site updated daily. Review listings online, and only apply through the web site directly into their resume data bank.   Many temps are hired thru their in-house agency, Tech Temps, @ 894-3245. HR department is located at
955 Fowler St NW, Atlanta GA 30332
(404) 894-3245 for instructions and general information; Fax 894-1235

GEORGIA LOTTERY CORPORATION (www.galottery.com)
Profile: Administers the Georgia lottery, employing 250+. Seeks experienced and entry level exempt in accounting/finance, sales/marketing, MIS operations (DEC VAX, LAN environment), et al.
Procedure: Check web site (updated daily) and email resume to HR
250 Williams St, Suite 3000, Atlanta GA 30303-1071
(404) 215-5000; ; Fax 215-8886
email resume to: hrjobs@galottery.com

GEORGIA MARBLE (www.georgiamarble.com)
Profile: Atlanta-based corporation involved in mining and quarrying of marble, which is then crushed or sawed into smaller sizes for end-user needs. Employs 48 at headquarters, one-half exempt. Hires a few recent grads each year in production management and engineering (IE, ME, mining). Hires experienced exempt in accounting/finance, sales, production management, engineering and MIS (IBM 38, AS400). Also seeks occasional geologist, trainee or experienced.
Procedure: Send resume to Human Resources Manager
PO Box 238, Tate GA 30177
(770) 735-2611; Fax (770) 735-2236
email resume to: jobs@georgiamarble.com

GEORGIA NATURAL GAS (www.gasguy.com)
Profile: Largest natural gas provider in GA, employing 60 at headquarters, 58 exempt.
Procedure: Send resume to human resources
5607 Glenridge Drive NE, Atlanta GA 30342
(404) 257-4000; Fax (404) 257-4118
email resume to: jobs@southstarenergy.com

GEORGIA POWER COMPANY (www.southernco.com)
Profile: Largest electric utility in Georgia and subsidiary of Atlanta-based Southern Company (see listing). Employs 5000+ in Atlanta, with 2000 exempt. Refer to Southern Company listing for employment needs and procedure.
Procedure: All hiring is conducted by parent Southern Company's East Coast Staffing Center at
270 Peachtree St, Atlanta GA 30303

(404) 526-6526; job line (800) 457-2981; Fax (404) 526-1630

GEORGIA STATE UNIVERSITY (www.gsu.edu)
Profile: Georgia's second largest and Atlanta's largest university, with more than 25,000 students, graduate and undergraduates. Employs 2100 non-faculty personnel (1300 exempt) and 980 faculty. Will need many experienced personnel, especially in general administration (office managers), MIS (Amdahl and Unisys), Advisors (student services) and trainers. Also seeks biology, chemistry and other science majors (including social science) for research positions. Experience in an academic setting is a definite plus. Job openings at web site.
Procedure: Job site updated daily. Call their Job Information Line and apply for a specific opening only; unsolicited resumes not accepted. If you are in Atlanta, you can apply in person; otherwise, mail your resume with a cover letter indicating for which opening you are applying.
Employment Office, University Plaza, Atlanta GA 30303
(404) 651-3330 for general information; 651-4270 for Job Information Line; Fax 651-2826
email resume to: jobapps@langate.gsu.edu

GEORGIA TECH RESEARCH INSTITUTE (www.gtri.gatech.edu)
Profile: Non-profit applied research unit of GA Institute of Technology; 80% of research is in electronics, but also has programs in aerospace, acoustics, physical, chemical, and materials sciences. Employs 1200 including 500 engineers and scientists and 300 graduate assistants. Hires 10 recent grads and 25 experienced exempt annually, mostly with technical backgrounds, especially EE and computer science, but also in ME, physics, chemistry, metallurgy, IE and environmental. Hires no office staff types, such as accountants, which are hired through the University (see listing.).
Procedure: E-mail resumes to employment@gtri.gatech.edu
400 Tenth Street NW, Atlanta GA 30332-0807
(404) 894-3245; Fax 894-3446

GEORGIA-PACIFIC CORPORATION (www.gp.com)
Profile: Atlanta-based Fortune 50 forest products company and Atlanta's largest Fortune 500 firm. Headquarters employs 3000 with 1500 exempt. Entry-level accountants and sales reps are hired mostly through campus recruiting, and experienced personnel in accounting/finance, sales, engineering (mostly environmental, ChE, ME, EE), logistics, transportation, MIS (several systems) and other corporate staff types are hired throughout the year. Up to 250 exempt employees are hired annually.

307

Procedure: (Note: Hires many temp-to-perm through their in-house temporary agency, Georgia Temps; call 652-5493.) Mail or email resume to
Manager of Corporate Staffing
133 Peachtree Street NW, Atlanta GA 30303
(404) 652-4000; 521-5211 job line; Fax (404) no faxes
email resume to: recruiting@gapac.com

GLOBAL PAYMENTS (www.globalpayments.com)
Profile: Atlanta-based payment processing company, recent spinoff from NDC. Most needs are for experienced accounting/finance, IT, sales, and administration.
Procedure: Send resume to human resources
Four Corporate Square, Atlanta GA 30329
(404) 325-9918; Fax (404)

GOLD KIST, INC. (www.goldkist.com)
Profile: Atlanta-based poultry processor, employing 17,500 nationally with 350 at Atlanta Hq (30% exempt). Will hire 20± entry-level management annually; degrees in poultry science, food science, agriculture, and business administration ideal. Occasional need for experienced exempt in engineering (ME, EE) and IT.
Procedure: Job site updated as needed. Send resume to Corporate Employment Director
244 Perimeter Center Pkwy, Atlanta GA 30346
(770) 393-5249; Fax (770) 393-5262
email resume to: jobs@goldkist.com

GOLDER ASSOCIATES (www.golder.com)
Profile: Corporate headquarters of consulting engineering firm specializing in geotechnical environmental engineering and hydrogeology employing 95. Seeks experienced and entry-level professionals with environmental related degrees at Master's level.
Procedure: Send resume to Human Resources
3730 Chamblee Tucker Road, Atlanta GA 30341
(770) 496-1893 (Phone calls are discouraged.); Fax (770) 934-9476

GOLIN/HARRIS INTERNATIONAL (www.golinharris.com)
Profile: Atlanta office for one of the 10 largest US public relations firms. Employs 14, all exempt. Has few needs annually, but offers one or two internships/quarter for journalism and PR majors and recent grads and these internships can lead to an entry-level PR position.
Procedure: Send resume to Office Manager
50 Hurt Plaza, Suite 1220, Atlanta GA 30303
(404) 681-3808; Fax (404) 681-9029
email resume to: spoole@golinharris.com

GOODY PRODUCTS (www.goodyproducts.com)
Profile: Atlanta-based and subsidiary of Atlanta-based Newell Rubbermaid.
             World's largest manufacturer of hair products and accessories.
             Headquarters employs 55, plus two manufacturing plants in GA
             employing 1200. Unable to determine employment projections.
Procedure: Send resume to Human Resources
             600 Westpark Drive, Peachtree City GA 30269
             (770) 486-1995; Fax (404)

GRADY HEALTH SYSTEM (FULTON-DEKALB HOSPITAL AUTHORITY)
(www.gradyhealthsystem.org)
Profile: Atlanta's largest hospital, employing 6,000 total, including part-time,
             2000 exempt. Hires 200+ exempt annually, recent grads and
             experienced, in accounting/finance, department management and MIS
             (IBM). Also seeks many health care specialists, especially RN, LPN,
             OT and PT. Seldom needs engineers.
Procedure: Send resume to Recruitment and Employment Services. If there is a
             current need for your background, you will be contacted.
             80 Butler Street SE, Atlanta GA 30335
             (404) 616-1900; Job line 616-5627; Fax (404) 616-7348
             email resume to: recruiter@gmh.edu

HANOVER INSURANCE/ALLMERICA FINANCIAL (www.allmerica.com)
Profile: Atlanta sales and customer service operations, employs 300 in Atlanta
             with 120 exempt. Hires recent finance and insurance grads, and
             experienced exempt in insurance specialties, finance, and mutual funds.
Procedure: Send resume to personnel
             1455 Lincoln Parkway, Suite 240, Atlanta GA 30346
             (770) 353-6134; Fax (770)
             email resume to: Resumes@Allmerica.Com.

HARLAND, JOHN H. COMPANY (www.harland.net)
Profile: Corporate headquarters for information solutions provider to the
             financial industry, and second largest check manufacturer in the world.
             Employs 500 (200 exempt) in headquarters, plus 650 in manufacturing
             locally. Experienced personnel are hired in accounting/finance, sales,
             and MIS. Also hires production managers for other locations, not
             Atlanta.
Procedure: Send or email resume to Manager of Corporate Employment
             P O Box 105250, Department HR, Atlanta GA 30348
             (770) 981-9460; Fax (770) 593-5599

HAVERTY FURNITURE COMPANY (www.havertys.com)

Profile: Corporate hq for retail furniture chain operating 105 stores, with 10 stores and region warehouse in Atlanta. Employs 460 in Atlanta, 130 exempt. Hires recent college grads for management and administrative positions, including manager trainees for store and warehouse, and then promotes from within. Also seeks entry level and experieinced exempt in accounting, finance, IS (AS 400, Cobol) and other headquarters staff.

Procedure: Job site updated frequently. For retail opportunities, send resume to PO Box 80606, Atlanta 30366; 404/454-3450. For corporate positions, send or email resume to HR Specialist
780 Johnson Ferry Road, Suite 800, Atlanta GA 30342
(404) 443-2900; Fax (404) 443-4170
email resume to: hr@havertys.com

HEERY INTERNATIONAL (www.heery.com)
Profile: Architectural, engineering, and construction management firm, specializing in commercial, institutional, industrial, and recreational facilities, including Turner Stadium. Employs 350 in Atlanta with 280 exempt. Most hiring (both recent grads and experienced) is for design- and construction-related engineers and architects.

Procedure: Send or email resume to Corporate Recruiter
999 Peachtree Street NE, Atlanta GA 30367
(404) 881-9880; Fax (404) 875-1283
email resume to: mbahns@heery.com

HEIDELBERG USA (www.heidelbergusa.com)
Profile: Atlanta-based subsidiary of German manufacturer of printing presses, finishing equipment and process technology, repaired and serviced in Atlanta. Employs 450 here, 200 exempt. Hires recent grads and experienced exempt in accounting/finance and management, plus experienced MIS(SAP).

Procedure: Send resume to Staffing Specialist
1000 Gutenberg Drive, Kennesaw GA 30144
(770) 419-6500; Fax (770) 419-6900
email resume to: miranda_renee@heidelburgusa.com

HEWITT ASSOCIATES (www.hewitt.com)
Profile: Atlanta's largest employee benefits and compensation consulting firm, employing 600, 540 exempt.

Procedure: E-mail resume to personnel through website
3350 Cumberland Circle, Suite 400, Atlanta GA 30339
(770) 956-7777; Fax (770) 956-8780

HEWLETT-PACKARD COMPANY (www.hp.com)
Profile: Business Center & Sales Offices, covering the Americas' field operations, for the second largest computer manufacturer. Employs

2300 in Atlanta, with 1300 exempt, and most are currently in sales, sales support, information technology and financial applications. Hires recent grads, mostly electrical engineers, MBA Finance, and computer science grads for sales and systems support, info technology, and training including UNIX backgrounds.

Procedure: Send resume to Employment Response Center, Mail Stop 20 APP, Hewltt-Packard, 3000 Hanover St., Palo Alto, CA 94304-1181. Or fax direct into computer at (415) 852-8138. Resumes are scanned into HP computer system and you are notified when your resume has been received and entered. Their Atlanta address is
20 Perimeter Summit Blvd, Atlanta GA 30319
(404) 648-0000; Fax (415) 852-8138

HILTON HOTELS (ATLANTA HILTON AND TOWERS) (www.hiltonhotels.com)
Profile: Atlanta's third largest downtown hotel with 1224 rooms and more than 817 employees (120 exempt). Most hiring is for Rooms and Food/Beverage divisions, and some experience is generally required. Will hire a few accountants annually, experienced preferred.

Procedure: When faxing resume, specify position sought. If in Atlanta, you can apply in person, Monday through Friday from 9 am to 3 pm. Prefer resumes to be faxed, but can accept through mail and e-mail as well.
255 Courtland Street, Atlanta GA 30303
(404) 659-2000; 221-6807 Job Hotline; Fax (404) 223-6787

HITACHI ELECTRONIC DEVICES (www.hedus.com)
Profile: Corporate headquarters support and sales office for Hitachi subsidiary that manufactures and sells TV's, VCR's, etc. Employs 190 with 130 exempt. Hires recent grads and experienced exempt in accounting/finance, sales, and MIS (AS400). No manufacturing or engineering here.

Procedure: Send resume to Human Resources
3890 Steve Reynolds Blvd, Norcross GA 30093
(770) 409-3000; Fax (770) 279-5648

HITACHI POWER TOOLS (www.hitachi.com/powertools)
Profile: North American headquarters for division that manufactures, markets, distributes and services a complete line of professional grade tools and accessories.

Procedure: Send resume to
3950 Steve Reynolds Blvd., Norcross GA 30093
(770) 925-1774; Fax (404)

HITACHI TELECOM (USA) (www.hitel.com)
Profile: US corporate headquarters for telecommunications operations of Tokyo-based Hitachi, employing 300+ here with 200 exempt. Manufactures

311

telecommunications equipment including PBX's, Ansyschronous Transfer Mode multiplexing and switching equipment, Synchronous Optical Network transmission equipment, and other advanced fiber optic-based products. Seeks software engineers, sales, product marketing, and engineers experienced in transmission products.

Procedure: Send resume to Human Resources Department
3617 Parkway Lane, Norcross GA 30092
(770) 446-8820; Fax

HOLOX (www.holox.com)
Profile: Atlanta-based supplier of industrial, medical and scientific gases, as well as welding materials and safety products. Employs approx. 1000 in Southeast, 350 in Atlanta. Some needs for technical backgrounds (ME, ChE). Occasional needs for accounting/finance and IS.
Procedure: Job site updated 2/mo. Fax resume to Human Resources
1500 Indian Trail Rd, Suite C, Norcross GA 30093
(770) 925-4640; Fax (770) 931-2735

HOME DEPOT, THE (www.homedepot.com)
Profile: Atlanta-based retailer of home improvement and building materials supplies; ranked by Fortune Magazine as America's most admired retailer. Currently operates 700+ stores in US and Canada, and is expanding rapidly. Corporate headquarters employs 2000+ and expects an increase. Recent grads and experienced personnel are hired in accounting/finance and IS, although not always in an exempt category. Personnel with home building products industry and/or retail experience are sought for managment positions.
Procedure: Non-exempt, in-store positions are hired at the individual stores. For corporate staff positions, send resume to The Home Depot Store Support Center, indicating on envelope Attn: [Information Services, Accounting/Finance, Human Resources, International, Imports/Logistics],
2455 Paces Ferry Rd NW, Atlanta GA 30339-4024
(770) 433-8211; job line x87677; Fax (770) 431-2685

HOMEBANC (www.homebanc.com)
Profile: Atlanta-based, largest mortgage lender in Atlanta and one of the Top 10 on-line mortgage lenders in the US. Needs for experienced mortgage professionals and other corporate staff.
Procedure: Email resume to human resources
55555 Glenridge Connector, Atlanta GA 30342
(404) 459-7400; Fax (404)
email resume to: careers@homebanc.com

HOOTERS OF AMERICA, INC. (www.hooters.com)

Profile: Atlanta-based, one of the fastest growing restaurant chains in the US, with 200+ units total, 80+ company-owned. Headquarters employs 85, 60 exempt, plus restaurant staffs here. Seeks both recent grads and experienced restaurant management (offers restaurant management training program for recent grads).

Procedure: Send resume to Corporate Recruiter - AJOBS
             1815 The Exchange, Atlanta GA 30339
             (770) 951-2040; Fax (770) 618-7031
             email resume to: arickey@hooters.com

HOSHIZAKI AMERICA (www.hoshizaki.com)

Profile: Manufacturer of commercial food service equipment, employing 525 with 200 exempt. Hires some recent grads in engineering (ME mostly), customer service, and accounting; and experienced exempt with 5+ years experience in manufacturing management, manufacturing engineering, accounting/finance, customer service, and sales.

Procedure: Send or email resume to Human Resources
             618 North Hwy 74, Peachtree City GA 30269
             (770) 487-2331; Fax (770) 487-8190
             email resume to: adramkissoon@hoshizaki.com

I B M (www.ibm.com)

Profile: World leader in information technology, employing 6200 in Atlanta. Most of IBM's hiring is for recent grads in technical sales and MIS-related positions. Accounting/finance is handled in NY headquarters, and although there are special programs for MBA's, they too are not in Atlanta. Engineering grads are hired to go into MIS, not engineering. Although IBM prefers to promote from within, and thus hires relatively few experienced exempt, there are special needs in MIS and for sales backgrounds from competitors or other IBM system experience. Web site has job information.

Procedure: You can obtain an application from the Atlanta Employment Office at 3200 Windy Hill Road in Marietta; call (770) 835-9000 for directions. Or call the central Job Line from touch-tone phone and follow instructions. Send resume to Staffing Services Center
             P O Box 12195, Research Triangle Park NC 27709
             (770) 835-9000 Atlanta Employment; (800) 964-4473 Job information;
             Fax (770) 835-8025

IMERYS (www.imerys.com)

Profile: British-owned company producing and marketing kaolin clay, employing 120 in Atlanta headquarters (90+ exempt), plus manufacturing facility in Sandersville, GA. Seeks experienced exempt in accounting/finance, sales, marketing, chemistry, and MIS (IBM).

Procedure: Send resume to Human Resources Manager

100 Mansell Ct. East, Suite 300, Roswell GA 30076
(770) 594-0660; Fax (770) 645-3348
email resume to: sharonpenn@ecc.com

IMMUCOR, INC. (www.immucor.com)
Profile: Atlanta-based manufacturer of in vitro diagnostic reagents for blood
banks and transfusion services. Develops, manufactures and sells
products used by hospital blood banks, clinical laboratories, and large
blood donor centers to test, detect and identify certain properties of
human blood prior to patient transfusion. Most recurring needs are for
lab technicians (certification not required), medical technologists [MT
(ASCP) and/or MLT certification required], production, and an
occasional need in manufacturing and sales.
Procedure: E-mail resume to
P O Box 5625, Norcross GA 30091-5625
(770) 441-2051; Fax (770) 441-3807
email resume to: hr@immucor.com

IN ZONE (www.in-zone.com)
Profile: Atlanta-based, manufactures beverageware, coffee tumblers, and soft-
sided lunchkits and coolers. #31 on Inc's list of fastest growing private
companies.
Procedure: Jobs listed on Monster. Send resume to
7775 The Bluffs, Suite H, Austell GA 30168
(678) 718-2000; Fax (404)

INDUS INTERNATIONAL (www.indusinternational.com)
Profile: World's largest provider of software for Enterprise Asset Management
(ie, keep down costs, raise production, and stay in regulatory compliance
by using software technology to manage assets).   Employs 400, 250
exempt. Most hires are MIS-related in marketing, customer service,
programming, and operations; has several systems – IBM, DEC, Oracle,
SQL. Some needs in accounting/finance.
Procedure: E-mail resume to Recruiting Manager
3301 Windy Ridge Pkwy, Atlanta GA 30339
(770) 952-8444; Fax (770) 989-4247
email resume to: recruiter_se@iint.com

INFINITY PROPERTY & CASUALTY CORP. (www.ipacc.com)
Profile: Atlanta-based provider of personal automobile insurance, emphasizing
nonstandard auto insurance, employing 700 with 350 exempt. Seeks
experienced insurance professionals (claims, adjusters, appraisers, etc.),
promotes heavily from within.
Procedure: Job site updated daily. Fax or email resume to Employment
11700 Great Oaks Way, Alpharetta GA 30022

(770) 951-5599; job line xJOBS; Fax (678) 627-7942
email resume to: recruiter@infinity-insurance.com

INGENICO (www.ingenico-us.com)
Profile: Regional office, employing 180 with 75 exempt. Develops,
             manufactures, and markets payment automation solutions to businessses
             and financial institutions, including debit, crdit and SmartCard payment
             technology; electronic benefit transfer systems; electronic signature
             capture and verification products; and MICR check readers and
             analyzers. Hires entry-level engineers (EE, ME, CompE), computer
             science and marketing grads; and experienced exempt in
             accounting/finance, engineering, computer science, and sales.
Procedure: Apply online or send resume to Human Resources
             1003 Mansell Road, Roswell GA 30076
             (770) 594-6000; Fax (770) 594-6027

INSTITUTE OF NUCLEAR POWER OPERATIONS (INPO)
(http://tis.eh.doe.gov/nsps/inpo)
Profile: Atlanta-based non-profit organization, whose members are electric
             utilities with nuclear interests. INPO's purpose is to strenghten the
             operational safety of nuclear plants. Employs 400, with 250 exempt.
             Does not hire recent grads, but seeks nuclear engineers with 10+ years
             commercial experience and experienced exempt in MIS (uses PC's and
             LAN).
Procedure: Send resume to Human Resources
             700 Galleria Pkwy, Atlanta GA 30339
             (770) 644-8000; Fax (770) 644-8763

INSTITUTE OF PAPER SCIENCE AND TECHNOLOGY (www.ipst.edu)
Profile: University information and research service for the pulp and paper
             industry. Employs 230 here, one-half exempt. Hires both recent grads
             and experienced exempt, mostly in chemistry, biology, and engineering
             (ME, EE, ChE or pulp and paper).
Procedure: If in Atlanta, obtain appliation from receptionist. Otherwise, send
             resume to Personnel Manager
             500 10th Street NW, Atlanta GA 30318
             (404) 894-5700; Fax (404) 894-5302
             email resume to: human.resources@ipst.edu

INTELLIGENT SYSTEMS CORP (www.intelsys.com)
Profile: Atlanta-based manufacturer of PC software and computer repair,
             employing 150 in Atlanta. This office hires for headquarters and
             subsidiaries; needs vary, but can include accounting, sales, engineering,
             etc.
Procedure: Send resume to personnel

4355 Shackleford Road, Norcross GA 30093
(770) 381-2900; Fax (770) 381-2808

INTERFACE, INC. (www.interfaceinc.com)
Profile: Atlanta-based, world's largest commercial carpet manufacturer.
Procedure: Job site under construction. Send resume to personnel
2859 Paces Ferry Rd, Ste 2000, Atlanta GA 30339
(770) 437-6800; Fax (404)

INTERLAND (www.interland.com)
Profile: Atlanta-based provider of business-class Web hosting to small and
medium businesses. Employs 500, mostly exempt. Hires experienced
exempt in accounting/finance, marketing, sales, and IT.
Procedure: Apply on-line at web site. Hq located at
303 Peachtree Center Ave., Suite 500, Atlanta GA 30303
(404) 260-2477; Fax (404)

INTERNATIONAL BANKING TECHNOLOGIES (www.intbantec.com)
Profile: Provider of branch-banking facilities and services within retail settings
such as supermarkets and super center stores.

Procedure: Jobs not online. Send resume to human resources
1770 Indian Trail Road, Suite 300 , Norcross GA 30093
(770) 381-2023 ; Fax (404)

INTERNET SECURITY SYSTEMS (www.issx.com)
Profile: Atlanta-based provider of total information security management for
networks, servers, applications and desktops. Employs 1200. Numerous
openings in sales, marketing, telemarketing, IT, and training, both entry-
level and experienced.
Procedure: Does not accept phone calls. Best to apply on line. Hq is located at
6303 Barfield Rd NE, Atlanta GA 30328
(404) 236-2600; Fax (404)

INVESCO PLC MANAGEMENT (www.invesco.com)
Profile: Atlanta-based money management advisory firm, employing 750 here
with 60% exempt. Hires entry-level finance and IT grads, and
experienced exempt in accounting/finance, MIS, and especially
backgrounds in money management and investments.
Procedure: Send resume to Human Resouces
1315 Peachtree Street NE, Suite 500, Atlanta GA 30309
(404) 892-0896; Fax (404) 962-8118

INVESCO RETIREMENT SERVICES (www.irps.invesco.com)

Profile: Retirement plan management firm based in Atlanta. Employs 400 with 80% exempt. Experienced exempt should have defined contribution experience, Series 6 preferred. Also hires recent grads for training program.

Procedure: Send resume to human resources
             1201 Peachtree St, NE, Suite 2200, Atlanta GA 30361
             (800) 538-6370; Fax (404) 575-3513
             email resume to: resumes@invesco.com

J. WALTER THOMPSON AND MINDSHARE (www.jwtworld.com)

Profile: Third largest advertising agency in the world and one of Atlanta's largest. Employs 150 total, mostly exempt. Rarely hires recent grads, but will hire advertising professionals with 1+ years experience.

Procedure: Send resume to Personnel,
             1201 Peachtree St NE, 400 Colony Sq, Ste 980, Atlanta GA 30361
             (404) 365-7300; Fax 365-7337

JONES LANG LASALLE (www.joneslanglasalle.com)

Profile: International real estate and investment management company. Employs 900+ with 450+ exempt in Atlanta. Seldom hires recent grads, but has needs for experienced exempt in accounting/finance, and for property management and commercial real estate backgrounds.

Procedure: Resumes only accepted via e-mail through their web site
             3424 Peachtree Road NE, Suite 300, Atlanta GA 30326
             (404) 995-2100; Fax (404) 231-3905

KPMG (www.kpmg.com)

Profile: One of the Big 5 international CPA firms. Employs 400 total with 320 exempt, and expects an increase. Has three divisions: tax and audit divisions hire mostly recent accounting/finance grads and MBA's (no recent MIS grads). Consulting division employs 90 in Atlanta and is national hq for KPMG Health Ventures; seeks some MBA's (accounting/finance or engineering undergrad good) with some work experience, especially in health care or employee benefits.

Procedure: For tax and audit position, send resume to Director of Personnel; for consulting positions, send resume to M. C. Managing Partner. Both at 303 Peachtree Center Avenue, Suite 2000, Atlanta GA 30308
             (404) 222-3000; Fax 888/one-kpmg
             email resume to: usjobs@kpmg.com

KAISER PERMANENTE (www.kp.com)

Profile: Nation's largest and Atlanta's largest health maintenance organization (HMO). Division Headquarters here employs 1300 with 450 exempt. Hires recent accounting/finance grads and experienced exempt with health care management backgrounds.

Procedure: Send resume to Human Resources
3495 Piedmont Road, Bldg 9, Atlanta GA 30305
(404) 364-7000; job info. (404) 364-4783; Fax 364-4789

KEANE, INC. (www.keane.com)
Profile: Provides information systems and applications development consulting; specializes in client/server mainframe environment. Employs 350 in Atlanta (97% exempt) and 10,000 nationwide, mostly exempt-level, and growing. Hires 90+ recent grads and experienced exempt annually (IBM mainframe, client/server).
Procedure: Send or email resume to Corporate Recruiter
200 Galleria Pkwy, Suite 400, Atlanta GA 30339
(770) 850-7270; Fax (770) 850-7280
email resume to: samuel_i_ezeilo@keane.com

KETCHUM (www.ketchum.com)
Profile: Atlanta's largest PR firm with 130 employees. Hires experienced PR professionals, plus interns and co-ops.
Procedure: Send resume to human resources
1230 Peachtree St NE, Suite 2100, Atlanta GA 30309
(404) 879-9000; Fax (404)

KEYLINK SYSTEMS (www.pios.com)
Profile: Newly acquired business unit of Pioneer Standard Electronics, selling IBM computers and employing 250+ here. Most hires, entry and experienced, are in sales and marketing.
Procedure: Send resume to Human Resources
1175 Northmeadow Pkwy, Suite 150, Roswell GA 30076
(770) 625-7500; Fax (770) 625-7525

KIMBERLY-CLARK CORP. (www.kcc.com)
Profile: Headquarters operations for Fortune 500 diversified manufacturer, supplying administrative support to several businesses. Employment is 1300 with 900 exempt. Hires mostly recent grads, mainly into research and engineering (ChE, EE and ME). Experienced needs are usually filled with transfers from other locations, but will have some openings for biology, chemistry and polymer backgrounds, including PhD's.
Procedure: Send resume to Human Resources Services
1400 Holcombe Bridge Road, Roswell GA 30076
(770) 587-8000; Fax (770) 587-7225

KING AND SPALDING (www.kslaw.com)
Profile: Atlanta law firm with many specialties, employing 900 attorneys and 400 support staff.
Procedure: Send resume to personnel

191 Peachtree St, Atlanta GA 30303
(404) 572-4600; Fax (404)

KLIKLOK-WOODMAN CORP. (www.kliklok-woodman.com)
Profile: Atlanta-based manufacturer of packaging equipment, employing 275
with 100 exempt. Hires experienced exempt in sales and engineering
(EE, ME).
Procedure: Send resume to Human Resources
5224 Snapfinger Woods Drive, Decatur GA 30035
(770) 981-5200; Fax (770) 987-7160

KROGER SUPERMARKETS (www.kroger.com)
Profile: Largest supermarket chain in Atlanta, with 33+% of market share.
Operates 100+ stores in Atlanta area. This office recruits only
management-level, mostly store management trainees. Occasional need
for engineers. No accounting or MIS here.
Procedure: Send resume via US mail to Recruiting Manager
2175 Parklake Drive NE, Atlanta GA 30345
(770) 496-7400; 496-7467 Job info; Fax (770) 496-5376

LANIER WORLDWIDE (www.lanier.com)
Profile: Atlanta Corporate Headquarters for subsidiary of Ricoh Corp. Sells and
services document management systems, including Copiers, fax
machines, printers, and scanners. Employs 1200 in Atlanta, one-half
exempt. Most needs are for accounting/finance, R&D engineering, and
information systems. Recent grads should have some experience, e.g.,
co-op or summer jobs. No manufacturing here. Sales personnel are
hired at the field offices.
Procedure: Email or send resume to Career Connections,
2300 Parklake Drive NE, Atlanta GA 30345
(770) 496-9500; Fax (770) 621-1403
email resume to: career@lanier.com

LAW COMPANIES GROUP (www.lawco.com)
Profile: Engineering and environmental consulting firm. Employs 450 in
Atlanta, 300 exempt. Most needs are for engineers (CE, ChE,
environmental, materials) and scientists (chemistry, biology, geology,
hydrology, natural resources), recent grads and experienced.
Procedure: Send resume to Corporate Recruiter
1105 Santuary Pkwy, suie 300, Alpharetta GA 3014430004
(770) 360-0600; Fax (770) 360-0670
email resume to: hr@lawco.com

LECRAW, JULIAN AND COMPANIES, INC. (www.lecraw.com)

Profile: Atlanta-based residential property leasing and management company, employing 350 (less than 75 exempt at Hq). Hires recent grads as leasing consultants, as well as experienced property managers. Hq seeks entry and experienced corporate staff types (accounting/finance, operations, admin, etc.) IS is outsourced.

Procedure: E-mail resume to Employment Rep
1575 Northside Dr NE, Gldg 100, Suite 200, Atlanta GA 30318
(404) 352-2800; Fax (404) 352-2836
email resume to: julies@lecraw.com

LEND LEASE REAL ESTATE INVESTMENTS (www.lendleaserei.com)

Profile: Headquarters in Atlanta, manages $38 billion in real estate assets throughout the world. Employs 300 total at headquarters, most of whom are exempt. Ony recent grads hired are for accounting/finance, although most hires are for accounting professionals with 2-3 yrs experience.

Procedure: Send resume to Director of Human Resources
3424 Peachtree Road, Suite 800, Atlanta GA 30326
(404) 848-8600; Fax (404) 848-8855
email resume to: resumes@lendleaserei.com

LEVEL 3 COMMUNICATIONS (www.level3.com)

Profile: Control and service center for fiber optics cable network, employing 300 over three shifts.

Procedure: Apply at web site
180 Peachtree St NW, Atlanta GA 30303
(404) ; Fax (404)

LIBERTY MUTUAL INSURANCE COMPANY (www.lmgproperty.com)

Profile: Southern division office covering nine southeastern states, employing 200 with 80 exempt. Hires recent grads as trainees in underwriting, claims, and loss prevention, and then promotes into upper management. No needs for experienced exempt.

Procedure: Each of the three areas has a recruiter. Send resume to Recruiter, [specify area]
200 Galleria Pkwy, Suite 100, Atlanta GA 30339
(770) 955-0003; Fax (770) 531-9680

LIFE OF GEORGIA/SOUTHLAND LIFE, ING GROUP (www.lifeofgeorgia.com)

Profile: Dutch-owned, Atlanta-based life and health insurance company, employing 1200 with 420 exempt. Will need numerous recent grads and experienced personnel in Sales, underwriting, claims, accounting/finance, and Information Technology.

Procedure: Send resume to Human Resources Department
5780 Powers Ferry Rd NW, Atlanta GA 30327-4390
(770) 980-5100; Fax (770) 618-3819

LIFE OFFICE MANAGEMENT ASSOCIATION (LOMA) (www.loma.org)

Profile: Atlanta-based trade association that sponsors education, training, and research to promote life and health insurance companies. Employs 185 with 125 exempt. Seldom hires recent grads but recruits experienced exempt with specific backgrounds when needed, including writers and editors.

Procedure: Do not send resume. LOMA does not maintain resume files, so you must call first to inquire if there are current openings for your background. (Web site includes LomaJobNet, which lists hundreds of openings with member companies)

2300 Windy Ridge Parkway, Suite 600, Atlanta GA 30339
(770) 951-1770; Fax (770) 984-3770
email resume to: jobs@loma.com

LITHONIA LIGHTING (www.lithonia.com)

Profile: Corporate headquarters for the nation's largest lighting firm, manufacturing all types of lighting fixtures for residential, commercial and industrial uses. Largest subsidiary of Acuity Brands, an Atlanta-based Fortune 500 corporation. Employs 1700 in Atlanta, with 800 salaried. Hires recent grads for marketing, engineering, mfg mgt, and information services trainees, plus 25+ entry- and experienced-level professionals in marketing, manufacturing, engineering, and information services.

Procedure: Send resume to Corporate Recruiter
1400 Lester Road, Conyers GA 30012
(770) 922-9000; Fax (770) 860-9403
email resume to: recruiter@lithonia.com

LOCKHEED MARTIN AERONAUTICAL SYSTEMS (www.lmasc.lmco.com)

Profile: Defense contractor that develops and manufactures aircraft; one of Atlanta's largest employers with 10,000 employees, including 5500 exempt. Seeks recent grads and experienced exempt in accounting/finance, manufacturing management, CS and engineering (ME, EE, IE, AE; CE's with stress applications, not construction). Has co-ops in engineering.

Procedure: Send resume to Employment Manager
86 S. Cobb Drive, Marietta GA 30063-0530
(770) 494-4411; 494-5003 - Employment Office; 494-5000 job info line; Fax (770) 494-6617
email resume to: stevehowser@lmco.com

LOGILITY, INC. (www.logility.com)

Profile: Atlanta-based supplier of suply-chain management solutions, employing
             175. IT positions look for SQL, Mercater and Windows/ NT
             backgrounds. Also seeks sales/marketing.
Procedure: Email resume to
             470 East Paces Ferry Rd, Atlanta GA 30339
             (404) 261-9777; Fax (404)
             email resume to: recruiting@logility.com

LUCENT TECHNOLOGIES (http://www.lucent.com)
Profile: Designs and delivers networks for the world's largest communications
             service providers. Sales office and most needs in sales or
             administration.
Procedure: Apply online.
             800 North Pointe Blvd, Alpharetta GA
             (770) unknown; Fax (404) 573-7306

M C I WORLDCOM (www.mci.com)
Profile: MCI is the nation's second largest long distance carrier and has several
             operations in Atlanta employing 3500. Atlanta is headquarters for
             Business Services, and that group employs approx. 75% of the personnel
             here. They seek both recent grads and experienced exempt in
             accounting/finance, sales, and telecommunications, and there is a
             separate program for MBA's.
Procedure: Send resume to Human Resources, or fax resume to Resumix at 1-800-
             691-6982
             Six Concourse Pkwy, Atlanta 30328
             (770) 668-6000 – switchboard; 800-274-5758 – employment
             information; Fax (770) 668-6475?

MAG MUTUAL INSURANCE COMPANY (www.magmutual.com)
Profile: Professional liability insurer to physicians and hospitals (malpractice
             insurance). Employs 130 with 95 exempt. Hires recent insurance grads
             and experienced insurance specialists (underwriters, claim specialists,
             etc).
Procedure: Fax or e-mail resume to Human Resources
             P O Box 52979, Atlanta GA 30355
             (404) 842-5600; Fax (404) 842-5614
             email resume to: recruitment@magmutual.com

MAGNET COMMUNICTIONS (www.magnetbanking.com)
Profile: Atlanta-based provider of e-commerce services to the banking industry,
             employing 125. Inc's list of fastest growing private companies.
Procedure: Jobs not on web site. Send resume to personnel
             1349 West Peachtree St, Suite 1300, Atlanta GA 30309
             (404) 892-9300; Fax (404)

MAKITA CORP OF AMERICA (www.makitatools.com)
Profile: Manufacturer of power driven hand tools, employing 1000 with 150 exempt. Hires recent grads for engineering; experienced exempt for engineering, account/finance and management.
Procedure: Send resume to Human Resources
2650 Buford Highway, Buford GA 30518-6054
(770) 932-2901 ; Fax (770) 932-2905

MANHATTAN ASSOCIATES (www.pkms.com)
Profile: Atlanta-based software developer and consulting firm to the retail and grocery industry, one of Inc Magazine's fastest growing companies. Employs 200 here, mostly exempt level, and expanding rapidly. Seeks entry and experienced technical backgrounds, especially engineering, logistics, and computer science degrees. Uses AS400 in Unix, C++, powerbuilder, RPG 400.
Procedure: Vacancies listed on web site. Email, fax or mail resume to Recruiting Director
2300 Windy Ridge Parkway, Atlanta GA 30339
(770) 955-5533; Fax (770) 955-0302
email resume to: mlarocca@pkms.com

MAPICS, INC (www.mapics.com)
Profile: Atlanta-based provider of collaborative, e-business enterprise applications for manufacturers. Has openings in IT and other corporate staff functions, including accounting/finance, sales/mktg, and administration.
Procedure: Send resume to human resources
1000 Windward Concourse Pkwy, Suite 100, Alpharetta GA 30005
(678) 319-8000; Fax (404)

MARINER HEALTH CARE (www.marinerhealth.com)
Profile: Atlanta-based, operates 300 nursing facilities and long-term acute care hospitals.
Procedure: Send resume to
1 Ravinia Drive, Ste 1500, Atlanta GA 30346
(678) 443-7000; Fax (404)

MARSH USA (www.marsh.com)
Profile: Atlanta office for international insurance broking and risk management company. Hires mostly recent grads.
Procedure: Send resume to human resources
3475 Piedmont Rd NE, Suite 1200, Atlanta GA 30305
(404) 995-3000; Fax (404)

MARTA (METROPOLITAN ATLANTA RAPID TRANSIT AUTHORITY)
(www.itsmarta.com)
Profile: Employs 5000 with 1000 exempt, mostly at headquarters. MARTA's staffing needs change often, and they suggest you call their Job Line or check their web site for current openings. Most needs occur in accounting/finance, police, administration, staff support management, and operations (including bus operators/mechanics).
Procedure: Job site updated bi-weekly. Send resume to Employment Division
2424 Piedmont Rd NE, Atlanta GA 30324-3324
(404) 848-5544 for information; 848-5627 Job Line; Fax 848-5687

MATRIA HEALTHCARE (www.matria.com)
Profile: Atlanta based Company, providing women's health services, diabetes supplies and services, cardiovascular and respiratory disease management services. Hires Clinicians, Sales Representatives, Diabetes Educators, Administrative, Operational, Financial, and other Professional personnel. Openings are loated throughout the continental US.
Procedure: Fax or e-mail resume to Human Resources
1850 Parkway Place, Marietta GA 30067
(770) 767-4500; Fax (770) 767-4521

MATRIX RESOURCES (www.matrixresources.com)
Profile: Atlanta-based search firm, handles both contract consulting and permanent placement of IT professionals, employing 700 in Atlanta.
Procedure: Review vacancies online or send resume
115 Perimeter Center Pl, Ste 250, Atlanta GA 30346
(770) 677-2400; Fax (404)

MCDONALD'S CORPORATION (www.mcdonalds.com)
Profile: Regional office for McDonald's Corporation, employing 170 (mostly exempt), and is directly responsible for company-owned units and provides consulting services for franchisees. Seeks mostly management trainees for their units, plus refers candidates to franchisees. Can apply via web site.
Procedure: Fax resume to Personnel Manager
5901 Peachtree Dunwoody Rd, Suite C-500, Atlanta GA 30328
(770) 399-5067; Fax (770) 392-0912

MCKENNEY'S INC. (www.mckenneys.com)
Profile: Atlanta-based plumbing, heating and air conditioning manufacturing company. Employs 550+ with 200 exempt in Atlanta. Hires experienced exempt in accounting/finance and engineering (ME, IE); some recent grads are hired in engineering.
Procedure: Send resume to Human Resources

1056 Moreland Industrial Blvd. SE, Atlanta GA 30316-3252
(404) 622-5000; Fax (404) 624-8751

McKesson Information Solutions (www.infosolutions.mckesson.com)
Profile: Atlanta-based, world's largest provider of computer systems and information services to health care organizations. Employs 2000 in Atlanta. Most entry-level hires have technical program or healthcare backgrounds, plus an occassional accountant. Any experiece in healthcare, especially from hospital and payor environment, is highly desirable, and experienced exempt are sought in accounting/finance, sales, customer service, technical support, and MIS (C/C++, Unix, Sybase, SmallTalk, local and wide area networks). No engineering function here.
Procedure: Send resume to Human Resources
5995 Windward Pkwy, Alpharetta GA 30005
(404) 393-6000; 393-6015 job info line; Fax (440) 393-6092
email resume to: careers@hboc.com

MEAG Power (www.meagpower.org)
Profile: Atlanta-based provider of wholesale electric power to 48 Georgia cities. Employs 150 in headquarters, 110 exempt. Seeks experienced personnel in accounting, finance, engineering (EE), and IT. MIS is client/server.
Procedure: Jobs listed on Monster &/or GA DOL site. Send or email resume to Human Resources
1470 Riveredge Parkway NW, Atlanta GA 30328
(770) 563-0300; Fax (770) 953-3141
email resume to: jobs@meagpower.org

Metro Atlanta Chamber of Commerce (www.metroatlantachamber.com)
Profile: Employs 80, 65 exempt. Has limited turnover, most often in entry-level administrative positions, and offers project internships for recent grads and rising seniors in several areas, including finance, public relations, sales/marketing, MIS, international business, et al.
Procedure: Job site updated as needed. Send resume to Human Resources
235 International Blvd NE, Atlanta GA 30303
(404) 880-9000; Fax (404) 586-8426
email resume to: recruiter@macoc.com

Microbilt Corporation (www.microbilt.com)
Profile: Atlanta-based, provider of terminals, PC software and information delivery systems to the credit industry, including technical support, training, software development (Basic, HTML, C/C++ in Windows 95/NT environments) and design, repair and deployment of POS terminals. Employs 300 in Atlanta, 100 exempt. Hires exempt

personnel in accounting/finance, management, human resources, and MIS.

Procedure: Call job line and respond to current openings, or send resume to Human Resources
1640 Airport Rd, Suite 115, Kennesaw GA 30144
(770) 218-4400; Job line (770) 218-4989; Fax (770) 218-4998
email resume to: jobs@microbilt.com

MICROTEK MEDICAL (www.orex.com)
Profile: (formerly Isolyser) Manufacturer of environmentally correct dissolvable hospital supplies, employing 100 with 75 exempt. Hires in accounting/finance, sales and engineering (ChE).
Procedure: Send resume to Human Resources
1850-E Beaver Ridge Cir., Norcross GA 30071
(770) 806-9898; Fax (770) 806-8876

MIRANT (www.mirant.com)
Profile: Global energy company that builds, owns and operates power and natural gas facilities, employing 1200 in Atlanta with 1000 exempt. Seeks some recent grads, but mostly experienced exempt in accounting, engineering (EE, ME, ChE) and IS.
Procedure: Job site updated daily. Can register online to be notified of appropriate vacancies, or send resume to Staffing,
1155 Perimeter Center West, Atlanta GA 30338
678-579-7000 ; Fax

MITSUBISHI WIRELESS COMMUNICATIONS (www.mitsubishiwireless.com)
Profile: Corporate sales and marketing office for cellular telephones, employing 75, 30 exempt. Most openings are for engineers (ME, EE, computer), as well as some in human resources, credit, accounting/finance, marketing/product development, and sales.
Procedure: Send resume to human resources
3805 Crestwood Pkwy, Suite 350, Duluth GA 30096
(770) 638-2100; Fax (770) 921-4522
email resume to: resume@mitsubishiwireless.com.

MOHAWK INDUSTRIES (www.mohawkcommercial.com)
Profile: Manufacturer of residential and commercial carpet, employing 150 at headquarters (50 exempt), plus 10,000+ employed in manufacturing. Hq rarely hires recent grads, but some experienced exempt in accounting/finance and marketing are needed. Manufacturing personnel are hired at the plants, including the management trainees.
Procedure: Send resume to Human Resources
500 Town Park Lane, Kennesaw GA 30144
(770) 792-6300; Fax (678) 355-5811

MOTOROLA ENERGY SYSTEMS GROUP (www.mot.com)

Profile: Group headquartered in Atlanta, designs and manufactures energy solution products including batteries and battery chargers for consumer electronics, such as cell phones, two-way radios, and lap top computers. Employs 1300 here, with 400 exempt. Most needs are for engineers (EE, ME), entry and exprienced.

Procedure: Send resume to Staffing
1700 Belle Meade Court, Lawrenceville GA 30243
(770) 338-3000; jobs (770) 338-3566; Fax (770) 338-3556
email resume to: epdstaff@email.mot.com

MURATA ELECTRONICS NORTH AMERICA (www.murata.com)

Profile: Atlanta-based manufacturer of wide variety of electronic components, employing 150 (100 exempt). Hires recent engineering grads (EE); experienced exempt needs are in engineering (EE), accounting, marketing, customer service, and MIS (several systems, including JD Edwards software, AS 400, client server, et al.).

Procedure: Send resume to personnel
2200 Lake Park Drive, Smyrna GA 30080
(770) 436-1300; Fax (770) 433-7605
email resume to: garesume@murita.com

N C R — RETAIL
(www.ncr.com)

Profile: Peachtree Distribution and Repair Center. Facility that handles national and international distribution of NCR parts. Employs 700 with 200 exempt. Hires mostly recent grads in engineering (EE), programming (NCR hardware) and purchasing (BBA best). Occasionally has need for experienced purchasing agents.

Procedure: Send resume to Human Resources
200 Highway 74 South, Peachtree City GA 30269
(770) 487-7000; Fax (770) 623-7222

N C R – RETAIL SYSTEMS GROUP (www.ncr.com)

Profile: Designs and develops integrated software and hardware computer solutions for retailers. Employs 750 here, 700 exempt. NCR's corporate philosophy is predominantly to hire recent grads and promote from within. Most needs are for engineers (EE, ME, Computer) computer science majors, and supply chain management. Offers internships in engineering, computer science, and other business-related majors. Jobs and applications at web site.

Procedure: E-mail resume to Human Resources
2651 Satellite Blvd, Duluth GA 30096
(770) 623-7175; Fax (770) 623-7222

email resume to: online application/resume
submittal@www.ncr.com/careers

N E C TECHNOLOGIES, INC. (www.nec.com)
Profile: Manufacturer of computer products, including color monitors, CD rom,
            and automotive electronics. Currently staffing within the
            manufacturing, warehouse, and technical areas. Employs 313 with 60
            exempt.
Procedure: Send resume to Human Resources Department
            1 NEC Drive, McDonough GA 30253
            (770) 957-6600; Fax (770) 957-6082

NAPA AUTO PARTS (www.napaonline.com)
Profile: Atlanta distribution center for Atlanta-based Genuine Parts Company, an
            automotive parts distributor and retailer. This distribution facility, plus
            the 28 retail stores in Atlanta, employs 500 with 140 exempt, and this
            office also hires for outside Atlanta. Seeks management trainees for
            Management Training Program: degree preferred + some business
            experience (any field).
Procedure: Send resume to Personnel Manager
            P O Box 2000, Norcross GA 30091
            (770) 447-8233; Fax (770) 246-4373

NATIONAL LINEN SERVICE (www.national-linen.com)
Profile: Atlanta-based, textile rental company, employing 750 (400 exempt) in
            Atlanta, which includes 2 plants + headquarters staff. Offers recent
            grads a Management Development Program that covers numerous
            corporate specialties, especially operations management and sales. Also
            seeks accounting/finance and experienced production/operations
            managers and sales representatives. (Note: Company is structuring.)
Procedure: Send resume to Manager of Personnel Administration
            1420 Peachtree St NE, Atlanta GA 30309
            (404) 853-1000; job info. (888) 729-4844; Fax (404) 853-6200

NATIONAL SERVICE INDUSTRIES (www.ndchealth.com)
Profile: Corporate headquarters support for five NSI divisions, which operate
            autonomously and handle their own hiring. Headquarters employs 90,
            45 exempt, and hires auditors and benefits specialists. (Note: NSI is
            currently restructuring.)
Procedure: Send resume to Personnel
            1420 Peachtree St NE, Atlanta GA 30309
            (404) 853-1000; 853-1282; Fax (404) 853-1420

NATIONAL VISION ASSOCIATES (www.nationalvision.com)

Profile: Atlanta-based optical retailing chain with 1100+ stores, mostly in Wal-Mart stores. Headquarters employs 350 with 60 exempt. Hires both recent grads and experienced exempt in accounting, distribution, and MIS (AS 400), marketing, merchandising, customer svc, HR, and optics.
Procedure: Send resume to personnel
            296 Grayson Hwy, Lawrenceville GA 30045
            (770) 822-3600; Fax (770) 822-6206
            email resume to: jobs@nationalvision.com

NDC HEALTH (www.ndcorp.com)

Profile: Atlanta-based company within the information services industry, providing data exchange, processing and telecommunications services to a variety of financial and health care clients. Employs 1800, including 1000 exempt, and anticipates hiring 200 exempt annually. Recent grads are hired mostly as programmers and customer service representatives (BBA or liberal arts majors). Experienced exempt are hired in a variety of areas: accounting, customer service; programming and all types of MIS professionals (Tandem and Unisys); engineers (EE, EET and MET); accountants and financial analysts; sales representatives with experience in banking (cash management or credit cards especially), and health care software systems.
Procedure: Send resume to Director of Employment
            NDC Plaza, Atlanta GA 30329
            (404) 728-2000; 728-2030 job info line; Fax (404) 728-3427

PLATO LEARNING (www.plato.com)

Profile: Markets software to schools, employing 60 here, with 40 exempt. Most need are for experienced software sales reps.
Procedure: E-mail resume to Human Resources
            100 Galeria Pkwy NW, Suite 1400, Atlanta GA 30339
            (770) 226-5000; Fax (770) 226-5010
            email resume to: hr@plato.net

NETWORK COMMUNICATIONS (www.livingchoices.com)

Profile: Atlanta-based printer and publisher of national real estate magazines and other commercial publications, employing 800 with 300 exempt. Hires both recent grads and experienced exempt in accounting, finance, sales, proofreading, and IS (Mac and PC).
Procedure: Send resume to Corporate Recruiter
            2 Pamblin Drive, Lawrenceville GA 30245
            (770) 962-7220; Fax (404) 822-4339

NEWELL RUBBERMAID (www.newellrubbermaid.com)

Profile: Newest of Atlanta's 13 Fortune 500 firms headquartered here,
             announcing plans to build signature building in north Fulton County.
             Diversified consumer products company, employs 300+ at headquarters.
Procedure: Review openings at web site
             undetermined at this writing, Alpharetta GA
             (770) ; Fax (404)

NORDSON CORPORATION (www.nordson.com)
Profile: North American Division Headquarters of Ohio-based Nordson Corp., a
             manufacturer of finishing and adhesive application equipment. This
             office provides marketing and technical support for several Nordson
             groups. Employs 500 with 225 exempt. Seldom hires recent grads, but
             seeks experienced exempt in sales, engineering (EE, ME), marketing
             specialties (analysts, product development, etc.) and technical training.
Procedure: Send resume to Sr. Recruiting Specialist
             12905 Pacific Drrrive, Norcross GA 30097
             (770) 497-3400; Fax (770) 497-3557
             email resume to: hwhaley@nordson.com

NORFOLK SOUTHERN CORPORATION (www.nscorp.com)
Profile: Norfolk, VA-based railroad and transportation company, parent of
             Norfolk-Southern Transportation Co. and North American Van Lines.
             Employs 2100 in Atlanta, 500 exempt, and adding 500 in 1999. Hires
             mostly recent grads, although there are needs for experienced computer
             programmers (MIS and CS) and systems analysts. Recent
             business/accounting/finance and CS/MIS grads are hired for Atlanta
             positions. Recent marketing grads are hired mostly for sales;
             engineers, transportation and industrial mgt grads are hired for
             management programs; may be relocated after training.
Procedure: Job site updated constantly. Hiring is conducted at headquarters. Send
             resume to Manager of Employment
             Three Commercial Place, Norfolk VA 23510-9214
             (800) 214-3609 - Job info line; Fax (757) 664-5069
             email resume to: careers@nscorp.com

NORTEL NETWORKS (www.nortelnetworks.com)
Profile: Nortel's two Atlanta locations employ approx. 1100, with 85% exempt-
             level. Alpharetta office is home to 800 employees and Bell Northern
             Research (BNR), Nortel's research and development subsidiary, is in
             Norcross with 300 employees. Alpharetta facility consists of Regional
             Sales and Customer Service, Broadband Networks, Switching, Wireless,
             and Enterprise Networks, and Customer Network Solutions, which is
             headquartered out of Atlanta. BNR's Atlanta lab is a center for
             development and support of Nortel's total access network solutions and
             products aimed at the North American marketplace. Hires sales,

marketing, engineering professionals, and personnel from other disciplines both recent grads and experienced, probably 150 annually.

Procedure: Although located in Atlanta at 5555 Windward Parkway, all exempt recruiting is handled from NC Resourcing Center. Send resume to Attn: US Resourcing
P O Box 13010, Dept 1175/NTP, Research Triangle Park NC 27709
(770) 661-5000; (800) 4NORTEL job info line; Fax (800) 546-8092

NORTHSIDE HOSPITAL (www.northside.com)
Profile: Atlanta general medical and surgical hospital. Employes over 3,500. Hires both recent graduates and experienced exempt. Hires account/finance, MIS, RN, MD and medical tech. positions.

Procedure: Send resume to Human Resources. Jobs are posted in the Sunday AJC
1000 Johnson Ferry Rd. NE, Atlanta GA 30342-1606
(404) 851-8078; job line (404) 303-3305 ; Fax (404) 851-6569
email resume to: employment@northside.com

NOVA INFORMATION SYSTEMS (www.novainfo.com)
Profile: Atlanta-based software developer, manages and transports payment and other information for retailers, banks, and financial instituions in US. Employs 425. Hires many recent grads, mostly in MIS but also in sales and customer service. Hires exempt in all areas, including accounting, sales, management, and MIS

Procedure: E-mail or fax to recruiting
1 Concourse Pkwy NE, Suite 300, Atlanta GA 30328
(770) 396-1456; Fax (770) 698-1028
email resume to: resumes@novainfo.com

OFS (www.ofsoptics.com)
Profile: (formerly Lucent Technologies, Network Systems) World's largest fiber optics communications cable manufacturing facility. Employs 1500, including 500+ exempt. Hires recent grads in accounting/finance, engineering (all types, especially EE, ME and ChE) and MIS, and experienced personnel in sales only. Offers internships in engineering.

Procedure: Complete online resume, or send resume to personnel
2000 Northeast Expressway, Norcross 30071
(770) 798-2000; Fax (770) 798-2589

OGILVY PUBLIC RELATIONS WORLDWIDE (www.ogilvypr.com)
Profile: Atlanta-based PR firm, employing 50. Hires experienced PR professionals, plus interns.

Procedure: Send resume to human resources
400 Colony Square, Suite 980, Atlanta GA 30361
(404) 897-2300; Fax (404)

OGLETHORPE POWER CORP. (www.opc.com; www.gasoc.com; www.gatrans.com)
Profile: Nation's largest power cooperative, based in Atlanta. Three divisions
             (generation, transmission , and operations) employ total 600 with 40
             exempt. Seldom hires recent grads, but seeks experienced
             accounting/finance, engineering (EE, IE mostly; few ME) and MIS.
Procedure: E-mail resume to Human Resources
             2100 East Exchange Place, Tucker GA 30085-1349
             (770) 270-7600; 270-7939 Job Line; Fax (770) 270-7676

OKI TELECOM, INC. (www.okitelecom.com)
Profile: Manufacturer of automotive electronic products. Employs 500+ with
             250 exempt. Most needs are for engineers (EE, IE, ME and software),
             both recent grads and experienced.
Procedure: Prefers that you not send resume until you have called the Job Line, then
             respond for a specific opening to
             437 Old Peachtree Rd, Suwanee GA 30174
             (770) 995-9800; 822-2701 Job Line; Fax (770) 822-5517

OLDCASTLE, INC. (www.oldcastle.com)
Profile: Atlanta-based manufacturer and distributor of pre-cast and architectural
             concrete and glass products.
Procedure: Send resume to personnel
             375 Northridge Rd, Ste 350, Atlanta GA 30350
             (770) 804-3363; Fax (404)

OXFORD INDUSTRIES (www.oxfordinc.com)
Profile: Atlanta-based international apparel manufacturing and marketing
             company, mostly for private and contract labels. Has manufacturing
             facilities throughout the Southeast, Latin America, and Asia. Corporate
             staff numbers 230, 115 exempt. Hires mostly recent grads in
             accounting/finance, customer service, and computer science (AS 400).
Procedure: Send resume to Manager of Human Resources
             222 Piedmont Avenue, Atlanta GA 30308
             (404) 659-2424; Fax (404) 525-3650
             email resume to: resumes@oxfordinc.com

PACTIV CORPORATION (www.tyco.com)
Profile: Manufactures and sells polyethylene (plastic films) and polystyrene
             (plastic foam) disposable products for consumer, industrial and
             institutional use. Consumer brand names include Baggies and Hefty.
             Employs 675 total with 100 exempt. Most needs are for experienced
             exempt in accounting/finance, sales, manufacturing and distribution
             management, and engineering (EE, ME, ChE). Also has occasional
             need for MBA's and in human resources.
Procedure: Send resume to Human Resources

9172 Industrial Dr., Covington GA 30014
(770) 786-5372; Fax 770-784-4395

PANASONIC (MATSUSHITA ELECTRIC CORPORATION OF AMERICA)
(www.panasonic.com)
Profile: Southeast region sales and service office, employing 360 with 250 exempt. Nearly all hiring is for experienced consumer and industrial sales representatives.
Procedure: Send resume to Recruiter
1225 Northbrook Pkwy, Suwanee GA 30174
(770) 338-6700; Fax (770) 338-6602

PANASONIC WIRELESS DESIGN CENTER (www.panasonic.com)
Profile: R&D of digital PCS handset utilizing TDMA standards. Future projections include the use of Bluetooth and EDGE. Employs 320. Seeks software, mechanical, test, RF and Logic engineers. Also growing IT, Business Operations and Product Planning departments. Hires entry level in Computer Science, Computer Engineering and Electrical Engineering, and has co-ops in software, hardware, and IT.
Procedure: Send or email resume to Human Resources
1225 Northbrook Pkwy, Suite 2-352, Suwanee GA 30024
(770) 338-6000; Fax (770) 338-6238
email resume to: recruiting@panasonic.atlanta.com

PEACHTREE SOFTWARE (www.peachtree.com)
Profile: Subsidiary of Best Software, provides software and applications development for small businesses. Employs 550 here, 250 exempt. Hires a few recent grads in telesales, support, accounting and computer science, and experienced exempt in many areas including accounting, marketing, software development, quality assurance, and product management.
Procedure: Job site updated daily or when needed. Send resume to Human Resources
1505 Pavilion Place, Norcross GA 30093
(770) 724-4000; Fax (770) 806-5166
email resume to: humanresources@peachtree.com

PEPSI COLA (www.pepsi.com)
Profile: Bottles and distributes Pepsi Cola brands of soft drinks. Employs 450 here, with 90 exempt. Hires both recent grads and experienced exempt for operations management and engineering. IS is handled at corporate headquarters in NY. Offers summer internships in operations management.
Procedure: Send resume to Director of Human Resources
1480 Chattahoochee Ave, Atlanta GA 30318

(404) 355-1480; Fax 352-6314

PER-SE TECHNOLOGIES (www.per-se.com)
Profile: Atlanta-based, national company providing software and management
services to the health care industry. Employs 500 at headquarters, plus
1000 at five branches in Atlanta, 30% exempt. Hires recent grads in
MIS, accounting, and physician practice management. Experienced
exempt sought includs accounting/finance (Big 5 or tax preferred),
medical-related sales, hospital administration, engineers (IE/systems),
and MIS (PC-based, client server; relational database, C++, UNIX,
Windows NT)
Procedure: Send resume to Corporate Employment Manager
2700 Cumberland Pkwy, Suite 300, Atlanta GA 30339
(770) 444-5300; Fax (770) 444-5626
email resume to: techjobs@per-se.com

PEREGRINE SYSTEMS (www.peregrine.com)
Profile: Marketing Group for end-to-end e-Business solutions software
development company, employing 140 with 120 exempt. Most needs
are for technical backgrounds (entry-level and experienced) in sales,
marketing, research/development, and support.
Procedure: Send resume to Human Resources
1055 Lenox Park Blvd, Atlanta GA 30319
(404) 841-4334; Fax (404) 848-2841

PHILIPS CONSUMER ELECTRONICS (www.philipsusa.com)
Profile: Division hq for world's third largest coonsumer electronics company,
develops and manufactures audio, video, TV, and PC peripherals.
Procedure: Send resume to human resources
64 Perimeter Center East, Atlanta GA 30346
(770) 821-2400; Fax (770) 821-3434

PHOTOCIRCUITS ATLANTA (www.photocircuits.com)
Profile: Manufacturer of print circuit boards, employing 1400 here with 250
exempt, and growing 20% annually. Hires recent grads and experienced
exempt in management and process engineering (ChE, ME, IE mostly).
Also has several IS interns.
Procedure: Send resume to Human Resources
350 Dividend Drive, Peachtree City GA 30269
(770) 487-8888; Fax (770) 487-7746
email resume to: ptcrecruiter@photocircuits.com

PIEDMONT HOSPITAL (www.piedmonthospital.org)
Profile: Fourth largest hospital in Atlanta, employing 2600. In addition to
medical specialties, has occasional needs in many administrative areas.

Procedure: Apply online or send resume to
1968 Peachtree Rd NW, Atlanta GA 30309
(404) 605-5000; Fax (404)

PIZZA HUT (www.yum.com)
Profile: Third largest fast food chain in the world, division of Yum Brands. Operates 115 stores in metro-Atlanta, employing 2,000 with 250 exempt. Most hiring here is for store operations and management, probably 30 recent grads and 125 experienced.
Procedure: Fax or e-mail resume to Staffing Manager
675 Mansell Road, Roswell GA 30076
(770) 990-2000; Fax (770) 552-1739
email resume to: jil.jordan@tricon-yum.com

PLANTATION PIPELINE CO. (www.kindermorgan.com)
Profile: Atlanta-based subsidiary of Kinder Morgan, interstate pipeline transporter of liquid refined petroleum products. Employs 120 in Atlanta, 80 exempt. Seeks recent grads and experienced exempt in accounting/finance and engineering (CE, ME, EE).
Procedure: Mail or fax resume to Recruiter at
1720 Windward Concourse, Suite 325, Atlanta GA 30005
(770) 751-4000; job line (770) 751-4295; Fax (770) 751-4131

PORSCHE CARS NA (www.porsche.com)
Profile: North American headquarters, employs 90, mostly exempt.
Procedure: Send resume to human resources
980Hammond Drive, Suite 100, Atlanta GA 30328
(770) 290-3500; Fax (404)

POST PROPERTIES (www.postproperties.com)
Profile: Atlanta-based developer and operator of upscale multi-family apartment communities. Prefers to hire entry-level and promote from within. Has openings in all corporate areas, plus property management. Offers landscaping internships.
Procedure: Apply online or email resume to Human Resources
4401 Northside Pkwy, Ste 800, Atlanta GA 30327
(404) 846-5000; Fax (404)
email resume to: careers@postproperties.com

PRICEWATERHOUSECOOPERS (www.pwcglobal.com)
Profile: International Big 5 CPA firm, employing 1000+ in Atlanta. Most hires are recent college grads in accounting/finance and MBA's. (See next listing for consulting.)
Procedure: Send resume to Recruiting
50 Hurt Plaza, Suite 1700, Atlanta GA 30303

(678) 419-7000; Fax (678) 419-8899

PRICEWATERHOUSECOOPERS (CONSULTING DIVISION) (www.pwcglobal.com)
Profile: Consulting division has 15+ seperate practices, each with own staffing
             function. Hires 50+ exempt annually, mostly with experience in
             implementing Oracle Financials, Peoplesoft HR or Financials, SAP R/3,
             and other package and custom software. Also seeks Supply Chain
             Managment Consultants, Manufaturing Consultants, and business
             process reengineering consultants.
Procedure: Send resume to Recruiting
             3200 Windy Hill Road, Suite 900 West, Atlanta GA 30339
             (770) 933-9191; Fax (678) 419-5959

PRIMEDIA BUSINESS MAGAZINES AND MEDIA (www.primediabusiness.com)
Profile: Publisher of 95+ trade magazines, plus trade shows and employing 120
             (90 exempt) in Atlanta in sales, editorial, graphics, and suport personnel.
             Nearly all hires are for journalism, advertising sales, or graphic arts
             positions.
Procedure: Fax or email resume to Human Resources Office
             6151 Powers Ferry Road NW, Atlanta GA 30339
             (770) 955-2500; Fax (770) 618-0126
             email resume to: tony_chimera@intertec.com

PRIMERICA FINANCIAL SERVICES (pfsfhq.com)
Profile: Atlanta-based company selling term life insurance and mutual funds.
             Employs 1500 here with 700 exempt. Seeks recent grads in accounting,
             management, journalism, and liberal arts for customer service positions.
             Seeks experienced exempt in accounting/finance, MIS (IBM), and
             insurance specialties.
Procedure: Send resume to Corporate Recruiter
             3120 Breckinridge Blvd, Duluth GA 30099
             (770) 381-1000; Fax (770) 564-6161

PRINTPACK, INC. (www.printpack.com)
Profile: Atlanta-based, nation's second largest converter of unprinted,
             unlaminated packaging film, employing 600 here with 260 exempt.
             Hires a few recent grads for sales training and seeks packaging degrees
             for management training. Most hires are experienced exempt with 3-5
             years experience in sales (industrial or packaging), manufacturing
             management and engineering, accounting/finance and MIS (IBM and
             HP — prefers manufacturing experience).
Procedure: Send resume to Corporate Recruiting Manager
             4335 Wendell Drive SW, Atlanta GA 30336
             (404) 691-5830; Fax (404) 699-7122

PROFIT RECOVERY GROUP (www.prgx.com)

Profile: Recovery auditing services for large companies and government egencies, employing 400 in Atlanta with most exempt. Seeks experienced exempt in all corporate support functions, IS, acctg/fin, operations, freight, telecom, personnel, etc.). Also hires recent grads in many areas.

Procedure: Check web site and send resume to human resources
2300 Windy Ridge Pkwy, Atlanta GA 30339
(770) 955-3815; Fax (770) 779-3250

PRUDENTIAL BANK (www.prudential.com/banking)

Profile: Subsidiary of Prudential Enterprises, issues and services credit cards, home equity loans, and other consumer financial needs. Employs 675 with 150 exempt. Most exempt-level hiring is for experienced accounting/finance, banking, and MIS (Macintosh).

Procedure: Send resume to Human Resources
1 Ravinia Drive, Suite 1000, Atlanta GA 30346
(770) 551-6700; Fax (770) 551-6885

PTEK (www.ptek.com)

Profile: Atlanta-based, rapidly growing telecommunications firm employing 225 with 150 exempt. Hires recent grads in computer related fields (programming, developmental, applications, etc.) and experienced exempt in all areas, including accounting/finance, sales, administrative, customer service, engineering, MIS, etc.

Procedure: Send resume to Human Resources
3399 Peachtree Rd NE, Suite 400, Atlanta GA 30326
(404) 262-8400; Fax (404) 487-8125
email resume to: hr@ptek.com

PUBLIX DIRECT (www.publixdirect.com)

Profile: Atlanta-based division offering on-line grocery shopping and delivery. Seeks IT (especially web design) and merchandising backgrounds.

Procedure: Send resume to human resources
3440 Preston Ridge Rd, Suite 500, Alpharetta GA 30005
(770) 772-7446; Fax (404)

PUBLIX SUPERMARKETS - DIVISION OFFICE (www.publix.com)

Profile: Atlanta's second largest supermarket chain, with 90+ stores here and growing. Has no formal training program; rather, most management started as non-exempt store clerks and worked to upper management. Publix also has large distribution facility in Atlanta employing 500, but generally hires only hourly positions and promotes up.

Procedure: Apply at individual stores, or send resume to Human Resources
(resumes are kept on file for one year)

2600 Delk Road, Marietta GA 30067
(770) 952-6601; Fax (404) 952-6558

QUEBECOR WORLD (www.world-color.com)
Profile: Atlanta-based printer that produces promotional games, lotteries, direct mail, directories, airline timetables, ticket jackets, pop-ups and specialty finishing. Employs 200 with 75 exempt in Atlanta, plus this office staffs the Oakwood, GA facility which employs 300 with 100 exempt. Hires a few recent grads in management and engineering (EE, ME, et al.) at their Oakwood facility, but most needs are for experienced exempt in all functions. Uses AS 400, IBM PC's, and IBM 4341 mainframe.
Procedure: Send resume to Human Resources Manager
3101 McCall Dr, Atlanta GA 30340
(770) 936-7100; Fax (404) 605-8768
email resume to: gina.inscoe@quebecorworld.com

QUEST DIAGNOSTICS (www.questdiagnostics.com)
Profile: One of the largest clinical reference laboratories in the US. Employs more than 1000 in Atlanta (150 exempt), plus 1500 additional in SE, mostly medical and laboratory specialists. Most needs are for medical technologists (entry-level and experienced; certification is required), lab workers, and administrative support (billing, customer service, etc). Offers on-site day care program.
Procedure: Send resume to Personnel
1777 Montreal Circle, Tucker GA 30084
(770) 934-9205; 621-7450 job line; Fax 621-7548

RACETRAC PETROLEUM, INC. (www.racetrac.com)
Profile: Corporate headquarters for rapidly expanding gasoline/convenience store retailer with 3700 employees and more than 400 stores in 13 SE states and expanding rapidly. One of Georgia's five largest privately held firms, employing 225 at headquarters, 125 exempt. Needs are for exempt and non-exempt personnel in accounting, finance, purchasing, legal, construction, engineering and design, real estate, retail operations and IS (AS 400, Unix, client server).
Procedure: Mail, e-mail, or fax resume to Human Resources
P O Box 105035, Atlanta GA 30348
(770) 431-7600; Fax (770) 319-7944
email resume to: hr@racetrac.com

RADIANT SYSTEMS (www.radiantsystems.com)
Profile: Atlanta-based, builds and delivers IT systems for managing site operations for retail and hospitality businesses, employing 1000 here. Hires entry and experienced exempt in all corporate areas, especially IT.
Procedure: Apply online for specific vacancy, or send/email resume to

3925 Brookside Parkway, Alpharetta GA 30022
(404) ; Fax (404)
email resume to: recruiting@radiantsystems.com

RANDSTAD NORTH AMERICA (www.randstad.com)

Profile: North American HQ for international staffing service operating 35 Atlanta branches. Has 600 permanent employees (500 exempt) and expects an increase. Positions available are a comination of sales and customer service and must have 10 yrs prior work experience. Branch managers are usually promoted from sales and customer service.

Procedure: Send resume Human Resources
2015 South Park Place, Atlanta GA 30339
(770) 937-7000; Fax (770) 937-7030

RARE HOSPITALITY (www.rarehospitality.com)

Profile: Atlanta-based, operates and franchises 200+ steak restaurants. HQ has exempt needs in HR, IS, Accountingfinance, Marketing, and restaurant management.

Procedure: Email or send resume to Employment,
8215 Roswell Road Building 600, Atlanta GA 30350
(770) 551-5464; Fax (404)
email resume to: careeropportunities@rarehospitality.com

RESPIRONICS, INC. (www.respironics.com)

Profile: Home care manufacturer of high-tech electronic medical equipment. Employs 500 here with 100 exempt. Hires recent grads and experienced accounting/finance, and experienced manufacturing managers (mostly with engineering degrees) and staff engineers (design, ME, EE and electronic). Also has need for non-exempt assemblers, solderers, and technicians.

Procedure: Send resume to Professional Recruiter
175 Chastain Meadows Court, Kennesaw GA 30144
(770) 499-1212; Fax (770) 429-2956

RICH'S-MACY'S DEPARTMENT STORES

Profile: See Federated Department Stores

RICOH ELECTRONICS (www.ricoh-usa.com)

Profile: Manufactures toner for copy machines and thermal media products. Employs 400 with 75 exempt. Most exempt needs are production supervisors and managers.

Procedure: Jobs updated monthly. Send resume to personnel
1125 Hurricane Shoal Rd, Lawrenceville GA 30043
(770) 338-7200; Fax (770) 338-7251
email resume to: hr@ricoh-usa.com

RIVERWOOD INTERNATIONAL (www.riverwood.com)

Profile: Atlanta-based manufacturer of paperboard,packaging, and packaging machinery, employing 82 in corporate headquarters with 70 exempt. Seeks recent grads in accounting/finance and engineering (P&P, EE, ME), and occasionally marketing MBA. Experienced exempt are needed in all corporate support functions, including accounting/finance, purchasing, HR, and MIS (Unix).

Procedure: Send resume to Corporate Staffing
3350 Riverwood Pkwy SE, Suite 1400, Atlanta GA 30339
(770) 644-3000; Fax (770) 644-2962
email resume to: pat.szall@email.riverwood.com

ROADWAY EXPRESS INC. (www.roadway.com)

Profile: Trucking company wwith regional headquaters in Atlanta. Employees 650 with 65 exempt. Hires some recent graduates for management training. Hire experienced exempt for account/finance and management.

Procedure: Send resume to Human Resources
2701 Moreland Ave. SE, Atlanta GA 3015-5710
(404) 362-9164; Fax (404) 361-0988
email resume to: hr@roadway.com

ROCK-TENN CO. (www.rocktenn.com)

Profile: Atlanta-based manufacturer of packaging products, merchandising displays and recycled paperboard. Has exempt needs in accounting/finance, IT (AS/400s and RS/6000s) and manufacturing.

Procedure:
504 Thrasher St, Norcross GA 30071
(770) 448-2193; Fax (404)

ROLLINS, INC. (www.orkin.com)

Profile: Corporate headquarters for diversified service corporation, including Orkin Exterminating Company. Employs 700 with 200 exempt, and will hire 50± exempt annually. Recent grads hired are usually entry accountants. Seeks experienced personnel for typical corporate headquarters types: sales, accounting/finance, insurance administration, distribution, MIS (AS400); etc.

Procedure: E-mail resume to Human Resources Department
2170 Piedmont Rd NE, Atlanta GA 30324
(404) 888-2000; job line: 888-2125; Fax 888-2672
email resume to: jobs@rollinscorp.com

ROSSER INTERNATIONAL (www.rosser.com)

Profile: Atlanta-based architectural/engineering design firm, employing 140 with 125 exempt. Offers career opportunities for both recent graduates and experienced professionals in architecture, planning, all disciplines of engineering (structural, mechanical, electrical, plumbing, and civil), accounting/finance, marketing, and administration.

Procedure: Job site updated monthly. Send resume to Human Resources
524 West Peachtree St. NW, Atlanta GA 30308
(404) 876-3800; Fax (404) 888-6863
email resume to: mfields@rosser.com

RTM RESTAURANT GROUP (www.rtminc.com)
Profile: Atlanta-based operator and franchisee of five restaurant chains with 500± units. Employs 125 at headquarters, plus individual stores. Unable to determine employment data.
Procedure: Send resume to Human Resources
5995 Barfield Road, Atlanta GA 30328
(404) 256-4900; Fax (404) 847-0284

RUSSELL CORP. (www.russellcorp.com)
Profile: International apparel company specializing in activewear, casualwear and athletic uniforms, dual HQ in Atlanta and AL.
Procedure: Vacancies not posted. Send or email resumes to
3330 Cumberland Blvd, Ste 800, Atlanta GA 30339
(678) 742-8000; Fax (404)
email resume to: Employment@russellcorp.com

RUSSELL, H. J. & COMPANY (www.hjrussell.com)
Profile: Fourth largest minority-owned business in the US, headquartered in Atlanta. Has five divisions, primarily in real estate, property management, construction, and construction management. Employs 375 in Atlanta area, with 50% exempt. Hires few recent grads, except for their interns. Experienced personnel hired include accounting/finance, property management, construction engineers, management services (e.g., personnel, PR, administration, etc.) and MIS (AS 400).
Procedure: E-mailresume to Human Resources Director
504 Fair Street SW, Atlanta GA 30313
(404) 330-1000; job line (404) 330-0996 ; Fax 330-0922
email resume to: bjshannon@hjrussell.com

S A P (www.sap.com)
Profile: World's largest inter-enterprise software company, providing e-business solutions. Most vacancies here are for Sales/Mktg and IT.
Procedure: Send resume to
5555 Glenridge Connector, Atlanta GA 30342
(404) 943-7400; Fax (404)

S I T A (www.sita.com)

Profile: French headquartered company that owns and operates the worlds's largest international data network, employing 450 in Atlanta, 100 exempt. SITA provides an extensive range of telecommunications and information processing services. Hires a few recent grads, but mostly experienced exempt in various positions – customer support, administration, operations, and technical.

Procedure: Send resume to Human Resources
3100 Cumberland Blvd., Suite 200, Atlanta GA 30339
(770) 850-4500; Fax (770) 303-3644

S1 CORP. (www.s1.com)
Profile: Atlanta-based, international leader in e-finance and transactional Internet banking solutions. Employs 700 here, 500 exempt. Will be expanding in 2002, seeking software developers, sales/mktg, IT, and CS engineers. Also has need for corp staff types, e.g. accounting/finance, admin, HR, etc.

Procedure: Email resume to
3500 Lenox Road, Suite 200, Atlanta GA 30326
(404) 812-6200; Fax (404)
email resume to: careers@s1.com

SAAB CARS USA (www.saabusa.com)
Profile: US corporate headquarters for Swedish car company. Hq employs 100 with 60 exempt. Does not hire recent grads, but seeks experienced exempt in accounting, finance, and automotive marketing. No needs for engineering or MIS.

Procedure: Send resume to Human Resources
4405-A International Blvd, Norcross GA 30093
(770) 279-0100; Fax (770) 279-6588

SAFECO INSURANCE COMPANY (www.safeco.com)
Profile: Major full-lines insurance company employing 300 in Atlanta, 240 exempt. Hires recent college grads, preferably with some professional work experience (insurance not necessary) for training programs in underwriting, claims and marketing.

Procedure: Send resume to Human Resources
2055 Sugarloaf Circle, Duluth GA 30097
(678) 417-0577; (800) 753-5330 job info line; Fax (678) 417-3370 879-3370

SAINT JOSEPH'S HOSPITAL OF ATLANTA (www.stjosephsatlanta.org)
Profile: 346-bed, tertiary care hospital, noted for its cardiac and cancer specialties, employing 1700. Nearly all needs are for medical and hospital specialties.

Procedure: Apply online or send resume to

5665 Peachtree Dunwoody Road NE, Atlanta GA 30342
(404) 851-7001; Fax (404)

SANDWELL ENGINEERING, INC. (www.sandwell.com)
Profile: US division headquarters of Canadian engineering consulting firm; this
            office specializes mostly in the power and pulp and paper industries, and
            employs 200 with 55 exempt. Hires some recent grads, plus experienced
            engineers (all disciplines, especially ME, EE, CE, structural).
Procedure: Send or email resume to Human Resources
            2690 Cumberland Pkwy, Suite 300, Atlanta GA 30339
            (770) 433-9336; Fax (770) 434-4995
            email resume to: hratlanta@sandwell.com

SCHWEITZER-MAUDUIT INTERNATIONAL (www.schweitzermauduit.com)
Profile: Atlanta-based manufacturer of cigarette papers and other fine specialty
            papers, employing 80 at headquarters, 60 exempt. Seldom hires recent
            grads, and seeks experienced exempt in all areas, especially finance and
            engineering (ChE mostly).
Procedure: Send resume to Human Resources
            100 North Point Center East, Alpharetta GA 30022
            (770) 569-4200; Fax (770) 569-4209

SCIENTIFIC ATLANTA (www.sciatl.com)
Profile: Largest high-tech company headquartered in
            Atlanta, employing more than 3000 (one-half exempt) in several
            divisions here. Corporate human resources recruits for all divisions, and
            seeks numerous backgrounds, entry and experienced, especially
            engineers (EE, ME, CS), MBA's (mktg, finance), accounting/finance,
            and MIS. Job vacancies and application included at web site.
Procedure: Send or email resume to Staffing
            4311 Communications Drive, ATL 30K, Norcross GA 30093
            (770) 903-5000; Fax (770) 236-3099
            email resume to: sa.staffing@sciatl.com

SCIENTIFIC GAMES (www.scigames.com)
Profile: Atlanta-based corporation that is the world's largest printer of lottery
            tickets for state-operated lottery games. Employs 550 in Atlanta,
            including headquarters and the manufacturing facility, with 200 exempt.
            Most needs are for programmers (Stratus) and experienced gravure
            printers for manufacturing.
Procedure: Send resume to Director of Human Resources
            1500 Blue Grass Lakes Pkwy, Alpharetta GA 30201
            (770) 664-3700; Fax (770) 664-3846
            email resume to: dirofrecruiting@scigames.com

SCIENTIFIC RESEARCH CORP. (www.scires.com)

Profile: Atlanta-based, engaged in system design, rapid prototyping, hardware and software integration, test, installation, and maintenance of systems. Employs 95 with 85 exempt in Atlanta. Seeks mostly multi-disciplinary engineers and scientists, especially with advanced technical degrees.

Procedure: Send resume to Human Resources
2300 Windy Ridge Pkwy SE #S-400, Atlanta GA 30339-5665
(770) 859-9161; Fax (770) 989-9438
email resume to: jobs@scires.com

SELIG ENTERPRISES (no web site)

Profile: Atlanta-based property management and parking-lot firm employing 500 here, 40 exempt. Hires recent grads and experienced exempt in accounting and parking lot management, plus experienced property and real estate management.

Procedure: Send resume to personnel
1100 Spring St NE, Suite 550, Atlanta GA 30309
(404) 876-5511; Fax (404) 875-2629

SEROLOGICALS CORP (www.serologicals.com)

Profile: Atlanta-based bio-tech corporation, employing 150 here, 75% exempt. Hires a few entry-level medical techs; Hq staff has exempt needs in all areas, including accounting/finance, medical specialties, MIS (WAN, Novell), etc.

Procedure: Send resume to Human Resources
780 Park North Blvd, #120, Clarkston GA 30021-1900
(404) 294-7700; Fax 404-508-1645
email resume to: HumanResources@serologicals.com

SIEBEL SYSTEMS (www.siebel.com)

Profile: Regional office for international provider of eBusiness applications software.

Procedure: Apply online for specific vacancy
1 Glenlake Pkwy, Atlanta GA 30328
(678) 319-4500; Fax (404)

SIEMENS ENERGY AND AUTOMATION - DISTRIBUTION CENTER
(www.sea.siemens.com)

Profile: One of three US distribution centers for Siemens' products, employing 125 here with 65 exempt. Seeks logistics-related backgrounds, entry and experienced, plus engineering (ME, IE), and IS.

Procedure: Send resume to Human Resources
3130 North Berkeley Lake Rd, Duluth GA 30096
(770) 495-9346; Fax (770) 418-1427

SIEMENS ENERGY AND AUTOMATION – DPD DIV. HQ (www.sea.siemens.com)
Profile: Distribution Products Division manufactures and markets products to
             control and distribute the flow of electricity for the industrial,
             construction, and residential markets. This is the division headquarters,
             employing 260 with 220 exempt. Most hires are ME an EE, both recent
             grad and experienced, plus some needs in marketing, software
             development, accounting/finance, and IS.
Procedure: Send resume to Human Resources
             5400 Triangle Parkway, Norcross GA 30092
             (770) 326-2000 ; Fax (770) 326-2355
             email resume to: cari.engert@sea.siemens.com

SIEMENS ENERGY AND AUTOMATION - HEADQUARTERS (www.sea.siemens.com)
Profile: North American Headquarters for Munich-based Siemens.
             Manufactures and designs electrical and electronic products. Employing
             300 with 250 exempt, headquarters houses accounting/finance and MIS
             (mostly Windows-based) functions only, and seeks entry- and
             experienced-level in those areas.
Procedure: Send resume to Human Resources
             3333 Old Milton Pkwy, Alpharetta GA 30005
             (770) 751-2000; Fax 770-740-3398
             email resume to: ga400career@sea.siemens.com

SIEMENS - RESIDENTIAL PRODUCTS DIVISION ()
Profile: Manufactures residential electrical loadsetters and meters, employing
             700 with 125 exempt, and adding 200 in 1996, mostly non-exempt.
             Hires for experienced exempt in engineering (ME) and manufacturing.
             No entry-level needs.
Procedure: Send resume to Personnel Manager
             2037 Weems Road, Tucker GA 30084
             (770) 939-7230; job line (770) 492-6295; Fax (770) 723-6600

SIMMONS COMPANY (www.simmons.com)
Profile: Atlanta-based manufacturer of bedding, with three facilities in Atlanta
             employing 300 total, 200 exempt; corporate staff nunbers 150 with 90
             exempt. Seeks recent grads for sales and management trainees, and
             experienced exempt in accounting/finance, sales, marketing,
             management, engineering (IE, ME mostly) and MIS (AS 400). This
             office hires for headquarters and the research center; manufacturing has
             their own personnel department.
Procedure: Send resume to Corporate Recruiter
             1 Concourse Parkway, Suite 600, Atlanta GA 30328
             (770) 512-7700; Fax (770) 392-2564
             email resume to: wsmith@simmons.com

SIX CONTINENTS HOTELS (www.sixcontinentshotels.com)
Profile: World's largest single-brand hotel chain, headquartered in Atlanta.
            Employs 1100 with 750 exempt at headquarters. Will seek all types of
            experienced exempt, including accounting/finance, sales, management,
            and Information Technology. This office hires for all corporate
            positions, plus the reservations and data centers.
Procedure: Send resume to Manager of Employment
            3 Ravinia Drive NE, Suite 2000, Atlanta GA 30346
            (770) 604-2000; Fax (770) 604-5548

SMITH, W H USA (www.whsmith.co.uk)
Profile: US Corporate Headquarters of British conglomerate. Owns and operates
            500+ retail gift shops located in airports and hotels nationwide.
            Employs 150 in Atlanta, with 75 exempt, plus managers and sales
            associates in several stores in Atlanta. Hires experienced exempt in
            accounting/finance, distribution, marketing and MIS, plus retail
            specialties (buying, merchandising, etc.).
Procedure: For Store Management, send resume to Director of Stores; for other
            positions, send resume to Employment Administrator
            3200 Windy Hill Road, Suite 1500 West Tower, Atlanta GA 30339
            (770) 952-0705; Fax (770) 661-9618
            email resume to: whsrecruiter@whsmithusa.com

SNAPPER PRODUCTS, INC. (www.snapper.com)
Profile: Atlanta-based manufacturer of outdoor power equipment. Employs 475
            with 75 exempt. Hires numerous recent grads in all areas,
            accounting/finance, manufacturing, engineering and MIS (AS 400)--
            sometimes in non-exempt positions to learn business basics, and then be
            promoted into exempt-level. Hires experienced personnel in all areas,
            especially manufacturing backgrounds.
Procedure: Jobs not on web site. Send resume to HR
            P O Box 777, McDonough GA 30253
            (770) 954-2500; Job line x444; Fax (770) 954-2583

SOLARCOM (www.solarcom.com)
Profile: Atlanta-based remarketer of IBM midrange computers and srvices,
            employing 260 with 130 exempt. Hires pert-time telemarketers and has
            occasional needs for experienced exempt in all areas.
Procedure: Send resume to Human Resources Director
            1 Sun Court, Norcross GA 30092
            (770) 449-6116; Fax (771) 582-7233
            email resume to: recruiting@solarcom.com

SOLUTIA, INC. (www.solutia.com)

Profile: (formerly Monsanto Company) Region office handling sales, customer service, and business fucntions. Employs 70 with 42 exempt. Hires entry-level sales, experienced sales reps, MBA's and customer service.

Procedure: Fax resume to Human Resources
3391 Town Point Dr., Suite 200, Kennesaw GA 30144
(770) 951-7600; Fax (770)951-7719

SOLVAY PHARMACEUTICALS (www.solvay.com)

Profile: Growing clinical research and development center for major pharmaceutical firm, employing 400 here with 300 exempt. Most hires are in pre-clinical, clinical research, and outside sales, generally with relevant experience.

Procedure: Send resume to Human Resources Department
901 Sawyer Road, Marietta GA 30062
(770) 578-9000; Fax (770) 578-5590

SONY ELECTRONICS (www.sony.com)

Profile: Sales and service office employing 150, 75 exempt. Hires no recent grads, but seeks experienced sales and sales support personnel with background in magnetic tape, electronics, or video equipment.

Procedure: Posts openings on Monster.com. Send resume to Personnel
3175-A Northwoods Pkwy, Norcross GA 30071
(770) 263-9888; Fax (770) 441-8870

SOUTHERN COMPANY (www.southernco.com)

Profile: Atlanta-based, owns electrical utilities throughout the Southeast, including Georgia Power, Alabama Power, Gulf Power, Mississippi Power, and Savannah Electric and Power. Conducts hiring for Georgia Power, for which needs are mostly engineering and other technical degrees, both recent grads and experienced exempt. Headquarters provides support functions for operating subsidiaries, and hires recent grads and experienced exempt in numerous areas including engineering, information resources, accounting/finance, PR/communications, and other administrative services. Also has many non-exempt needs, especially in office support, customer service, and line repair. Has 200 engineering co-ops, which are hired through college placement departments, not through this ofice. No job information is included at their web site.

Procedure: All staffing for Georgia Power and Southern Company is conducted thru their East Coast Staffing Center. Unsolicited resumes are not accepted. Hires heavily through campus recruiting for entry positions, and co-ops often fill these positions as well. Otherwise, for both entry and experienced positions, you must check first with the Job Information Line, then respond to a specific opening including the job code for which you are applying. Staffing center is located at

270 Peachtree St, Atlanta GA 30303
(404) 506-5000; (800) 457-2981 Job Info Line; Fax

SOUTHERN ELECTRONICS DISTRIBUTORS (www.sedonline.com)

Profile: Atlanta-based distributor of computers, computer equipment, and cellular equipment, employing 250. Hires entry-level and experienced accounting/finance; also seeks experienced telemarketers in computer sales with backgrounds in computer and cellular phone telemarketing.

Procedure: Job site updated monthly. Send resume to Human Resources
4916 North Royal Atlanta Drive, Tucker GA 30085
(770) 491-8962; Fax (770) 938-1235

SOUTHTRUST BANK OF GEORGIA, NA (www.southtrust.com)

Profile: Birmingham-based bank, operating 85+ branches in Atlanta, employing 1300 with 300 exempt. Hires recent grads and experienced exempt in management and accounting/finance. MIS only at HQ in Alabama.

Procedure: Send resume to Human Resources
2000 RiverEdge Parkway, Atlanta GA 30328
(770) 951-4000; 951-4010 job info line; Fax (770) 951-4287

SOUTHWIRE (www.southwire.com)

Profile: Corporate headquarters for the nation's largest privately held wiremaker. Employs 1800 at this location, with 500 exempt. Will hire co-ops, recent grads and experienced exempt in all areas, including accounting/finance, sales, management, MIS (Unisys A series) and especially engineering (EE, ME, ChE and IE).

Procedure: Send resume to Professional Employment
1 Southwire Drive, Carrollton GA 30119
(770) 832-4242; Fax (770) 832-4355
email resume to: employment@southwire.com

SPRINT CORPORATION (www.sprint.com)

Profile: Third largest long distance telephone carrier, employing 2000 in Atlanta, 900 exempt. Personnel with experience in telecommunications or other large systems (e.g., computers) are needed for marketing and sales positions, plus engineers with network communications experience and MIS (IBM system) professionals.

Procedure: Send resume to Staffing Department (they respond to all resumes)
3100 Cumberland Circle, Atlanta 30339
(770) 859-5000; Fax (770) 859-6288

SPRINT PCS (www.sprintpcs.com)

Profile: Wireless telecommunications carrier, employing 250 in Atlanta. Vacancies in sales/marketing, finance, and IT.

Procedure: Apply online or build online resume, or send resume to personnel

3330 Cumberland Blvd, Atlanta GA 30339
(678) 589-1222; Fax (404)

St. Paul Fire and Marine Insurance (www.stpaul.com)
Profile: Provider of property-liability insurance to businesses and other
organizations. Most needs are for experienced claims adjusters,
underwriters, and account execs.
Procedure: Apply online or send resume to personnel
3097 Satelite Blvd, Ste 600, Duluth GA 30096
(770) 497-5700; Fax (404)

Starband Communications (www.starband.com)
Profile: High-tech firm that designs, manufactures and monitors VSAT
equipment used to provide digital data services via satellite. Seeks
VSAT-related experience, experienced MIS, plus sales and hardware
and software engineers with datacomm and/or circuit design experience.
Procedure: Send or email resume to
840 Franklin Court, Marietta 30067
(770) 426-4261; Fax (770) 514-3447
email resume to: jobs@starband.com

State Farm Insurance Companies (www.statefarm.com)
Profile: Regional office handling support operations for State Farm policy
holders in Georgia. Employs 1900 with 800 exempt. Prefers to hire
entry-level and then promote up; thus, will seek many recent grads for
trainee programs in underwriting, claims, and administration.
Procedure: Send resume to Human Resources Specialist
11350 John Creek Pkwy, Duluth GA 30098
(770) 418-5600; Fax (770) 418-5627
email resume to: jobopps.georgia@statefarm.com

Sterling Commerce (www.stercomm.com)
Profile: Atlanta-based software developer of RemoteWare remote access utilities
that deliver enhanced performance, manageability of all applications for
remote and mobile users who work off-line. Employs 270, mostly
exempt. Seeks experienced technical backgrounds in software
development; uses PC's, LAN. Lists job openings at web site, and can
apply on web or via email.
Procedure: Send resume to Human Resources
3340 Peachtree Road NE, Suite 300, Atlanta GA 30326
404-760-8200; Fax 404-760-8250

Stevens Graphics (www.stevensgraphicsinc.com)
Profile: Subsidiary of BellSouth, second largest printer in Atlanta, and prints
mostly directories, catalogues, and business forms. Employs 375 with

95 exempt. Hires recent grads for manufacturing management, engineering and MIS, and seeks experienced exempt in the same areas (printing experience preferred) plus accounting.

Procedure: Send resume to Human Resources Manager
713 Ralph D. Abernathy Blvd SW, Atlanta GA 30310
(404) 753-1121; Fax

STRATEGIC TECHNOLOGIES (www.strategictech.com)

Profile: Atlanta-based software marketer. Employs 400 in Atlanta, all exempt. Nearly all needs (about 50 each year) are in MIS, some recent computer science grads, but mostly for experienced UNIX and Windows, OS2 systems professionals, experienced C programmers, and relational data base backgrounds.

Procedure: Send resume to Human Resources
3445 Peachtree Road NE, Suite 1400, Atlanta GA 30326
(404) 841-4000; Fax 841-4115

SUNGARD INSURANCE SYSTEMS (www.sungardinsurance.com)

Profile: Atlanta-based insurance systems division of SunGard Financial Systems; develops software for investment and accounting applications in the financial services industry. Employs 105, 100 exempt. Seeks experienced exempt in accounting/finance/investment and MIS (PC-based).

Procedure: Send resume to Recruiting Manager
1357 Hembree Road, Suite 200
, Atlanta GA 30076
(770) 587-6800; Fax (770) 587-6808
email resume to: ccunningham@net.sungard.com

SUNTRUST BANKS, INC. (www.suntrust.com)

Profile: Subsidiary of Atlanta-based SunTrust Banks (see separate listing). Employs 6000 in Atlanta, 2000 exempt. Generally hires for more entry level positions than experienced, and recent grads interested in a banking career can enter one of several training programs. Experienced personnel are hired in all areas, especially accounting/finance, MIS, banking professionals, telecommunications, etc.

Procedure: Send resume to Career Center
303 Peachtree Center Ave, 2nd Floor, Mail Code 0636-G, Atlanta GA 30308
(404) 588-7251 Job Info Line; Fax (877) 266-0777

SUNTRUST ROBINSON-HUMPHREY CAPITAL MARKETS
(www.robinsonhumphrey.com)

Profile: Full-service financial services firm, specializing in the southeast region, selling institutional and individual investment opportunities. Corporate headquartered in Atlanta, and subsidiary of Atlanta-based SunTrust Banks. Employs 600 in Atlanta. Recent MBA grads are hired as Corporate Financial Associates and recent undergrads (usually finance) are hired as Corporate Financial Analysts, a two year training program. More often, recent grads are hired for non-exempt administrative positions (research; sales, trading, and operations assistants) to learn business basics first; they are not hired as brokers, unless they have three years prior sales experience. Broker training program available for individuals with 3+ years sales or entrepreneurial experience.

Procedure: Send resume to Director of Human Resources
3333 Peachtree Road NE, Mezzanine, Atlanta GA 30326
(404) 266-6300; Fax 266-5986
email resume to: careers@rhco.com

SUPER DISCOUNT MARKETS, INC. (D/B/A CUB FOODS) (www.sdm-cub.com)
Profile: Corporate headquarters for franchise operator of 18 Georgia supermarkets. Employs 2100 in Atlanta, 270 exempt. Hires 15± recent grads in supermarket management, MIS (AS 400) and accounting/finance. Seeks experienced supermarket management personnel. Hourly hired at stores.

Procedure: Send resume to Director of Human Resources
420 Thornton Road, Suite 103, Lithia Springs GA 30122
(770) 732-6800 (press 5 for personnel); Fax (770) 941-1334

SWEETHEART CUP (www.sweetheart.com)
Profile: Manufacturing facility for plastic foam products, employing 500 with 30 exempt. Does not hire entry-level exempt, but seeks experienced engineers (ME, ChE) and production managers.

Procedure: Send resume to human Resources
1455 Highway 138 NE, Conyers GA 30013
(770) 483-9556; Fax (770) 918-5572
email resume to: lsphillips@sweetheart.com

SYNAVANT (www.synavant.com)
Profile: Interactive mktg services and e-business software to medical services industry. Employs 400 in Atlanta, all exempt. Nearly all needs are in IS, some recent computer science grads, but mostly for experienced UNIX and Windows, OS2 systems professionals, experienced C++ programmers, and relational database backgrounds.

Procedure: Send resume to Human Resources
3445 Peachtree Road NE, Suite 1400, Atlanta GA 30326
(404) 841-4000; Fax (404) 841-4115

T B S — CORPORATE HEADQUARTERS (www.turner.com; www.turnerjobs.com)

Profile: Headquarters for Turner Broadcasting System, Inc. and its divisions, including CNN, TBS Superstation, TNT, Cartoon Network, CNNfn, CNN Interactive, CNN International, Headline News, the Atlanta Braves, Hawks and Thrashers, and many more. Hires entry and experienced exempt in all areas, permanent and temporary. Posts jobs at www.turnerjobs.com; the day I checked, there were more than 200 jobs available in Atlanta!

Procedure: All Turner subsidiaries conduct hiring through a central staffing department. Best to check job web site and follow directions. Located at 100 International Blvd, CNN Center, Atlanta GA 30303 (404) 827-1700; Fax 827-1600

T B S — ENGINEERING DEPARTMENT ()

Profile: Provides engineering services all TBS companies and employs 265, 25 exempt. Hires 10± recent BS and AS grads (EET mostly) to work in quality control engineering and maintenance. Also needs 8± experienced engineers annually, preferably with broadcast experience.

Procedure: Send resume to Director of Engineering Services 1 CNN Center, P O Box 105366, Atlanta GA 30348 (404) 827-1700; Fax (404) 827-1835

TECHNICAL ASSOCIATION OF THE PULP AND PAPER INDUSTRY (www.tappi.org)

Profile: Atlanta-based international association employing 95 with 50 exempt. Most exempt needs are in marketing, publications, communications, and education, both recent grads and experienced.

Procedure: Send resume to Human Resources 15 Technology Parkway South, Norcross GA 30092 (770) 446-1400; Fax (770) 446-6947 email resume to: hr@tappi.org

TENSAR CORPORATION, THE (www.tensarcorp.com)

Profile: International, Atlanta-based company involved in the production and sale of geosynthetics for structural soil reinforcement technology, environmental applications, and various other uses. Employs 250 with 150 exempt. Nearly all exempt hires are for civil engineers with soil improvement/reinforcement experience, sales and marketing personnel, or for manufacturing engineers with polymer extrusion experience.

Procedure: Job site updated as needed. E-mail resume to Personnel Manager 1210 Citizens Parkway, Morrow GA 30260 (770) 968-3255; Fax (770) 960-0984 email resume to: hr-tet@tensarcorp.com

TJ MAXX (www.tjmaxx.com)

Profile: Largest off-price apparel retailer in US with 600 stores. Employs 900 full- and part-time in Atlanta, including 60 managers. Hires no recent grads, but will hire 25 experienced managers for Atlanta and 70 for the SE; also seeks loss prevention and audit positions. Offers summer internships for college juniors in retail or business management.

Procedure: Send resume to Regional Recruitment Manager
1600 Parkwood Circle, Suite 610, Atlanta GA 30339
(770) 980-1114; Fax (770) 980-1972
email resume to: mtague@tjx.com

TOWERS PERRIN COMPANIES (www.towers.com)

Profile: Fifth largest international consulting firm, specializing in actuarial, insurance, retirement, diversity, compensation, communications, and general management. Employs 300 here, 250 exempt. Atlanta personnel office hires only entry-level, and seeks degrees in finance, economics, math and communications/journalism, plus MBA's. Experienced exempt are hired either through headquarters in NYC or by individual department managers here.

Procedure: Send resume to Human Resources Department
950 E. Paces Ferry Rd NE , Atlanta GA 30326-1119
(404) 365-1600; Fax (404) 365-1662

TOYS 'R' US (www.toysrus.com)

Profile: World's largest toy retailer with nine stores in Atlanta employing 425 (100 exempt) + 500 in warehouse. Exempt needs here are for store mgt and distribution mgt, trainee and experienced.

Procedure: Send resume to Human Resources, or go to their web site careers and email with job source code.
830 Highway 42 South, McDonough GA 30253
(770) 898-5815; Fax (770) 898-3561
email resume to: employment@toysrus.com

TRANSUS INTERMODAL (www.transus.com)

Profile: Southeastern common carrier and transportation service, corporate headquartered in Atlanta. Employs 800 here, 200 salaried. Hires recent grads and experienced personnel for accounting/finance, operations management, sales, MIS (AS 400) and technical school grads.

Procedure: Send resume to Employment Office
2090 Jonesboro Rd, Atlanta GA 30315
(404) 627-1124; Fax 622-5896

TRAVELERS PROPERTY AND CASUALTY COMPANY (www.travelers.com)

Profile: Provider of full range of insurance products for homeowners, auto insurance, and commercial markets, employing 400+ here and hires approximately 20-25 positions annually. Seeks recent grads in insurance and risk management, and experienced in claims, underwriting and customer service. Travelers' products are sold through independent brokers.

Procedure: Job site updated frequently. Email resume to Human Resources, Subject line should indicate "Atlanta Jobs"
4400 North Point Pkwy, Alpharetta GA 30222
(770) 521-3626; Fax (770) 521-3536
email resume to: alpharettaresume@travelers.com

TRX (www.trx.com)

Profile: Atlatna-based travel processing and outsourcing for travel agents, airlines, and corporate clients, employing 300+. Has exempt needs in all corporate functions, including accouting/finance, HR, training, sales/marketing, IT, plus numerous non-exempt support positions.

Procedure: Apply to online vacancies, or email resume for future consideration to
6 West Druid Hills Drive, Atlanta GA 30329
(404) 929-6100; Fax (404) 929-5270
email resume to: hratlanta@trx.com

TYCO HEALTHCARE (www.tyco.com)

Profile: Manufacturer of adult incontinence and feminine hygiene products. Employs 480 with 40 exempt. Seeks both recent grads and experienced exempt in all disciplines when needed.

Procedure: Send resume to Human Resources
1169 Canton Road, Marietta GA 30066
(770) 422-3036; job line (770) 422-3036 x331; Fax (770) 422-4350

U. S. FRANCHISE SYSTEMS (www.usfsi.com)

Profile: Atlanta-based, rapidly expanding hotel company with 900 hotels open or under development. Corporate headquarters employs 75, 62 exempt. Hires both recent grads and experienced exempt in all corporate areas, especially with hotel management experience. Each hotel conducts own hiring for managers.

Procedure: Send resume to personnel
13 Corporate Square, Suite 250, Atlanta GA 30329
(404) 321-4045; Fax (404) 235-7465
email resume to: roberta.weisshaut@usfsi.com

UCB PHARMA (www.ucb-group.com)

Profile: Belgium-owned pharmaceutical and chemical company, with US headquarters in Atlanta employing 900, 800 exempt. Hires recent grads in accounting/finance, general business, and science (bio, chem), and experienced exempt in same areas, including MBA, MS, and PhD level.

Procedure: Job site updated weekly. Send resume to Human Resources
1950 Lake Park Drive, Smyrna GA 30080
(770) 434-6188; Job line (770) 333-6996; Fax (770) 801-3270

UNISYS CORPORATION (www.unisys.com)

Profile: Region headquarters center for sales/marketing, research and development, engineering, and service, employing 400, all exempt. Hires for MIS and computer science backgrounds, both recent grads and experienced, and experienced computer sales reps and information services consultants.

Procedure: Send resume to Planning and Recruiting
5550-A Peachtree Parkway, Norcross GA 30092
(770) 368-6000; Fax (770) 368-6134
email resume to: work@unisys.com

UNITED HEALTHCARE (www.uhc.com)

Profile: Health care and insurance provider, employing 275+ in Atlanta. Hires entry and experienced exempt in numerous areas, including accounting/finance, sales, admin, nursing, customer service, and MIS.

Procedure: Send resume to human resources
2970 Clairmont Road NE, Atlanta GA 30329
(404) 982-8800; Job line: (404) 982-8847; Fax (404) 320-8342

UNITED PARCEL SERVICE (www.ups.com; www.upsjobs.com)

Profile: Number 9 on Fortune Magazine's most admired US firms. UPS has corporate headquarters in Atlanta and employs 2000 at that location, 75% exempt. Although there are needs for experienced exempt, a career with UPS in all areas (accounting/finance, management, engineering, human resources, etc.) often starts in an hourly operations position, such as sorting packages or driving a delivery truck, with promotion into higher positions when an opening occurs. These entry positions are generally filled at the district level, and you may wish to direct your efforts there, rather than at the corporate level. Management positions at the corporate level require a minimum of a bachelor's degree, with most requiring a master's. Corporate job vacancies at www.upsjobs.com

Procedure: Two methods: (1) For entry-level positions, including part-time seasonal, UPS hires extensively through the Georgia Department of Labor, especially the offices in Smyrna and Decatur (see Public Agencies section). (2) Experienced personnel applying for Hq positions can create "job profile" at www.upsjobs.com, and review job vacancies. Or send resume to
990Hammond Drive, Atlanta GA 31146
404-828-6000; 888-967-5877 Job Employment Line; Fax (770) 828-6440

UNITED WAY OF METROPOLITAN ATLANTA (www.unitedwayatlanta.org)

Profile: Non-profit agency, employing 160 with 85 exempt. Most needs are in administration.

Procedure: Jobs site updated when needed. Send resume to human resources
100 Edgewood Ave , Atlanta GA 30303
(404) 527-7200; Fax (404) 527-7354
email resume to: tlimehouse@unitedwayatl.org

UPS SUPPLY CHAIN SOLUTIONS (www.ups-scs.com)
Profile: Subsidiary of UPS that offers a full spectrum of supply chain services
and logistics expertise throughout the world. Most needs require
background in logistics or transportation.
Procedure: Complete online resume, or send resume to
12380 Morris Rd, Alpharetta GA 30005
(678) 746 4100; Fax (404)

VERIZON ENTERPRISE SOLUTIONS (www.verizon.com)
Profile: National headquarters location for Verizon subsidiary that sells, installs
and services telecommunications equipment. Employs 150 here (100
exempt), including district office, plus this office handles staffing needs
nationwide. Growing approx. 30% annually. Seldom hires recent grads,
but seeks experienced exempt in accounting, purchasing, human
resources and other central office support types. No MIS.
Procedure: Send resume to Manager, Human Resources for advertised positions
only. Does not accept unsolicited resumes.
5897 Windward Parkway, Suite 300, Alpharetta GA 30005
(770) 772-5700; Fax (770)
email resume to: jobs@verizon.com

VERIZON WIRELESS (www.verizon.com)
Profile: Provider of cellular communications services to businesses and
individual users. Employs 580 in Atlanta, 175 exempt, and growing
rapidly. Seeks business accoount reps, part-time and full-time retail
sales reps, customer service, engineering, and information services.
Procedure: Send resume to Human Resources Manager
1 Verizon Place, Alpharetta GA 30004
(678) 339-4012; (678) 339-4400 - job line; Fax (404) 257-5081
email resume to: jobs@verizon.com

VERSO TECHNOLOGIES (www.verso.com)
Profile: Atlanta-based developer and marketer of computerized Property
Management Systems to hotels and cruise lines, employing 140. Seeks
experienced exempt with hotel operations experience, plus programmers
(UNIX C) and other MIS.
Procedure: Send resume to Human Resources
400 Galleria Pkwy, Suite 300, Atlanta GA 30339
(770) 612-3500; Fax (770) 951-6880

VIDEO DISPLAY CORP (www.videodisplay.com)
Profile: Atlanta-based manufacturer of cathode ray tubes and electronic optic components, employing 80 in Atlanta, 40 exempt. Most needs are for tech school grads, plus some accounting/finance.
Procedure: Send resume to personnel
1868 Tucker Industrial Blvd, Tucker GA 30084
(770) 938-2080; Fax (770) 493-3903
email resume to: rebecca@videodisplay.com

VISIONARY SYSTEMS (www.visionarysystemsinc.com)
Profile: Atlanta-based provider of marketing, software development, and consulting services using an ASP environment. #15 on Inc's fastest growing private companies.
Procedure: Send or email resume to
550 Pharr Rd NE, Atlanta GA 30305
(404) 504-9006; Fax (404)
email resume to: Careers@VisionarySystemsInc.com

VISITING NURSE HEALTH SYSTEM (http://www.vnhs.org)
Profile: Atlanta-based home health care agency, employing 650 here with 300 exempt. Hires recent grads in administration (accounting/finance, customer service) and seeks many experienced health care backgrounds (pharmacists, nurses, social workers, certified nursing assistants, therapists).
Procedure: Vacancies on ajcjobs.com. Fax resume to personnel
6610 Bay Circle, Suite A, Norcross GA 30071
(404) 936-1052;job line (770) 451-4044; Fax (770) 936-1044

VOLVO OF NORTH AMERICA (www.volvocars.com)
Profile: Southern Region Office employing 45. Most needs are for experienced sales and parts/service reps.
Procedure: Send resume to personnel
1125-A Northbrook Park, Suwanee GA 30174
(770) 995-1675; Fax (770) 995-5355

W S B - TV CHANNEL 2 (www.wsbtv.com)
Profile: Subsidiary of Atlanta-based Cox Enterprises, operates TV Channel 2 (ABC). Employs 190, most of whom are in broadcast positions. Hires no entry-level positions and very rarely has exempt-level administrative positions. Broadcast applicants must have prior experience, internships OK. Hires several interns for summer and school year programs; must be enrolled in college broadcast or journalism program.
Procedure: Hiring is done by department heads, so check web site for specific openings. Send resume with cover letter to
1601 West Peachtree St NE, Atlanta GA 30309

(404) 897-7000; Fax 897-6444

WACHOVIA BANK (www.wachovia.com)
Profile: Largest bank in Georgia, and subsidiary of Charlotte, NC-based Wachovia (formerly First Union), one of the largest bank holding companies in the Southeast. Operates 100+ branches in the Atlanta area. Conducts campus recruiting with corporate human resources department, and will hire 20 recent grads for management training classes beginning in January, May and September. Will also seek 40± experienced personnel, including accountants and banking professionals.
Procedure: Email or send resume to Human Resources
P O Box 740074, Personnel Mail Code 9048 (Located at 999 Peachtree St NE, Suite 1050, but use the P O box for mail.), Atlanta GA 30374
(404) 827-7119 HR Dept.; (800) 386-4473 job info line; Fax 827-7902
email resume to: apply.careers@wachovia.com

WAFFLE HOUSE (www.wafflehouse.com)
Profile: Atlanta-based operator of restaurants, employing 250 in headquarters (200 exempt) plus stores. Seeks many Management Trainees and assistants for store operations, plus other headquarters staff personnel.
Procedure: Send resume to Vice President People
5986 Financial Drive NW, Norcross GA 30071
(770) 729-5700; job line (770) 729-5809; Fax (770) 729-5834

WAGA-TV (www.fox5atlanta.com)
Profile: Fox affiliate, channel 5. Has needs in sales, experienced broadcasters, and other corporate areas. Offers internships in Community Affairs, News, Weather, Sports, Production, Sales, Graphics, Promotions, and Human Resources.
Procedure: Send resume and non-returnable tape (if applicable) to Human Resources
1551 Briarcliff Road, NE, Atlanta GA 30306
(404) 875-5555; Fax (404) 724-4426
email resume to: hratlanta@foxtv.com

WASHINGTON MUTUAL (www.wamu.com)
Profile: Rapidly growing banking and finance company, with 50 branches in metro-Atlanta. Seeks entry and experienced exempt in all areas of banking, plus mortgage backgrounds.
Procedure: Apply online or send resume to Recruitment Center
340 Interstate North Pkwy, Ste 160, Atlanta GA 30339
(770) 661-8502; Fax (404)

WAUSAU INSURANCE COMPANIES (www.libertymutual.com)

Profile: SE region headquarters for sixth largest US commercial property and casualty insurance company, employing 325 in SE with 180 exempt (170 in Atlanta, 85 exempt). Seeks a few recent grads in business, accounting, and risk management, but most current needs are for experienced risk underwriters, environmental engineers, and sales reps.

Procedure: Send resume to Human Resources
            4425 Alexander Drive, Stuie 100, Alpharetta GA 30022
            678-566-0600; Fax 770-667-6014

WEATHER CHANNEL, THE (www.weather.com)

Profile: 24-hr international weather network, headquartered in Atlanta. Employees 800 with 550 exempt. Employment opportunities in IS, media/cable TV, sales/mktg, meteorology, and corporate operations.

Procedure: Best to review vacancies at their web site (www.weather.com/jobs) and then respond to specific opening. Does not accept resumes via USPO.
            300 interstate North Parkway, Atlanta GA 30339
            (770) 226-0000; ask for job line and follow instructions; Fax (770) 226-2959
            email resume to: jobs@weather.com

WELLSTAR HEALTH SYSTEM (www.wellstar.org)

Profile: Five-hospital health care system and 60+ physician proactices employing 8000 with 30% exempt. Hires medical personnel, especially nurses and therapists, plus some experienced accounting, administration, MIS, environmental techs, dietary and other support positions..

Procedure: Send resume to Human Resources
            805 Sandy Plains Pd NE, Marietta GA 30339
            (770) 792-7600; Fax (770) 792-4976

WENDY'S OLD FASHIONED HAMBURGERS (www.wendys.com)

Profile: Fourth-largest fast food chain in the world, Wendy's operates 64 units in Atlanta. Atlanta office employs 50, all exempt-level. Plans to hire 25 recent grads and 125 experienced exempt into operations management. This office hires for Georgia and Florida.

Procedure: Send resume to Human Resources Representative
            375 Franklin Road, Suite 400, Marietta GA 30067
            (770) 425-9778; x109 Job Line; Fax (770) 421-2118

WESTWAYNE INC. (www.westwayne.com)

Profile: Atlanta-headquartered and largest privately-owned advertising agency in Atlanta. Employs 170 in Atlanta, 35 exempt, and hires only experienced advertising professionals. Seldom needs accounting or MIS.

Procedure: Send resume to Personnel
            1100 Peachtree St NE, Atlanta GA 30309
            (404)347-8700; Fax 347-8919

WGCL-TV (www.cbs46.com)
Profile: Atlanta's CBS affiliate. Numerous vacancies for experienced broadcasters.
Procedure: Send resume and demo tape where applicable to Human Resources Mgr
425 14th Street NW, Atlanta GA 30318
(404) 325-4646; Fax (404) 327-3075

WHEREHOUSE MUSIC (www.wherehouse.com)
Profile: Retailer of records, tapes and videos, operating 300+ stores in the Southeast, including 60+ in Atlanta. Eastern Division office employs 20, most exempt. Hires Management Trainees and experienced retail management, 50+/year, for several SE cities, including Atlanta.
Procedure: Send resume to Human Resources
2155 Post Oak Tritt Road NE, Marietta GA 30062
(678) 560-4320; Fax 678-560-4351

WINN-DIXIE SUPERMARKETS (www.winndixie.com)
Profile: Division office and warehouse for largest supermarket chain in the SE, third largest in Atlanta, operating 68 stores here. Office here employs 50 with 30 exempt. Recent grads are hired mostly for mangement training positions (BBA best but others OK). Winn-Dixie promotes heavily from within. MIS function at Hq in Jacksonville, FL.
Procedure: Send resume to Human Resources Manager
5400 Fulton Industrial Blvd, Atlanta GA 30336
(404) 346-2400; Fax

WITNESS SYSTEMS (www.witness.com)
Profile: Atlanta-based, provides a business-driven multimedia recording, performance analysis and e-learning management solutions, employing 280. Most exempt needs in accounting/finance, IT, and training.
Procedure: Fax or email resume to
300 Colonial Center Pkwy, Roswell GA 30076
(770) 754-1900; Fax (770) 754-8729
email resume to: jobs-atl@witness.com

WORLDSPAN TRAVEL AGENCY INFORMATION SERVICES (www.worldspan.com)
Profile: World's second-largest travel reservations system, based in Atlanta, and employing 1800. Seeks experienced exempt in all areas, including accounting/finance and marketing, and especially programmers (IBM, TPM), airline background ideal.
Procedure: Send resume to Human Resources
300 Galleria Pkwy, Atlanta GA 30339
(770) 563-7400; jobline x1; Fax (770) 563-7892

WXIA-TV (www.11alive.com)

Profile: Atlanta NBC affiliate. Numerous openings for experienced broadcasters in reporting, editing, writing, and sales; occasional need in web content and IT. Internships available in News, Promotion, Sports and Web.

Procedure: Email resume or send to Human Resources
1611 West Peachtree Street NE, Atlanta GA 30309
(404) 892-1611; Fax (404)
email resume to: Jobs@11alive.com (no attachments)

Y K K USA (www.ykkamerica.com)

Profile: Atlanta-based, world's largest manufacturer of zippers, employing 100 here with 25 exempt. Most exempt needs are for experienced sales reps.

Procedure: Send resume to personnel
1306 Cobb Industrial Dr, Marietta GA 30066
(770) 427-5521; Fax 770-422-8527

YAMAHA MOTOR MANUFACTURING CORP. (www.yamaha.com)

Profile: Manufacturing facility that makes golf cars, atv's and water vehicles. Employs 600 with 320 exempt. Hires both recent grads and experienced exempt in accounting, manufacturing and engineering (mostly ME, some IE).

Procedure: Send resume with cover letter indicating the specific discipline for which you are applying, to Human Resources
1000 Georgia Hwy 34, Newnan GA 30265
(770) 254-4000; Fax (770) 254-4041

YOKOGAWA CORPORATION OF AMERICA (www.yca.com)

Profile: Atlanta-based joint venture company, supplies advanced instrumentation and control systems for continuous batch and discrete process industries; and is involved in the design, manufacture, sales, and service of industrial control products, and sales and support of Distributed Control Systems (DCS). Employs 320 in Atlanta (685 nationwide), with 200 exempt. Most needs are for engineers (ChE, EE, ME) with 3-5 years experience in process control instrumentation, control engineering, DCS engineering, and/or Process Control Sales/Marketing; experienced accountants, manufacturing managers and MIS (IBM and HP).

Procedure: Jobs updated monthly. Email resume to Employee Relations Specialist
2 Dart Road, Newnan GA 30265-1040
(770) 254-0400; Fax (770) 253-8174
email resume to: beth.styron@yca.com

YUM! BRANDS (www.yum.com)

Profile: Parent company of Pizza Hut, Taco Bell, and KFC with hundreds of restaurants in the Atlanta area. Many needs for management, trainee and experienced.

Procedure: For quicker attention, fax or e-mail resume direct to Staffing at Atlanta Region Office, or apply online
675 Mansell Rd, Suite 200, Roswell GA 30076
(404) 770-990-4000; Fax (770) 552-1739
email resume to: jason.hughes@yum.com

ZEP MANUFACTURING COMPANY (www.zepmfg.com)

Profile: Corporate headquarters in Atlanta, unit of Atlanta-based Acuity Brands (see listing). Manufactures and sells specialty chemicals, cleaning agents and agricultural chemicals, primarily for the hospitality, health care and maintenance industries. Employs 450 in Atlanta + 175 in Smyrna office, with 325 total exempt. Hires recent grads in accounting/finance, sales, engineering (ChE and ME), operations, information systems, R&D, and management training. Seeks experienced personnel in accounting/finance, sales, manufacturing management, distribution, engineering, MIS (HP), and laboratory assistants and chemists. Has interns in Chemical Engineering.

Procedure: Send resume to Manager of Employment
1310 Seaboard Industrial Blvd, Atlanta GA 30318
(404) 352-1680; ask for job line; Fax 404-603-7764
email resume to: webmaster@zepmfg.com

Updates to these companies and many more, plus links to more than 500 companies and their web sites are available on www.ajobs.com. The site for updates is password protected, so have your copy of _Atlanta Jobs_ available.

Appendix D

ATLANTA PERSONNEL AGENCIES

Permanent Employment Agencies

Most of these are members of the Georgia Association of Personnel Services, but as I stated in Chapter IV, many good agencies are not members of the association, and so I urge you to follow my suggestions in choosing a personnel agency. Refer back to "Chapter IV, Tool #4: Personnel Agencies."

Not all agencies represent only fee paid positions, so I recommend you ask the agency on you first contact wheat their fee policy is.

Should you have a complaint regarding the ethics of a specific agency, you may seek redress through the Georgia Association of Personnel Services. Members of GAPS supposedly adhere to a code of ethics and you can register your complaint by calling their Atlanta office at (770) 952-3178, or contact them online through ajobs.com

Temporary Employment Agencies

Many temporary agencies have more that one location, some agencies even have twenty or more offices in the Atlanta area. For that reason, I have not listed every location and you will need to check your phone directory for the location nearest you, or call the one I have listed and ask for the s closest office.

Should you have problems with a temporary agency, you can reach their professional association, Georgia Staffing Association, at (770) 392-1411.

PERMANENT EMPLOYMENT

ACCOUNTANTS & BKKPRS
1841 Montreal Road, Suite 212
Tucker, GA 30084
(770)938-7730; fax (770) 938-7826
actg, book, credit, exec, fin, temp

ACCOUNTANTS ONE, INC.
1870 Independence Square, Suite C
Atlanta, GA 30338
(770) 395-6969; fax (770) 395-0398
actg, book, fin, temp-to-perm

ACCOUNTING ALTERNATIVES
1200 Ashwood Parkway, Suite 190
Atlanta, GA 30338
(770) 671-9647; fax (770) 671-1341
actg, book, entry, fin, staff, temp

ACCOUNTING SOLUTIONS
1050 Crown Pointe Pkwy, Suite 1640
Atlanta, GA 30338
(770) 352-0010; fax (770) 352-0888
actg, bank, comp (IT), credit, entry,
exec, fin

ACT 1 TECHNICAL SVCS
400 Embassy Row, Suite 570
Atlanta, GA 30328
(770) 522-9880; fax (770) 522-0618
comtec, comp, hi tech, tech

A.D. & ASSOCIATES
5589 Woodsong Drive, Suite 100
Atlanta, GA 30338-2933
(770) 393-0021; fax (770) 393-9060
actg, data, exec, hi tech, mkt, sales

ADMINISTRATIVE SOLUTIONS
PO Box 536
Fayetteville, GA 30214
(770) 460-7280; fax (770) 460-7262

adm, cus ser, hr, legal, oa

ALLISON ASSOCIATES
550 Pharr Road Ne, Suite 207
Atlanta, GA 30305
(404)233-8836; fax (404) 233-3287
actg, cus srv, oa, ofc-st&sup, sec,temp

AMERICA EMPLOYMENT
1950 Spectrum Circle, Suite 400
Atlanta, GA 30067
(770) 980-3401; fax (770) 919-2039
cus ser, fin (trnee), legal support, mfg,
oa, sales

ANITA G. FREEDMAN, INC
3190 Northeast Expressway, Ste 210
Atlanta, GA 30341
(770)458-0400; fax (770) 263-7361
actg (bk)(h),adm (mktg, hr,
adm,exec)(h) cus ser, it(h),oa, ofc-sup

ARGENTA FINANCIAL
P.O. Box 1566
Fayetteville, GA 30214
(770) 599-1941; fax (770) 599-1447
actg, exec, fin, intl, mfg

ASHLEY-BURNS GROUP,
900 Old Roswell Lakes,#220
Roswell, GA 30076
(770)650-0056; fax (770) 650-5960
const, eng, full, lgl, mfg, secrt

ASK GUY TUCKER, INC.
4990 High Point Rd.
Atlanta, GA 30342
(404) 303-7177; fax (404) 303-0136
adv, multi, pr

ASK STAFFING
Suite 204, 3327 Hwy 120
Duluth, GA 30096-3339

(770) 813-8947; fax (770) 813-8376
comp

ATC HEALTHCARE SVCS
2141 Kingston Court, Suite 110-A
Marietta, GA 30067
(770) 991-2515; fax (770) 991-1557
adm, health, med, oa

ATWATER CONSULTING, INC
5179 Browning Way
Liburn, GA 30047
(770)806-0864; fax (770) 925-8739
full svc

BANKPRO
3812 Cumberland Court
Lithonia, GA 30038
(770) 987-5322; fax (770) 987-8834
bank

BASILONE-OLIVER EXEC SCH
1080 Holcomb Bridge Rd, Bldg 200
Suite 130,. Roswell, GA 30076
(770)649-0553; fax (770)649-0565
actg(h), dist, eng (h), fin, mfg, oper, qc

BELL OAKS COMPANY
3390 Peachtree Road, Suite 1124
Atlanta, GA 30326
(404) 261-2170; fax (404) 261-4885
actg, comp, eng, fin, mfg, sales

BOLTON GROUP
3500 Piedmont Rd NE, Ste 215
Atlanta, GA 30342
(404)228-4280; fax (404)228-2060
actg, eng, exec, fin, it, rs

BOWSER SCIENTIFIC ASSOC
3208 Wicks Creek Trail
Marietta, GA 30062
(770) 977-6658; fax (770) 977-4742
IT, med (device, diag), pharm (no
sales), biotech

BRADLEY-MORRIS, INC.
1701 Barrett Lakes Blvd., Suite 280
Kennesaw, GA 30144
(770) 794-8318; fax (770) 794-8242
jmo, mfg, eng, oper

BRADSHAW & ASSOCIATES
1850 Parkway Place, Suite #420
Marietta, GA 30067
(770) 426-5600; fax (770) 993-6777
chem, dist (logistics), eng, a/f, mgt,
mfg, sales

BROCK & ASSOCIATES
3190 Northeast Expressway, Suite 210
Atlanta, GA 30341
(404) 525-2525; fax (770) 454-8292
actg, adm, book, ofc-sup, secrt, wp

BUSINESS PROF.GROUP
3490 Piedmont Rd., Suite 212
Atlanta, GA 30305
(404) 262-2577; fax (404) 262-3463
eng, entry (0-2 yrs exp, all)

C-PECK COMPANY
169 Interlochen Drive
Atlanta, GA 30342
(404) 843-3183; fax (404) 255-9359
ins, mgt

CALVERT MEDICAL ASSOC
5304 Panola Industrial Blvd, Ste O
Decatur, GA 30035-4065
(770)322-9131; fax (770)322-8698
phy(int & emerg med), staff, temp

CHAMBERLAIN ASSOCIATES
1000 Johnson Ferry Rd, SteE-200
Marietta, GA 30068
(678)560-8085; fax (678)560-8622

CHRIS KAUFFMAN & CO
P.O. Box 53218

Atlanta, GA 30355
(404) 233-3530; fax (404) 262-7960
exec, food, hosp, mkt, pd, rest, rs

CHRISTOU & ASSOCIATES
1401 Johnson Ferry Rd., Bldg. E47,
Suite 328
Marietta, GA 30062-8115
(770) 565-8998; fax (770) 565-2522
comp (contract & perm)

CLAREMONT-BRANAN
1298 Rockbridge Road, Suite B
Stone Mountain, GA 30087
(770) 925-2915; fax (770) 925-2601
arch, eng (consulting only), int des

COMMONWEALTH CONSULTS.
5064 Roswell Rd., Suite B-101
Atlanta, GA 30342
(404) 256-0000; fax (404) 256-3625
comp (sales, consulting, mgt),data

COMPUTER SEARCH
P.O. Box 8403
Atlanta, GA 31106-0403
(404) 231-0965; fax (404) 607-0902
comp

CONSULTING RESOURCE
100 Galleria Parkway, Suite 400
Atlanta, GA 30339
(404) 240-5550; fax (404) 240-5552
comtec, comp, data, mgt, tele

CORP. DEVELOPMENT SVCS
400 Perimeter Ctr Terrace, Suite 900
Atlanta, GA 30346
(770) 392-4295; fax (770) 392-4297
entry (mkt, mgmt, comp, eng, int'l)

CORP. SEARCH
47 Perimeter East, Suite 260
Atlanta, GA 30346
(770) 399-6205; fax (770) 399-6416

all

DATA MANAGEMENT & STAFF
3490 Piedmont Road, Ste 310
Atlanta, GA 30305
(404)233-0925; fax (404)231-9778
comp, IT

DDS STAFFING/
MEDICAL STAFFING
9755 Dogwood Rd. Suite 200
Roswell, GA 30075
(770) 998-7779; fax (770) 552-0176
credit, dental, med, ofc-st, temp

DENISE HASTY & ASSOC
430 River Close
Roswell, GA 30075
(770) 992-1069; fax (770) 992-1070
adm, oa, ofc-st, out, secrt

DELTA STAFFING
1002 Virginia Ave., Suite 100
Atlanta, GA 30354
(404) 715-4300; fax (404) 715-4002
adm, comtec,cus ser, tech, travel

DIALOGUE CONS. GROUP
782 Bayliss Drive, Ste C
Marietta, GA 30068
(770)579-6050; fax (770)536-4072
comp, exec, fin, sales(software), staff

DISCOVER STAFFING
12850 State Hwy 9 Ste 1700
Alpharetta, GA 30004
(678)393-9313; fax (678)393-8898
adm, cuse ser, oa, st/sup, tech, temp

DOCTOR'S CHOICE, INC.
5250-A Highway 9
Alpharetta, GA 30004
(770) 475-0504; fax (770) 475-1117
med (med office staff, clinical, admin)

366

DON RICHARD ASSOCIATES
3475 Lenox Rd., N.E., Suite 210
Atlanta, GA 30326
(404) 231-3688; fax (404) 364-0124
actg, book, fin, temp

DOSHAN & ASSOCIATES
1980 Annwicks Drive
Marietta, GA 30062
(770) 977-7482; fax (770) 578-4670
comtec, comp, data, exec, hi tech, tech, tele

DSA - DIXIE SEARCH ASSOC
501 Village Trace, Building 9
Marietta, GA 30067
(770) 850-0250; fax (770) 850-9295
food, rest

DUNHILL SEARCH OF WEST ATLANTA
2110 Powers Ferry Rd., Suite 110
Atlanta, GA 30339
(770) 952-0009; fax (770) 952-9422
mfg, eng, hr, pkg, mat-mgt, pur, qc

EDEN GROUP, INC.
1837 Mallard Lake Drive
Marietta, GA 30068
(770) 640-9577; fax (770) 993-9268
inv, inv sales

SOLIANT HEALTH
100 Crescent Centre Pkwy, Suite 360
Tucker, GA 30084
(770) 908-2113; fax (770) 908-2203
health, med

EMERGING TECH SEARCH
1080 Holcomb Bridge Rd., Bldg. 200, Suite 305
Roswell, GA 30076
(770) 643-4994; fax (770) 643-4991
IS (programmer to v.p.), hi tech, tele
actg, cus ser, eng, exec, mfg, print

EVANS & JAMES EXEC SRCH
P.O. Box 862232
Marietta, GA 30062
(770) 992-4299; fax (770) 992-4496
chem, pkg, plastics

EXECUME PLACEMENTS, INC
3400 Peachtree Rd, NE Ste 549
Atlanta, GA 30326
(404)233-1467; fax (404)262-3814
res

EXECUTIVE PLACEMENT SVCS
1117 Perimeter Ctr West, #302 East
Atlanta, GA 30338
(770) 396-9114; fax (770) 393-3040
game, hosp, retail

EXECUTIVE STRATEGIES
11205 Alpharetta Highway, Suite C
Roswell, GA 30075
(770) 552-3085
comp (mis), exec, fin, mgt

GCB - EXECUTIVE SEARCH
3655 Canton Highway
Marietta, GA 30066
(770) 517-9017; fax (770) 517-9016
actg, bank, fin, health, real, tele

GEORGIA TEMP, INC
133 Peachtree St NE, Ste 2300
Atlanta, GA 30303
(404)652-5493; fax (404)656-1013
actg, adm, oa, ofc, sup, tech, temp

GEORGE MARTIN ASSOC
12 Executive Park Drive, N.E.
Atlanta, GA 30329
(404) 325-7101; fax (404) 633-3888
comp, fin

G H & I, RECRUITING
1200 Ashford Pkwt, Ste 300

Atlanta, GA 30338
(770)352-9374; fax (770)395-0694
acctg, bkkpg, fin, hr, mkt, oper, sales

GRAPHIC RESOURCES
2265 Roswell Rd., Suite 100
Marietta, GA 30062-2974
(770) 509-2295; fax (770) 509-2296
multi, pkg, print (sales & mgt)

GRAYSON INS. RECRUITERS
8097-B Roswell Road
Atlanta, GA 30350
(770)350-7856; fax (770)350-7589
Ins (p&c)

GREENSEARCH
6690 Roswell Rd., Suite 310-157
Atlanta, GA 30328
(770) 392-1771; fax (770) 392-1772
agr, arch, const, hr, mgt, sales

GROBARD & ASSOC
2370 Ridge Bluff Lane
Suwanee, GA 30024
(770) 271-1828; fax (770) 271-4026
health, sales

G.T. PROF EXECUTIVE SRCH
2775 S. Main St, Ste G
Kennesaw, GA 30144
(770)420-7440; fax (770)420-7126
comp, exec, hi tech, sales, staff, tech

HIRE POWER STAFFING
3525 Piedmont Rd
7 Piedmont Ctr, Suite 300
Atlanta, GA 30305
(404) 298-5520; fax (404) 298-7637
book, health, ins, med, ofc-sup, secrt

H&A CONSULTING, INC.
875 Old Roswell Road, F-100
Roswell, GA 30076
(770) 998-0099; fax (770) 993-7406

comp (contract, perm)

HR SOLUTIONS
400 Perimeter Ctr Terr, Suite 900
Atlanta, GA 30346
(770) 804-6400; fax (770) 804-6401
hr

HUEY GERALD ASSOC
3636 Autumn Ridge Pkwy, Suite 100
Marietta, GA 30066
(770) 973-8944; fax (770) 977-8837
comp (is)

HYGUN GROUP, INC.
P.O. Box 70635
Marietta, GA 30007-0635
(770) 973-0838; fax (770) 973-0877
eng (civil, trans, traffic, env)

INSURANCE OVERLOAD SYS
5901 P'tree-Dunwoody, Bldg C # 35
Atlanta, GA 30328
(770)668-9991; fax (770)668-0255
ins

INSURANCE PERSONNEL
8097-B Roswell Road
Atlanta, GA 30350
(770) 730-0701; fax (770) 730-0703
ins (p&c, l&h, emp benefits)

INT'L TRNG &PLACEMENT
770 Old Roswell Place, Suite J 100B
Roswell, GA 30076
(770)399-0462; fax (770)522-0452
actg, div, draf, eng, exer, hr, ind, intl,
mat-mgt, mfg, out, pd, plastics, qc

INVESEARCH
750 Hammond Drive Building6,
Suite 100
Atlanta, GA 30328
(404)255-8822; fax (404) 236-0300
actg(h)(payro(h), adm, bank, book, fin

IPR GROUP, INC.
8097-B Roswell Rd.
Atlanta, GA 30350
(770) 235-9429; fax (770)
hr

ISC OF ATLANTA, INC.
4350 Georgetown Square, Suite 707
Atlanta, GA 30338
(770) 458-4180; fax (770) 458-4131
actg, eng, exec, fin, mfg, pharm, phy,

IT INTELLECT, INC
1026 Towne Lake Hills East
Woodstock, GA 30189
(77)926-1674, fax (770)926-8764
comp(h), data, hi tech(h), intl, tech

JACKIE GLOVER ASSOC
1150 Lake Hearn Drive, Suite 200
Atlanta, GA 30342-1506
(404) 250-1538; fax (404) 250-1222
book, oa, ofc-st, ofc-sup, secrt, wp

JAG GROUP, THE
860 First Union Plaza
999 Peachtree Street
Atlanta, GA 30309
(404) 874-9910; fax (404) 874-8446
comtec, comp, data, hitech, tele

JAN SEARCH GROUP
315 Gorham Close, Suite 310
Alpharetta, GA 30022
(770) 642-1926; fax (770) 642-9326
ins, sales

JES SEARCH FIRM, INC.
3475 Lenox Rd., Suite 970
Atlanta, GA 30326
(404) 262-7222; fax (404) 266-3533
comp (information technology), tech

JUDGE, INC
2500 Northwinds Pkwy, Suite 300
Alpharetta, GA 30004
(678) 297-0800; fax (678) 297-9014
dist, eng, food, mfg, retail, sales, trans

KEY BUSINESS SOLUTIONS
Alpharetta, GA 30022
(770) 619-0438; fax (770) 619-0439
cus ser, hitech, mgt, mkt, sales, tele

K. MURPHY & ASSOCIATES
2557 Burnt Leaf Lane
Decatur, GA 30033
(404) 315-9859; fax (404) 315-9918
eng, env, risk, safe

CORP SOLUTIONS
6 Piedmont Center, Suite 210
Atlanta, GA 30305
(404)816-6911; fax (404)816-8631
actg, adm, cus ser, oa, ofc-st, ofc-sup

LPH PROSEARCH
P.O. Box 813596
Smyrna, GA 30081
(770) 384-1022; fax (770) 384-1022
career, hosp, mgt, rest, res, retail, rs

LUCAS GROUP
3384 Peachtree Road, Suite 700
Atlanta, GA 30326
(404) 239-5620; fax (404) 239-5688
actg, fin, jmo, mkt, sales

MANAGEMENT DECISIONS
4940 Peachtree Indus Blvd., Suite 310
Norcross, GA 30071
(770) 416-7949; fax (770) 416-7323
comp, tech

MANPOWER
3175 Satellite Blvd, Ste 110, Bldg600
Duluth, GA 30096
(770)622-8148; fax (770)623-0442

cus ser, full, ind, ofc-st, staff, tech ,
temp

MED PRO PERSONNEL, INC.
1955 Cliff Valley Way, Suite 116
Atlanta, GA 30329
(404) 633-8280
med (temp & perm)

MERIDIAN HEALTHCARE
24 Perimeter Center East, Suite 2414
Atlanta, GA 30346
(770) 351-0500; fax (770) 351-0400
health, med

MILLENIUM TECH SOLUTIONS
5825 Glenridge Dr, Bld3, Ste101
Atlanta., GA 30342
(404)250-6514; fax (404)843-9344
comp, comtec, hi tech, intl, staff, tech,
tele

MILLER RAY & HOUSER
3060 Peachtree Rd., NW, Suite 800
Atlanta, GA 30305
(404) 365-1400; fax (404) 365-1410
actg, book, exec, fin, oa, ofc-sup, secrt

MORE PERSONNEL SVCS
4501 Circle 75 Parkway, Suite A-1190
Atlanta, GA 30339
(770) 955-0885; fax (770) 955-0767
all: cus ser, entry, fin, ins, mgt, sales

MSI CONSULTING
6151 Powers Ferry Rd., Suite 545
Atlanta, GA 30339
(770) 850-6465; fax (770) 850-6468
actg, comp

MSI PERIMETER ATLANTA
1050 Crown Pointe Pkwy, Suite 100
Atlanta, GA 30338
(770) 394-2494; fax (770) 394-2251
const, eng, mfg

MSI INTERNATIONAL
245 Peachtree Center Ave., N.E.
2500 Marquis One Tower
Atlanta, GA 30303
(404) 659-5050; fax (404) 659-7139
actg, bank, const, fin, med

NELL RICH & ASSOCIATES
P.O. Box 6363
Marietta, GA 30065
(770) 974-7567; fax (770) 974-7567
const, fin, real (dev)

OSI - OLIVER SEARCH
P.O. Box 81092
Conyers, GA 30013
(770) 760-7661; fax (770) 760-7729
food (mfg, sales, mkt), sr&d

OEM TECS, INC.
890-F Atlanta Street, suite 231
Roswell, GA 30075
(678) 461-3452; fax (678)461-3462
metal (die casting & fabrication), pkg,
plastics

OMNI RECRUITING GROUP
1950 Spectrum Circle, Suite A-405
Marietta, GA 30067
(770) 988-2788; fax (770) 988-2789
hr (recruiters, managers, exec), sales

PACES PERSONNEL SVCS
235 Peachtree Street, N.E., Suite 217
Atlanta, GA 30303
(404) 688-5307; fax (404) 688-5312
secrt - paralegal (exec sec), nurse

PATHFINDERS, INC.
229 Peachtree Street, N.E., Suite 1500
Atlanta, GA 30303
(404) 688-5940; fax (404) 688-9228
oa, ofc-sup, secrt

PEACHTREE PEOPLEWARE
4351 Shackleford Rd.
Norcross, GA 30093
(770) 564-5585; fax (770) 564-5584
comtec, comp, eng (sw/hw), mkt

PERFECT SEARCH
1100 Circle 75 Parkway, Suite 950
Atlanta, GA 30339
(770) 226-0055; fax (770) 226-0303
actg, adm, book, cus ser, hr, ins, mgt,

PERIMETER PLACEMENT
24 Perimeter Cnt E. , Ste 247
Atlanta, GA 30346
(770)393-0000; fax (770)393-4370
actg, oa, ofc-st, ofc-sup, secrt

PERSONALIZED MGT ASSOC
1950 Spectrum Circle, Suite B-310
Marietta, GA 30067-6059
(770) 916-1668; fax (770) 916-1429
exec, food, hosp, hr, rest, retail, sales

P.J. REDA & ASSOCIATES
1955 Cliff Valley Way, Suite 117
Atlanta, GA 30329
(404) 325-8812; fax (404) 325-8850
hospitality & food svc mgmt

PROGRESSIVE PERSONNEL
Two Midtown Plaza, Suite 1625
1349 W. Peachtree St., N.E.
Atlanta, GA 30309
(404) 870-8240; fax (404) 249-9014
legal (support - temp & perm)

PRO STAFF
1349 W. P'tree, 2 Midtown Pl, # 1880
Atlanta, GA 30309
(404) 898-0370; fax (404) 898-1788
actg, comp, cus ser , IT, ofc-st, secrt

QUANTUM SEARCH, INC
3235 Satelliite Blvd, Bldg300, Ste300

Duluth, GA 30096
(770)291-2118; fax (770)291-2119
actg, exec, fin, health, hr, med, oper

RANNOU & ASSOCIATES
1900 The Exchange, Suite 370
Atlanta, GA 30339
(770) 956-8225; fax (770) 951-2362
pkg (corrugated industry)

RESOURCE 360
3081 Holcomb Bridge Road Suite A-1
Norcross, GA 30071
(770)734-9943; fax (770)724-0443
comp, fin'acct, hi tech (h), hr, tech

RICHARD LEWIS &ASSOC
1511 Old Mill Crossing, Ste 200
Marietta, GA 30062
(678)498-4000; fax (678)498-4000
actg, bank, fin, inv, mor

RIGHT CHOICE STAFFING
294 S. Main St, Ste 100
Alpharetta, GA 30201
(770)664-8790; fax (770)664-7649
exec, food, oa, hosp. rest, temp

ROWLAND MT. ASSOCIATES
4 Executive Park Northeast, Suite 100
Atlanta, GA 30329
(404) 325-2189; fax (404) 321-1842
sales, mkt

SALES GROUP, THE
3000 Northwoods Pkwy #285
Norcross, GA 30071
(678) 421-1950; fax (770)
sales

SANFORD ROSE ASSOCS.
One Medlock Crossing, Suite 204
9650 Ventana Way
Alpharetta, GA 30022
(770) 232-9900; fax (770) 232-1933

comp, mkt, tele (wireless: sale, mgmt)

SCI OF ATLANTA, INC.
1874 Independence Square, Suite B
Atlanta, GA 30338
(770) 396-7788; fax (770) 396-7803
chem (sales), comp, HVAC, env, med

SNELLING PERSONNEL SVC
3555 Koger Blvd, Suite 370
Duluth, GA 30096
(770) 381-2838; fax (77)381-0631
adv, full (h), oa, secrt, temp
SOFTWARE SEARCH
2163 Northlake Pkwy, Suite 100
Tucker, GA 30084
(770) 934-5138; fax (770) 939-6410
comp, hi tech

SONDRA SEARCH
P.O. Box 101
Roswell, GA 30077
(770) 552-1910; fax (770) 552-7340
sales (incl mgt -all outside, all levels)

SPECIALTY EMPLOY. GRP.
5920 Roswell Rd., Suite B 107-118
Atlanta, GA 30328
(770) 399-9350
hr, ofc-st,trvl, wp

SPHERION PROFESSIONAL
RECRUITING GROUP
3333Peachtree Rd, Ste 310
Atlanta, GA 30326
(404)364-4660; fax (404)364-4650
comp, dist, eng, fin, hr, mat-mgt, mfg

STAFFINGIT, INC
4880 Lower Roswell Rd, Suite 40,
Marietta, GA 30068-4375
Copm(h), comtec, eng, hi tech (h), pd,
tech, tele

STAFFLINK SERVICES, INC

431 Commerce Drive
Peachtree City, GA 30269
(770) 487-4001; fax (770) 654-0138
temp (office automation, ofc-st, light
industrial, techinical)

STERLING LEGAL SEARCH
5180 Roswell Rd., N.W.
South Bldg., Suite 202
Atlanta, GA 30342
(404) 250-9766; fax (404) 250-9765
legal

CORBAN GRP
4405 International Blvd, Suite B-117
Norcross, GA 30093
(678) 380-6005; fax (678) 380-6006
exec, hitech, hr, print, retail, sls, tech

STRATEGIC STAFFING, INC.
183 Norcross Street, Suite 400
Roswell, GA 30075
(770) 587-0107; fax (770) 587-1483
actg, health, ins

SUPER SYSTEMS, INC.
6075 Roswell Rd., Suite 425
Atlanta, GA 30328
(404) 843-0770; fax (404) 843-9270
staff, tech

THORNE CONSULTING
4067 Riverlook Pkwy
Marictta, GA 30067
(770) 951-8075; fax (770) 951-1823
exec, health, hr, ins, mgt, med

TOAR CONSULTING, INC.
1176 Grimes Bridge Rd., Suite 200
Roswell, GA 30075
(770) 993-7663; fax (770) 998-5853
bank, eng, mfg, print, rs, sales, tele

TRILOGY EXEC SEARCH
10945 State Bridge Rd., Suite 401-267

Alpharetta, GA 30022
(678) 319-9833; fax (678) 319-9818
ins

TSI/FUTURE STAFF
7513 Roswell Road
Atlanta GA 30350
(678)443-9088; fax (770)306-9226
book, full, hr(h), ca(h),ofc-st, wp

WHITTAKER AND ASSOCS
1000 Johnson Fry Rd, Ste B120
Marietta, GA 30068
(678) 285-2222; fax (678) 285-0547
food industry - all disciplines

TEMPORARY EMPLOYMENT

Access Personnel Services, Inc.
200 Galleria Parkway, Suite 420
Atlanta, GA 30339
770/988-8484; fax 770/988-8522

Adams, Evens & Ross, Inc.
4757 Canton Highway, Suite 201
Marietta, GA 30066
770/928-4525; fax 770/928-4539

ADECCO
100 Galleria Parkway, SE, Suite 450
Atlanta, GA 30339-3165
770/612-2540; fax 770/612-2545

All Medical Personnel
1961 N. Druid Hills Rd, Ste 201-A
Atlanta, GA 30329
404/320-9125; fax 404/320-9182

Alternative Staffing
PO Box 957268
Duluth, GA 30095-9522
770/381-7710; fax 770/381-6112

Always-Care Nursing Service
PO Box 52248
Atlanta, GA 30355

404/266-8773; fax 404/233-8098

Careers USA
8881 Roswell Road,
Atlanta, GA 30350
770/642-8000; fax 770/642-9595

DDS Staffing Resources, Inc.
9755 Dogwood Road, Suite 200
Roswell, GA 30075
770/998-7779; fax 770/552-0176

Delta Staffing Services
1007 Virginia Avenue, Suite 100
Atlanta, GA 30354
404/715-4600; fax 404/715-4000
Durham Staffing, Inc. of GA
1343 Canton Road, Suite D2
Marietta, GA 30066
770/499-1665; fax 770/499-8407

firstPRO, Inc.
5607 Glenridge Drive, Suite 340
Atlanta, GA 30342
404/252-9422; fax 404/252-9146

Georgia TEMP, Inc.
133 Peachtree Street, NE, Suite 200
Atlanta, GA 30303
404/652-5493; fax 404/230-7876

Hire Intellect, Inc.
2401 Lake Park Drive, Suite 260
Smyrna, GA 30080-7609
770/435-2111; fax 770/435-2177

Horizon Staffing
5975 Roswell Road, Suite 109
Atlanta, GA 30328
770/961-0751; fax 770/961-1528

Legal Resources, Inc.
11285 Elkins Road, Suite J-8
Roswell, GA 30076
770/475-0739; fax 770/475-0879

Maristaff, Inc.
5901-C Peachtree Dunwoody Road,
Suite 50
Atlanta,, GA 30328
770/393-2718; fax 770/393-8321

Spherion
3535 Piedmont Road, #15C
Atlanta, GA 30305
404/240-3907; fax 240-3980

NovaCare Occupational Health Svcs.
2625 Cumberland Parkway, Suite 310
Atlanta, GA 30297
770/433-3400 x. 104

NPS of Atlanta, Inc.
3305 Breckinridge Boulevard
Duluth, GA 30136
770/931-0611; fax 770/493-4946

Paces Personnel, Inc.
235 Peachtree Street, NE, Suite 217
Atlanta, GA 30303
404/688-5307; fax 404/688-5312

Price Waterhouse Coopers LLP
1100 Campanile Building, 1155
Peachtree Street
Atlanta, GA 30309
404/870-1102

Pro Staff
1349 W. Peachtree Street, Suite 1880
Atlanta, GA 30309
404/898-0370; fax 404/898-1788

Quality Employment Service
315 5th Avenue, SE
Moultrie, GA 31768
912/891-3458; fax 912-891-2538

Quality Employment Service, Inc.
115-A S. Elm Street

Adel, GA 31620
912/896-5270; fax 912/896-5270

Quest Temporary Services, Inc.
1475 Atlanta Industrial Parkway
Atlanta, GA 30331
404/699-7447; fax 404/699-7533

Randstad Staffing Services
2015 S. Park Place
Atlanta, GA 30339
770/937-7045; fax 770/937-7044

Randstad Staffing Services
585 Franklin Road, Suite 250
Marietta, GA 30067
770/427-3575; fax 770/514-8009

Royal Staffing, Inc.
5675 Jimmy Carter Blvd, #685
Norcross, GA 30071
770/263-8111; fax 770/263-8868

Sizemore Personnel
1369 Reynolds Street
Augusta, GA 30901
706/724-5629; fax 706-722-0592

Southern Crescent Personnel
7179 Jonesboro Rd, Ste 101, Marrow
30260
770/9684602; 770/968-4606 fax
temp to perm, legal, medical, admin

Southern Home Care Nursing Service
1225 August West Parkway
Augusta, GA 30909
706/860-3835; fax 706/854-9640

Southern Home Care Services, Inc.
PO Box 2797,
Valdosta, GA 31602
912/242-2797; fax 912-242-2358

Staffing One
3312 Piedmont Road, Suite 210

Atlanta, GA 30305
404/467-8850; fax 404/467-9606

Staffing Options
8560 Holcomb Bridge Rd, Suite 103
Alpharetta, GA 30022
770/643-0034; fax 770/998-9138

Staffing Resources
4275 Shackleford Road, Suite 250
Norcross, GA 30093
770/638-8100; fax 770/638-1758

Staffing Resources
4275 Shackleford Road, Suite 250
Norcross, GA 30093
770/638-8100 x 122

Staffing Solutions
1050 Crown Pointe Pkwy, Ste 1650
Atlanta, GA 30338
770/671-9333

Staffing Systems
3330-G Peachtree Corners Circle
Norcross, GA 30092
770/368-8556; fax 770/368-8511

StaffMark
200 Galleria Parkway, Suite 905
Atlanta, GA 30339
770/955-0112; fax

Sterling Legal Search, Inc.
5180 Roswell Rd, Ste 202, So Bldg.
Atlanta, GA 30342
404/250-9766; fax 404/250-9765

Technical Resource Staffing, Inc.
2555 Cumberland Parkway, Suite 275
Atlanta, GA 30339
770/438-7601; fax 770/799-1504

Temp Choice, Inc.
5150 Buford Highway, Suite 1306

Norcross, GA 30071
770/447-4199; fax 770/447-4089

TempWorld
1810 Highway 20, Suite 174
Conyers, GA 30208
770/760-8828; fax 770/785-2375

The Personnel Factory, Inc.
406-A Main Street
Forest Park, GA 30297
404/366-8060; fax 404/366-5070

Top Notch Personnel, Inc.
4360 E Commerce Circle
Atlanta, GA 30336
404/691-4500; fax 404/699-9010

TRC Staffing Services, Inc.
5226 Highway 78, Suite B
Stone Mountain, GA 30087
770/879-9090; fax 770/879-1867

Trimark Health Services, Inc.
1649 Tullie Circle, Suite 105
Atlanta, GA 30329
404/633-1935; fax 404/636-8023

Volt Services Group
2964 Peachtree Road, Suite 105
Atlanta, GA 30305
404/231-5656; fax 404/231-5902

Westaff
6351-A Jonesboro Road,
Morrow, GA 30260
770/960-8166; fax 770/960-8633

Venturi
100 Colony Square, Suite 760
Atlanta, GA 30361
404/815-0440; fax 404/815-6666

APPENDIX E:

PROFESSIONAL AND TRADE ASSOCIATIONS

I have included here 50 of the largest associations, and more are included at ajobs.com, with links to both national and local chapters. Nearly all associations and most local chapters list job vacancies online.

Do not underestimate the assistance available through these organizations. Most industries are represented by more than one association, and the following list is only a modicum of the total number of national organizations with Atlanta chapters. If your representative association is not included here, call the national headquarters and ask for the local contacts.

Even associations that do not offer direct job assistance are often excellent network sources, especially at their meetings. I have spoken with many persons who found their jobs this way.

Remember that many of the officers and contacts are not paid, but have volunteered their time to help the association. Do not ask to have long-distance phone calls returned and avoid taking up too much of the volunteer's time.

I have included the names of the most recent officers here, but since they are elected for a limited time, they may have changed. If so, ask this past official for the new slate of officers, or go online to **ajobs.com** to their local link which often lists the current slate. In case you are not able to locate the new officers, I have also included the phone number of the national headquarters. Call them, ask for "Membership Services," and then inquire the name and phone number of the current president for their Atlanta chapter or another city, if you are open for relocation.

List of associations and organizations included

Please let me know of other associations that I have not listed here and who offer job assistance, so that I can include them in future editions. I would also appreciate comments on how useful and successful they are for you.

Human Resources
American Society for Training and Development
Atlanta Human Resources Planning Group
International Society of Certified Employee Benefits Specialists
International Society for Performance Improvement
Society for Human Resource Management
Working in Employee Benefits

MIS/Data Processing
Association for Information Technology Professionals
Black Data Processing Associates

Ethnic/Minority
Association for Women in Communications
National Society of Women Accountants
Financial Women International
Georgia Association of Women Lawyers
Insurance Professionals of NWGA
National Association of Black Accountants
National Association of Women in Construction
Black Data Processing Associates
National Black MBA Association

Manufacturing/Distribution
APICS (American Production and Inventory Control Society)
American Society for Quality
Institute for Supply Management
National Contract Management Association

Engineering/Technical
American Society of Heating, Refrigerating, and Air Conditioning Engineers
American Society of Mechanical Engineers
Georgia Society of Professional Engineers
Society of Logistics Engineers

Communications
American Institute of Graphic Arts
Association for Women in Communications
Atlanta Ad Club
Business Marketing Association
Creative Club of Atlanta

International Association of Business Communicators
Public Relations Society of America
Society for Technical Communication

Accounting/Finance
American Institute of CPA's/Georgia Society of CPA's
American Society of Women Accountants
Financial Executives International
Financial Women International
Institute of Internal Auditors
Institute of Management Accountants
National Association of Black Accountants
National Association of Business Economists
Strategic Leadership Forum

Management/Administration
American Society for Public Administration
Association of Records Managers and Administrators
Georgia Society of Association Executives
International Association of Administrative Professionals
Meeting Professionals International
National Association of Legal Secretaries
Non-Profit Resource Center
Project Management Institute

Medical
American Association of Occupational Health Nurses
American Nursing Association

Sales/Marketing
American Marketing Association
Commercial Real Estate Women
International Customer Service Association
National Society of Fund Raising Executives
Society for Marketing Professional Services
Sales and Marketing Executives

Appendix E:

Professional and Trade Associations

Note: I would greatly appreciate information on other associations not listed here and that offer job assistance for their membership. Email to jobguru@ajobs.com or send the information to
CareerSource Publications
P O Box 52291, Atlanta, GA 30355.

APICS (www.apicsatlanta.com)
(formerly American Production and Inventory Control Association)   Membership comprised of companies and individuals engaged in manufacturing management and inventory control; current membership in Atlanta is more than 1000. Publishes monthly newsletter listing job openings and job seekers, and maintains a file for prospective employers. No charge. Membership is required. Has two group meetings monthly for dinner: Northside meets on third Tuesday and Southside meets on third Thursday. Contact Jon Harvill, Placement Coordinator, c/o Dunhill Professional Search, 2110 Powers Ferry Rd, Suite 110, Atlanta, 30339; (770)952-0009;fax(770)952-9422;e-mail-www.dunstaff.com/watga.htm Reservations, call (770)333-6502.
President: Loretta L. David, CPIM, CIRM, (404) 495-9233
Membership: Bill Howell, CPIM, (770) 475-8010
National Headquarters- (800) 444-2742
E-mail: dswatlga@mindspring.com

AMER. ASSOC. OF OCCUPATIONAL HEALTH NURSES (www.aaohn.org)
Corporate headquarters in Atlanta. Publishes monthly newsletter that includes both job openings and job seekers, usually five of each; for a copy, call Trish McCants, Communications Specialist, at (770) 455-7757x113. Maintains a file for interested employers, and applicants are coded to preserve anonymity; listing information must be received by the fifth of the month prior to publication. Cost is $350 up to 175 words for companies and $150 for an ad for two consecutive months for non-members, but is free to members. Posting on the website for an additional fee. Does not meet monthly; rather, has large, national meeting in April or May and smaller, leadership conference in September. Employment information board is available at annual meeting. For information, contact Jerry Williamson, Associate Executive Director at 2929 Brandywine Road, Suite 100, Atlanta, GA 30341. (770)455-7757); fax (770)455-7271
E-mail: aaohn@aaohn.org.

AMERICAN INSTITUTE OF CPA'S (www.aicpa.org)
Excellent source for CPA's and non-CPA's. Has seven chapters in the metro-Atlanta area, representing geographic areas, and each meets monthly; visitors are welcome. Georgia headquarters maintains a Job Bank file which includes job seekers and job openings. Membership is not required, nor is certification – there are many openings for

non-CPA's. The Job Bank is updated monthly, with jobs deleted after two months; resumes, after three months. Call for current service charges. For information concerning the various chapters and their meeting times and places, as well as for Job Bank information, contact Membership Services Coordinator, Julie Anderson, at 3340 Peachtree Rd NE, Suite 2700, Atlanta, GA 30326-1026. (404)231-8676 x 817; fax -(404)237-1291; E-mail: janderson@gscpa.org. Also publishes monthly newsletter called "Current Accounts" which contains a classified ad section. Companies and individuals may advertise there for a fee of $40 for 50 words. Job referral service for members includes postings on web page. To place an ad or obtain a copy of the newsletter, contact the Communications Department or ask for Julie Jackson at the above address and phone number (x 814). Deadline is first of month.
National Headquarters: (212)569-6299
Local- www.gscpa.org

AMERICAN INSTITUTE OF GRAPHIC ARTS (www.aiga-atl.org)
The Atlanta chapter has 600 members, mostly creative and art directors and graphic designers, a few illustrators. Meets monthly, but not on a specific date. Contact the Administrative Assistant, at Point B, King Plow Arts Center, 887 W. Marietta St, Atlanta, GA 30318; (404) 888-1700.
President: Kathi Roberts; Membership: Julie Campbell @ julie@pointb.cc
National Headquarters- (212) 807-1990
E-mail: aiga.atlanta@mindspring.com

AMERICAN MARKETING ASSOCIATION (www.ama.org)
The Atlanta chapter is one of AMA's largest, with more than 900 members. Members are from marketing-related backgrounds, mostly research, advertising, planning, and analysis, with some sales reps also. Meets second Thursday at 11:30 at the Villa Christina Restaurant. Also has group called "Young Professionals," which meets monthly for career enhancement seminars. Offers job seekers several excellent programs under their Employment Referral Service and you can refer to the website for specifics; most are free to members or low cost for non-members.
Executive Director:Cindi Miller, at (404)299-7735; fax: (404) 299-7740
7070 Wittshire Drive, Avondale Estates, GA 30002
E-mail: amaatlanta@mindspring.com
National Headquarters - (312) 648-0536; (800) 262-1150;
Local website- www.ama-atlanta.com;

AMERICAN NURSING ASSOCIATION (www.georgianurses.org/)
Members are registered nurses in all practice settings.
Staff admin: Debbie Hackman - ceo@georgianurses.org (404) 325-5536

AMERICAN PLANNING ASSOCIATION (www.planning.org)
Represents planners, officials, and citizens involved with urban and rural planning issues, 2/3 of whom work for state and local government agencies. Atlanta chapter web site lists

job openings in GA. Publishes newsletter that lists job vacancies; for copy, email Lucy Jenkins at lucyjenkins@georgiaplanning.org.
President: Lisa Hollingsworth, lisahollingsworth@georgiaplanning.org
Local site: www.georgiaplanning.org; national: 312/431-9100

AMERICAN SOCIETY FOR PUBLIC ADMINISTRATION
(www.aspanet.org) Members are public service and government employees. Does not include job openings in their newsletter, since most government openings are posted elsewhere; or job seekers, since they have excellent networking at meetings. President, Robert Sanders, (770) 836-4572, bsanders@westga.edu
Local website: www.aspanet.org/chapsec/chapter/georgia.htm
National Headquarters - (202) 393-7878

AMERICAN SOCIETY FOR QUALITY (www.asqc.org)
Membership comprised of quality administrators, including governmental, manufacturing, administrative, etc.; Atlanta chapter has 2200 members. Meets monthly, usually for dinner on the second Thursday, and non-members can attend. Publishes monthly newsletter for members, and includes job listings and job seekers. Generally, however, all employment assistance goes through one person who handles both job listings and job seekers, and also maintains a resume file. Membership is preferred for list.
Employment: Art Geist @ (678)-482-3803, employment@asqatlanta.org
Chapter Chair: Jay Jones, chair@asqatlanta.org
Voice mail for meeting information or to leave a message: (770) 717-4506
(414) 272-8575; (800) 248-1946

AMERICAN SOC. FOR TRAINING AND DEVELOPMENT (www.astdatlanta.com)
An educational society of human resources and training managers, both corporate and consultants; Atlanta chapter has 1300 members. Meets for dinner and program. Time and location varies and is announced in the monthly newsletter and on voice mail and webpage. Register for dinner meeting attendance through webpage. Jobline is listed on their web page; members only. For information, call voice mail and follow prompts. Laura Weiss (404)845-0522 Chapter Administrator at the local ASTD office at 325 Hammond Drive NE, Suite 104, Atlanta, GA 30328-5026.
(404) 845-0522 (also voice mail information); fax (404) 845-0521;
National Headquarters (703) 683-8100; (800) 628-2783

AMERICAN SOCIETY OF HEATING, REFRIGERATING AND AIR-CONDITIONING ENGINEERS, INC. (www.ashrae.com)
Society headquartered in Atlanta, and publishes monthly magazine with classified section in which individuals may at their own expense include a classified ad. Local chapter publishes monthly newsletter which lists both job openings and synopses of job seekers, available free to members only. Meets second Tuesday monthly at Marriott Century Center at 5:00 for social hour, dinner, and program. To receive the newsletter and submit your synopsis, contact Clint Knudson, 770-425-1500, cknudson@lincolnassoc.com.

President: Chris Page, 770-425-1500, cpage@lincolnassoc.com
National office: 1791 Tullie Circle NE, Atlanta, GA 30329.
(404) 636-8400

AMERICAN SOC. OF MECHANICAL ENGINEERS INT'L(www.asme.org)

Has 1500 members in greater Atlanta. Publishes monthly newsletter ; editor Bob Cuneo @ (404)325-2807, or email b.h.cuneo@worldnet.att.net.   Coordinates job referrals through Dallas, TX region office, which maintains job bank for members only; call Judy Cobb at (800) 445-2388. Maintains resume file for prospective employers and announces job openings at meetings on second Monday each month, except summers and publishes job info on website.
President: Brian Dietz (817) 276-9256
Membership Development: Fred Apple @ (770) 552-4207
Southern region office - (800) 445-2388
National Headquarters (212) 705-7722; (800) 843-2763;
Southern Region- www.asmesro.org

AMERICAN SOCIETY OF SAFETY ENGINEERS(www.asse.org)

Members are individuals whose employment, education and experience are safety-related. Meets second Monday each month all year. Publishes monthly newsletter which contains both job openings (from companies and personnel agencies) and job seekers. No charge for members. For information, contact the president, Michael Belcher, CSP, (404) 236-5732, mike.belcher@cingular.com
Membership: Sandra Mann, (404) 529-0411, sandy.mann@bellsouth.com
National Headquarters- (847) 699-2929
Atlanta Chapter -www.asse-ga.org

AMERICAN SOCIETY OF WOMEN ACCOUNTANTS(www.aswa.org)

Publishes monthly newsletter that includes job seekers and openings. Local membership is preferred, but not required, especially for individuals relocating to Atlanta. Their service is not available to personnel agencies. Usually meets on the third Tuesday of each month for supper, including a speaker and then the business meeting. Yearbook is published for members, including companies and job titles of their membership.
President: Carol Hayes @ 770-426-7330, cahayes@bellsouth.net
Local chapter phone for meeting info and messages- (770)242-4844
National Headquarters - (800) 326-2163

ASSOCIATION FOR WOMEN IN COMMUNICATIONS

Represents women in print and broadcast journalism, television and radio production, film, advertising, public relations, marketing, graphic design, multi-media design, and photography.
President: Erin Bransford, 770-206-9929, bransfords@mindspring.com

ASSOCIATION OF FUNDRAISING EXECUTIVES
(www.accessatlanta.com/community/groups/nsfre   )

Membership comprised of 300+ professionals in the non-profit fund raising industry. Offers annual conference and meets on the third Monday of each month. Events open to non-members. For membership info, call the national headquarters. Produces a monthly newsletter that lists job openings; available to members only. For info, call Gina Grantham at (770) 516-0207, afp_atl@bellsouth.net.
National Headquarters –(703) 684-0410 or (800) 666-FUND
E-mail: nsfrega@bellsouth.net

ASS"N OF INFORMATION TECHNOLOGY PROFESSIONALS

(http://www.aitpatlanta.homestead.com/) Members are CIO's, VP's, Senior Technicians, IS Managers and university level students. Meets monthly third Thursday at 6pm for technical session, followed by social hour, dinner and speaker.
President: Donald Gonsalves, Jr., (O) 770-237-4002, Don.gonsalves@per-se.com
M'ship: Shelly M. Steele, 770-993-5591, Shelly.Steele@ccagents.net

ASS'N. OF RECORDS MGRS. AND ADMIN.(www.arma.org/hq)

Usually meets third Tuesday of each month for lunch and speaker, but may vary to accommodate exceptional speaker. Publishes monthly newsletter "Flaming Peach," which lists job openings and occasionally applicants. A confidential file of job seekers is maintained, and applicants are notified before being referred to a company.
President: Dana Moore, 404-572-4552, dmoore@pgfm.com
National Headquarters- (913) 341-3808; (800) 422-2762

ATLANTA AD CLUB(www.atlantaadclub.org)

Membership of 400 comprised of companies and individuals in advertising and advertising-related businesses. Has monthly luncheon usually on third Tuesday. Publishes monthly newsletter which includes employment columns "Positions Wanted" and "Positions Available". For $200, ad will post in both newsletter and website. For information, contact Sandra Stockman, Executive Director, at PO Box 500846, Atlanta, GA 31150.
(770)649-8872; fax (770) 642-8580; e-mail atlantaadclub@mindspring.com
National Office – (800)999-2231

ATLANTA HUMAN RESOURCES PLANNING GROUP

Also known as Human Resources Leadership Forum. 130 members representing senior-level HR professionals in corporate succession planning, both corporate and consultants. Meets bi-monthly, usually third Thursday.
President: Lynn Slavenski with Equifax @ (404) 836-2200
Chapter Administrator: Denise Grant at (770) 840-8251

BLACK DATA PROCESSING ASSOCIATES (www.bdpa.org)

The Atlanta chapter has 165 members and is growing rapidly. Meets monthly on the third Wednesday at the Marriott Northeast (Clairmont x I-85) at 6:00. Has job coordinator who receives job openings and maintains resume file. Members can send resume to be circulated, and request to be added to the mailing list for the monthly newsletter. For other information, leave a message on their voice mail service and your call will be returned.

President: Perry Chase, president@atlantabdpa.org
Membership: Cheryl Sams, vp_membership@atlantabdpa.org
Voice mail- (404) 681-6025(also includes general information, meeting dates and speaker, special events, etc.)
National Headquarters (301)429-2702; Local website www.atlantabdpa.org

BUILDING OWNERS AND MANAGERS OF ATLANTA (www.boma-atlanta.org)

Membership consists of building owners, developers, managers, service companies, investors, and brokers. Meets for lunch and program usually on second Wednesday. Maintains resume file for prospective employers and prints job openings when available in monthly newsletter and website. Membership not required. Contact Alan Fisher, Executive Vice President,
6855 Jimmy Carter Blvd, Suite 2830, Norcross, GA 30071.
(770) 825-0116; fax (770)825-0139; E-mail: suehuey@boma-atlanta.org;
National Headquarters (202) 408-2662

BUSINESS MARKETING ASSOCIATION (www.marketing.org)

Members are corporate marketing communicators, representatives of media, agency personnel, and industry suppliers (sales), that are involved in business-to-business marketing (generally not consumer marketing). Meets monthly (except summers) for lunch and program; call (770)673-0834 for information and reservations. Maintains Professional Assistance Network (PAN) to help members with job search; contact membership chairperson. Publishes quarterly newsletter, but does not list job openings or seekers. For information, contact the chapter president, Dave Owen, hello@imageserve.com
VP Membership: Mike McClellan (770)390-9692, x202
E-mail: bmaatlanta@mindspring.com
National Headquarters- (312)409-4262 or (800)664-4262;
Local website: www.bmaatlanta.com /

COMMERCIAL REAL ESTATE WOMEN(www.crewnetwork.org)

Membership of 315 and meets first Thursday for lunch and program. Maintains Job Bank newsletter which includes company vacancies and job seekers, available at meetings and mailed to membership. Contact Chapter Administrator, Erika Marshall (404) 471-1110;(404)-471-1109-fax.
P.O.Box 191546, Atlanta, GA 31119-1546
Local website- www.crewatlanta.org-local

CORENET GLOBAL (www.corenetglobal.org)

Atlanta-based, represents corporate real estate executives. Meeting dates and activities vary. List job vacancies online and members can post resume on the site.
Chair: Matt Fanoe with Coca-Cola Enterprises, mfanoe@na.cokecce.com;
M'ship: Don Buchanan with IBM, buchanan@us.ibm.com

CREATIVE CLUB OF ATLANTA(www.creativeclub.org)
Members are creative advertising types: art directors, illustrators, photographers, copy-writers, production, etc. Meets monthly, but time and place varies with speaker availability. Publishes regular newsletter, and includes job information when available. Contact Chris Bradley, Director, at
P O Box 190016, Atlanta, GA 31119. (404) 874-0908; E-mail creativeclub@msn.com

FINANCIAL EXECUTIVES INTERNATIONAL(www.fei.org)
Membership comprised of senior financial executives – controllers, treasurers, VP's of finance and CFO's. Meets at 6:00 monthly on fourth Tuesday for dinner and speaker; does not meet during the summer. They also sponor "Career Transition Breakfasts" for those between jobs. Has "Member Career Services Committee" which serves as liaison with executive search firms, companies, and applicants, as well as with the national office job assistance program. Membership required. Contact Roger Haggerty @ oblassoc@mindspring.com
Membership Counselor: Roger Haggerty @ (770)521-9303
Executive Director: Norene Quinn @ (404)681-9878; fax-(404)522-0132
National headquarters- (201) 898-4600
E-mail: feiatl@mindspring.com

FINANCIAL WOMEN INTERNATIONAL (www.fwi.org)
Metro chapter has 61 members associated with financial service industries, and meets 8/year on third Tuesday for dinner and program. Offers no formal job assistance programs, but excellent networking system. Publishes quarterly newsletter, but seldom includes job information.
Membership: Mitzi Saxton (770) 521-9303
National Headquarters (703)807-2007

GEORGIA ASSOC OF WOMEN LAWYERS(www.lar.emory.edu/gawl)
Atlanta chapter has 600 members, including corporate attorneys, judges, and private practice attorneys. Meets the third Wednesday of each month at various law firms in Atlanta. Has a Job Bank. Contact President Kim Warden @ (404)656-2382.

GEORGIA SOCIETY OF ASSOCIATION EXECUTIVES (www.gsae.org)
Represents the paid employees of more than 450 professional associations in Georgia. Send resume to their office, and it will be kept on file for 90 days for perusal by interested employers. Publishes monthly newsletter which sometimes lists job openings. For information, contact Beth Abbott, Member Services at
2965 Flowers Road South, Suite 155, Atlanta, GA 30341
(770) 934-2555; fax (770) 934-6210

GEORGIA SOCIETY OF PROFESSIONAL ENGINEERS (www.gspe.org)

13 chapters in Georgia have over 1500 members; three chapters located in Atlanta. Publishes bi-monthly magazine that lists job openings. Maintains resume bank and refers resumes on file to interested employers. Has monthly meetings and major semi-annual meetings; potential members welcome. Must be member to receive magazine, and prefers membership in order to retain resume. For more information, including meeting dates, places, and slate of local officers call (404) 521-2324; fax (404)521-0283.
Executive Director: Tom Leslie @(404)521-2324.
250 Williams, Suite 2112, Atlanta, GA 30303-1032.
National Headquarters- (703) 684-2800
E-mail: gspe@mindspring.com

INSTITUTE FOR SUPPLY MANAGEMENT
(formerly National Association of Purchasing Management) Members are in purchasing and materials management. Has more than 700 local members and meets second Thursday for dinner and speaker; membership is not required, but encouraged. The national headquarters sponsors a for-profit placement company, whose profits go to NAPM's education programs, and this agency maintains a list by state of job vacancies. For local openings and information, contact Employment Development Services, Bart Crispen @ (770)410-7501, or send resume to chapter address:
NAPM - GA, Inc., PO Box 870785, Atlanta, GA 30087-0020.
For information regarding NAPM services contact President Sondra Bradford (770) 486-6101. Local chapter phone: (770)493-4806
There is also a West Georgia Chapter that has a resume referral service. This chapter meets the first Thursday of each month.
President: Barbara Olsavksi (770)486-6101
West Georgia Contact: Jon Harvill @ (770)952-0009
National Headquarters - (602) 752-6276
Local website- www.napmga.org

INSTITUTE OF INTERNAL AUDITORS(www.theiia.org)
Members are auditors and accountants in private and public organizations. Grants the CIA designation. Averages 40 at monthly meetings on second Monday, except summers and October (first Monday) at 5:00; visitors are welcome ($25, includes supper). Publishes monthly newsletter which includes job opportunities. Maintains resume file, and matches applicants and openings; no charge. Contact Pat Lincoln, job coordinator, @ (404)249-3566.
Chapter president: Jackie Geyer @ (770)803-2814
National Headquarters-(407)830-7600
Local website- www.theiia.org/atlanta/atliia.htm

INSTITUTE OF MANAGEMENT ACCOUNTANTS
Atlanta chapter has 900 members and meets on the third Tuesday monthly, except summers, for social hour and dinner. Has Employment Director who maintains resume file and matches resumes with company job requests. Contact Kristen Russum at (770)395-0014; email- kristenr@acsysatlant.com; membership preferred but not required.

Chapter president: Robert Coons, (770) 650-7558, rcoons@randallpaulson.com
National Headquarters - (201) 573-9000

INSURANCE PROFESSIONALS OF NWGA (www.naiw.org)

Three chapters in the Atlanta area: Atlanta, NE Atlanta and Cobb County. Membership is comprised of companies and individuals in insurance and insurance-related businesses, and includes both men and women. Each chapter has an Employment Chairman who announces current openings at meetings and will refer interested persons to existing openings. Monthly newsletter also includes current openings. NE Atlanta chapter meetings are held monthly on the second Thursday; Cobb, on third Tuesday.
Atlanta Pres.: Madge Betenbuagh (770) 439-7991
Northeast Pres.: Penny Daniel (770) 439-7991
Cobb Pres.: Robin Johnson @ 770/422-4511
National Headquarters: (800)766-6249

INT'L ASSOC. OF ADMINISTRATIVE PROFESSIONALS

www.iaap-hq.org) Awards designation "Certified Professional Secretary." Meets third Monday monthly @ 6:15 for social hour, dinner, and program at Sheraton Hotel Buckhead. Has Job Placement officer who accepts job openings and lists them in monthly newsletter and announces them at meetings; Tava Kirk with Cox Radio at 404)843-5248; fax (404)843-5586. There are several chapters within Atlanta, check the local website for chapter info.
Atlanta Chapter President: Cathy Fox @ (770) 395-3911;
fax- (770) 395-3904
International Headquarters: (816)891-6600
Local website- www.accessatlanta/community/groups/iaap

INT'L ASSOC. OF BUSINESS COMMUNICATORS(www.iabc.com)

Members are professionals in all areas of communications over public relations, working for corporations, as consultants or as freelancers; more than 200 members here. Alternates monthly meetings between lunch and dinner, usually on fourth Tuesday. Publishes monthly newsletter distributed to many companies in Atlanta, and that includes an employment section listing job seekers and job openings. The service is free to local members and employers, and costs $15 for non-members. All communication from job seekers except renewals is to be in writing. Deadline is the 20th of each month. Send 40-word ad (plus contact data) + fee (if applicable) to P.O.Box 80768, Atlanta, GA 30336. E-mail: iabc@mindspring.com

President: Tammie Addison, tammie.addison@bellsouth.com
Executive Director: Kathy Zamora @ (770)457-2358
National Headquarters- (415) 433-3400 or (800) 776-4222
Local website: www.iabcatlanta.com

INT'L CUSTOMER SERVICE ASSOCIATION

Meets second Tuesday monthly, alternating between breakfast and dinner. Headquarters maintains resume bank and forwards all local openings to Atlanta chapter. Chapter here

also maintains resume bank for employers to review. For more information including next meeting time, call voice mail at 621-2586.
President: Christopher Kocks, 678-376-5197, ckocks@customerleaders.com
National Headquarters- (312)644-6610; 800/360-4272

INT'L SOC. OF CERTIFIED EMP. BENEFIT SPEC. (www.ifebp.org/ceiscebs.html)
Members work in the field of employee benefits. Usually meets third Thursday for breakfast or dinner nine times per year; call for dates/location. Has Career Develop-ment Chair who announces job openings at meetings or over the phone, including openings through personnel agencies, and who maintains a resume file for prospective employers; membership is required. Contact Chapter Administrator for details.
President: Catherine Jackson, @ (404) 233-2200 cjackson@tbc-atl.com
Chapter Administrator: Denise Grant at (770) 840-8696; fax (770)449-6589 –; E-mail: iccepsga@aol.com
National Headquarters – (414)786-6710

INT'L SOCIETY FOR PERFORMANCE IMPROVEMENT
(www.ispi-atlanta.org) Members are professionals in performance and instructional technology, with emphasis on increasing employee's performance and productivity; more emphasis on program design and instructional technologies, and less on platform instruction. Dues are $40/year. Meets monthly, and much networking is done then; past Membership Chairman found her job this way! Cost is $15 for non-members; $12 for members. Informal job assistance among members, and monthly newsletter includes company openings. Pres: Donald T. Tosti
Contact: Anita Pitts (404) 332-1019; E-mail anita.pitss@wachovia.com
National Headquarters- (202) 408-7969
E-mail: ispiatlanta@hotmail.com

MEETING PROFESSIONALS INTERNATIONAL (www.mpi.web.org)
Membership comprised of meeting planners and individuals whose companies supply goods or services to meeting planners. Meets for lunch third Tuesday monthly. Has "Resume Library" that collects resumes from members and non-members, and makes them available to potential employers; Planners contact Carolyn Hellerung with Siemens @ (770) 973-0071. Suppliers contact Russell LoPinto @ (770)457-0966.
President: Ken Jones, CMP, kenneth.jones@aspenproductions.com, 770-955-6656
Membership Chair: Michele Woodward, mwoodwar@cnsopo.hyatt.com
Executive Director: Jim Folwer, GA office: (404)869-0606, (404) 249-8831-fax.
National Headquarters: (972) 702-3000

NAT'L ASSOCIATION OF BLACK ACCOUNTANTS (www.nabaatl.org)
Has monthly and quarterly newsletter that lists openings and job seekers, available for members only. Maintains "Job Bank" of resumes for interested employers. Meets third Wednesday each month, and printed agenda includes job openings.
President: Angela Murphy, (404) 927-7584, amurphy01@msn.com

Chapter Voice Mail: (404)221-3192
National Headquarters -(301)474-6222

NATIONAL ASSOC. FOR BUSINESS ECONOMICS (www.nabe.com)
Atlanta affiliate is "Atlanta Economics Club." Meets third Tuesday (except summers) for lunch and visitors are welcome; cost for non-members is $20. No formal job assistance locally, but excellent networking--the day I called they had just secured employment for someone! National office publishes monthly newsletter that includes several pages of job vacancies, including Atlanta.
President: Carol E. Shipley, 404-506-2226, ceshiple@southernco.com
National Headquarters- (202) 463-6223
Local website- www.atlantaeconomics.org

NAT'L ASSOC. OF AFRICAN AMERICANS IN HUMAN RESOURCES
Atlanta chapter meets second Wednesday at 5pm for social time, followed by program/dinner at 6pm. President William Riddick, Jr., PHR, wriddick@naaahr-atlanta.org. VP of Plans & Programs: Jesse Owens, jowens@naaahr-atlanta.org

NAT'L ASSOC. OF LEGAL SECRETARIES (www.nals.org)
www.atlantalsa.idsite.com
Several metro-Atlanta chapters. The Atlanta chapter meets third Monday evening at 6:00 pm for dinner and program. Has Employment Chair, who announces current openings at meetings and will refer applicants to existing openings.
President: Sally Stenger, (404) 541-6821; fax (404) 815-6555; E-mail stenger@kilpatrickstockton.com
National Headquarters (918) 493-3540;
Local website: www.NALSofAtlanta.org

NAT'L ASSOC OF WOMEN IN CONSTRUCTION (www.nawic.org)
Membership comprised of women in construction-related positions and industries. Operates very successful Occupational Research and Referral Service, matching jobs and applicants. Also publishes monthly newsletter which includes job openings and applicants, and maintains applicant file for interested employers. Also offers information on EEO-related positions. National Headquarters has computerized Job Data Bank. Awards annual scholarship in Atlanta area. Meets first Tuesday each month at 6:30 for dinner, program and business meeting; membership not required. Important: when sending resume, indicate WIC on envelope.
Contact Lisa Simmonds (800)552-3506 x 14
National Headquarters- (817)877-5551; (800)552-3506 –
E-mail: nawic@onramp.net

NATIONAL BLACK MBA ASSOCIATION (www.bmba.org)
More than 500 members in Atlanta. Meets fourth Monday of each month. Has book of openings for perusal at these meetings and job networking is encouraged. Maintains Job Hot Line for members only and publishes a list of recommended personnel recruiters.

Sponsors annual job fair each September. Non-members can attend meetings for a $5 fee. For information, leave a message on the chapter voice mail, and your call will be quickly returned.
C J Bland, POB 54656, Atlanat, GA 30308-0656
National Headquarters- (312) 236-2622

NATIONAL CONTRACT MANAGEMENT ASSOCIATION (www.ncmahq.org)
Has 180 members, involved in contracting with government and industry. Meets monthly, generally third Thursday (off summers), and offers career enhancement seminars throughout the year. Publishes monthly newsletter that occasionally lists job openings, not seekers. Has Employment Chair who maintains resume file and refers to interested employers; membership required.
Chapter president: Phillip King (404) 331-4620
National Headquarters- (703) 448-9231; (800) 344-8096
Local website- www.knfcon.com/atl-ncma

NON-PROFIT RESOURCE CENTER (www.nonprofitgeorgia.org)
Lists job openings (internships, administrative, professional, and executive) with Atlanta's non-profit sector. Maintains resume bank for up to three months free of charge. Job assistance is called "Opportunity 'NOCS", a bi-monthly newsletter that lists job openings, and is available by ordering a subscription.Contact Managing Editor, Ricky Hyde, The Non-Profit Resource Center, 50 Hurt Plaza SE, Suite 220, Atlanta, 30303; (404)688-4845; fax (404)521-0487

PROJECT MANAGEMENT INSTITUTE (www.pmi.org)
Members are individuals practicing and studying project management in many different industry areas. Meets second Monday at 5:00 for check-in, and dinner must be pre-paid online at local site. Numerous Atlanta jobs listed at local site.
Pres: Frank Polack, president@pmiatlanta.org; Katrinda McQueen, Mem'ship, Avery Chesser, Programs programs@pmiatlanta.org
Local web site: www.pmiatlanta.org

PUBLIC RELATIONS SOCIETY OF AMERICA (www.prsa-ga.org)
Meets monthly on first Thursday for lunch. Monthly newsletter includes a section called "People Pointers," which lists job openings and job seekers for full-time, part-time, freelancing, and internships and is available at their web site in 1999; lists an average of 10 openings, 5+ internships, and six job-seekers each month. Members receive the newsletter free and can list at no charge, plus a file of resumes is kept for interested employers. Non-members can list in "People Pointers" and on the website for $25 and their resume also will be kept on file, and they will receive that monthly letter with their listing. All chapter information, including meetings, membership and employment is published on the website. Procedure: send a 40-word synopsis of yourself (including name and contact data), your resume and $25 fee (if applicable) to Denise Grant, Executive Director, at 4971 Staverly Ln, Norcross, GA 30092; E-mail: djgpr@aol.com. Important: Deadline for job listing is the fifth of the month.

Chapter office: (770)449-6369, fax (770)449-6589;
National Headquarters (212) 995-2230

RETIRED OFFICERS ASSOCIATION
Composed of veteran and active members of tehe armed forces. Meets third Wednesdays at Vinings Library. National site has job listings and career services, but must be member to access. Pres: LTC Melvin Wilkerson, (770) 996-4505, http://shelmiller.home.mindspring.com/index.html
National: 703/549-2311; www.troa.org

SALES AND MARKETING EXECUTIVES (www.SME-Atlanta.org)
Has 200 members and meets monthly at the Atlanta Marriott Perimeter Center on the second Monday. At 5:00 there is an open round table for disucssion; at 5:30 a social hour, followed by dinner and program at 6:30. Focus is primarily on educational seminars, but much networking at meetings also. Works closely with Phi Sigma Epsilon, professional sales and marketing fraternity.
President: John Fayad
Chapter administrator: Stacey Trainer 678-432-0803;
e-mail smersvp@earthlink.net

SOCIETY FOR HUMAN RESOURCE MANAGEMENT (www.shrmatlanta.org)
The Atlanta chapter has 2400+ members and generally meets first Monday each month; non-members can attend two meetings, after which membership is required. Has outstanding "SupportNet" group for members only, meets third Tuesday. Offers Resume Referral Service that maintains a resume file for interested employers and publishes a list of job openings (average 50+ monthly) that is published on the website. Because of SHRM's size, avoid calling the volunteer officers when possible. Instead, first call the Business Manager, Linda Lefebvre at (770) 886-1800, fax (770)886-1900, or write 3651-E Peachtree Pkwy, Mailbox 367, Suwanee, GA 30024.
Information and chapter office: (770) 886-1800; email: shrmatl@mindspring.com
National Headquarters- (703) 548-3440
Note: There are more than 20 HR professional associations with chapters in Atlanta, most of which specialize in a specific HR function. All offer excellent networking opportunities. Begin your networking efforts with SHRM or one of the other associations listed here, then add the others as your efforts expand.
Local website: www.shrmatlanta.org

SOCIETY FOR MARKETING PROFESSIONAL SVCS (www.smps.org)
Membership comprised of companies and individuals in architecture, engineering, planning, and construction, and who are responsible for marketing their organization's services; local chapter has 140+ members. Provides marketing education process for people in the "built" environment. Offers Employment Opportunity Committee under Membership Director that maintains file of job openings and applicants. Contact Tina Hayes @ (770)514-6082-phone and fax. Quarterly newsletter includes job information in

a "classified section" with job openings and job seekers; contact Laura Long @ (770)360-8888. Meets for lunch on the third Tuesday each month.
President: Peggy Henderson, CPSM, phenderson@cdai.com, 404.633.8861
National Headquarters - (703)549-6117

SOCIETY FOR TECHNICAL COMMUNICATION (www.stc.org)
World's largest association of technical communicators, with 750 members in Atlanta. Meets third Wed. monthly from 6:00 to 8:00 pm.at the Marriott Perimeter. Maintains resume database available to companies; contact Frank Harper, Employment Chair, 678.525.8420, hfharper@mindspring.com.
President: Lori Brown, 404.236.2771, lbrown@iss.net
Membership: Karen Docherty
National headquarters- (703)522-4114
Local website- www,stcatlanta.org Also sponsors a special interest group information is located on their web site.

SOCIETY OF LOGISTICS ENGINEERS (www.sole.org)
Promotes logistics education and technical activities. Atlanta chapter has 60 members and meets third Wednesday for lunch at 11:30. Membership chairman maintains resume bank, and monthly newsletter lists job openings and job seekers. Headquarters has central job bank for members only, accessible with touch-tone phone 24 hours/day. All information including Atlanta workshops also available through website.
Chairperson: Paul Williams with Lockheed at (770) 793-0507; fax (770)793-0581
Membership Chair: Bob Shively @ (770)793-0535
National headquarters - (301) 459-8446, (800) 695-7653
Local website- www.soleatlanta.org

STRATEGIC LEADERSHIP FORUM
Atlanta chapter has 100 members, mostly corporate planners and consultants, involved in financial planning, strategic management, and business development. No formal job assistance, but excellent networking. Meets monthly on second Monday, except during summer, alternating between lunch and dinner; visitors are welcome. Offers additional workshops and seminars.
President: Elizabeth Moore
Co-Chairperson: Eric Hutchinson with A T. Kearney @ (770)393-9900
Chapter Administrator: Wanda Rivera with A T Kearney also @ (770)393-9900
National Headquarters - (800) 873-5995

WEB NETWORK OF BENEFITS PROFESSIONALS (www.webenefits.org)
Mission is benefits education and networking, and members are from human resources backgrounds, consultants, and vendors. Has 150 members, and meets third Thursday for lunch at 103 West restaurant. Has two Job Bank Coordinators: employers should call Beth Riccio @ (770) 384-2731 to list a job vacancy; job seekers, call Jane Van Valzah @ (404) 329-5757 to have resume included, or fax resume to (404) 636-2317. Monthly

ewsletter lists both openings and individuals seeking employment. Offers reduced membership fee for unemployed!

resident: ANDREA BAILEY 404/525-2585

Membership: Bill Lund, (770) 993-4358, lundw@bellsouth.net

ational headquarters – (414)821-9080

APPENDIX F: GOVERNMENT OFFICES

(1) U. S. (Federal) agencies

(2) State of Georgia

(3) Local counties and City of Atlanta

Federal:

Department of the Army Civilian Personnel Office
    See "Appendix C," the list of companies

ajobs.com
Links to many gov't sites and job lists.

Office of Personnel Management (OPM)
    75 Spring St SW, Suite 956, Atlanta, GA 30303-3309
    (404) 331-4315 for recorded message; 331-4531 for assistance

Largest federal agencies in Atlanta:
    Environmental Protection Agency
    61 Forsyth St. SW, Atlanta, GA 30303
    (404) 562-8182
    (employs 1100+ in Atlanta)

    Federal Aviation Administration - Southern Region
    1701 Columbia Avenue
    College Park, GA 30337
    (404) 305-5300
    info at www.jobs.faa.gov or automated fax line 405/954-0250
    (Employs 900 here)

    Dept of Health and Human Services (Social Security)
    61 Forsyth St, SW, Suite 22T64, Atlanta, GA 30303
    (404) 562-1200

    General Accounting Office
    2635 Century Pkwy, Suite 700, Atlanta 30345
    (404) 679-1900
    Job announcements listed on the web page and applications are taken from September through April. Hires recent grads and experienced.
    www.gao.gov

    General Services Administration--Southeast Region Office

Note: This office conducts all hiring for the Southeast. Prefers to hire recent grads under the "outstanding scholar" authority, which requires graduation in the upper 10% of class or 3.5 GPA.
401 West Peachtree St, Suite 2802, Atlanta, GA 30365
(404) 331-3186; (404) 331-5102 Job Information Line updated each Tuesday; employs 600 in Atlanta
www.gsa.gov

Department of the Treasury--Internal Revenue Service, Atlanta Service Ctr.
4800 Buford Highway, Chamblee, GA
(770) 455-2455 - Job Information Line

Department of Labor
61 Forsyth St SW, Suite 6B50, Atlanta, GA 30303
(404) 562-2008   Ask for "Chief of Employment Branch," currently Marilyn Vanne. (employs 500 in Atlanta)

U S Forestry Service – Southern Region Office
1720 Peachtree Road NW, 7th Floor
Atlanta, GA 30309
(404) 347-2384
(employs 250 here)
www.r8web.com

Federal Bureau of Alcohol, Tobacco and Firearms
2600 Century Parkway, Atlanta, GA 30345
(404) 679-5170
www.atftreas.gov

US Postal Service
3900 Crown Rd, Atlanta, GA 30304
(404) 765-7234

tate of Georgia

tate Merit System
200 Piedmont Ave, Room 418, West Tower, Atlanta, GA 30334
(404) 656-2724 - Two minute information recording, plus directions to their office.

epartment of Audits
Financial Division: Hires mostly recent grads with accounting major, probably 15 each year, and 3.0 GPA is required. Send resume to Director of Finance Division, 254 Washington St, Room 214, Atlanta, GA 30334.

(404) 656-2180

Performance Audits Division: Hires mostly MBA's and accounting grads, but also seeks a few economics and public administration grads; good GPA is important. Send resume to Director of Performance Audits, 254 Washington St, Room 314, Atlanta, GA 30334.
(404) 657-5220

Medicaid Division: Hires 7± accountants each year; 3.0 GPA required. Send resume to Ed Kemp at 254 Washington St, Suite 322, Atlanta, 30334.
(404) 656-2006

Local

Atlanta, City of
Profile: Government for City of Atlanta, employing 8000+ and expecting an increase. Hires both recent grads and experienced personnel in accounting/finance, administration and MIS.
Procedure: Send your resume with Social Security Number and cover letter requesting to be placed on their mailing list for a certain job classification (*e.g.*, accounting, administration, engineering, etc.) and they will notify you of openings for which you can apply. If you are in Atlanta, you can go to their office and review the "Specifications List," which includes all current openings. Mail information or go to Employment Services Division, 68 Mitchell Street SW, Ste. 2107, Atlanta, GA 30335.
(404) 330-6369 to check on job information and resume status; 330-6456 for professional-level Job Hot Line.

Clayton County
Profile: Smallest of the five major metro-Atlanta counties, with 1600 employees. Publishes a Job Announcement List of current needs, which can be reviewed at their offices; they will not mail copies. You can call their office and ask if there is a job vacancy for your specialty, and if so, they will mail you an application form. Both recent grads and experienced personnel are needed.
Procedure: Contact or visit their office at
112 Smith St., Jonesboro, GA 30236.
(770) 477-3239

Cobb County
Profile: Third largest metro-Atlanta county and growing rapidly. Currently employs 4000 total. In a "normal" year, hires approximately 50 recent grads and 25 experienced exempt, primarily in accounting/finance, engineering (CE

mostly) and MIS, plus social work and urban planning. Seeks experienced managers in accounting and engineering.

ocedure: Send resume to Employment Manager,
Cobb County Personnel Department, 100 Cherokee St., Ste. 350, Marietta, GA 30090-9614.
(770) 528-2544; 528-2555 job info line

eKalb County

ofile: Second largest metro-Atlanta county, employing 5000+. All applicants are hired through the county merit system.

ocedure: Write for application from DeKalb County Merit System, 1300 Commerce Dr., Decatur, GA 30030.
(404) 371-2331 - Job Hot Line

ulton County

ofile: Largest metro-Atlanta county, employing 9000+. Has many openings in all areas. Must go to their office to review current job listing, then apply for employment. Most exempt positions require a proficiency test, which is given twice weekly.

ocedure: Go to their Personnel Office at 141 Pryor St. S.W., Ste. 3030, Atlanta, GA. 30303
(404) 730-6700; 730-5627 job info. line

winnett County

ofile: For several years, Gwinnett County had been the fastest growing county in the entire nation, and is now the fourth largest metro-Atlanta county. Employs 2500, and expects an increase in hiring, both for recent grads and experienced personnel, especially civil engineers, accountants and other disciplines.

ocedure: Send resume to Personnel Department,
75 Langley Dr, Lawrenceville, GA 30045.
(770) 822-7940 - Job Hot Line; 822-7930 - information

About the author . . .

STEPHEN E. HINES has been involved in career counseling and assessment, and personnel recruitment and placement in Atlanta since July, 1970. He is the founder and owner of HINES RECRUITING ASSOCIATES, a professional-level personnel placement service, established in 1975. For more information, call (404) 262-7131 or email JobGuru@ajobs.com.

The author wishes to thank the following for their contributions to this book:

Anne Kraft
Dick France
Katie Baer
Jeffrey Smith
Ken Vaughn
Ray Osborne
Harvey Brickley